ARTS
AND
CRAFTS
GARDENS

With photographs by
MARTIN CHARLES

Dedication

For Greysteil and Matty - the number one boys.

First published in the United States of America in 1998 by
RIZZOLI INTERNATIONAL PUBLICATIONS, INC.
300 Park Avenue South, New York, NY 10010

First published in Great Britain by
Pavilion Books Limited
26 Upper Ground
London SE1 9PD

ISBN 0-8478-2084-X
LC 97-69460

Art direction and design by Janet James

Color reproduction by Anglia Graphics
Printed and bound in Spain by Graficas Reunidas

Frontispiece:
William Robinson's garden, Gravetye Manor in Sussex.

CONTENTS

Preface

In writing this book I did not set out to make a comprehensive survey of Arts and Crafts gardens. That would have required a much longer text and it would have duplicated the material in David Ottewill's excellent book, *The Edwardian Garden*. I wanted to get at the ideas that shaped the gardens, the social environment that determined the way in which they were worked and enjoyed, and to look at their planning and planting as expressions of the commitment and philosophies of their designers. In order to do this I have chosen to look at a few gardens in detail. A broader selection would have embraced a wider range of Arts and Crafts ideals, in a movement that was distinguished by its diversity. There is a long list of designers whose work, barely mentioned here, would qualify for more extensive study: C.E. Mallows, Thomas Mawson, Mervyn Macartney, Ernest Newton, E.S. Prior, R.W. Schultz and W.R. Lethaby, to name only the most obvious. By packing too many gardens into the itinerary, however, I felt that there would be a risk, as with booking too many sights into a coach tour, of finishing with an incoherent catalogue of names and half-digested impressions. I hope that the gardens discussed in this book, and the patterns and personalities that link them together, will cast light on the movement as a whole. There will be other studies, I know, to compensate for my most glaring omissions.

Wendy Hitchmough

Author's Acknowledgements

My children, Greysteil and Matthew, must be first in line for thanks for putting up with all the times that I wasn't quite with them during the writing of this book. Ken Baker was unstinting in his support and my parents were interested and encouraging, as always.

I would like to thank Colin Webb for his enthusiasm when the project was first mooted and for making it happen. I have been especially fortunate to have worked with Martin Charles again. His comments on the draft manuscript as well as the gardens themselves played a part in shaping the book. His photographs need no acknowledgement from me. Helen Castle gave valuable time when it was in short supply to an incisive reading of the text. The 'signposts' are dedicated to her. I am grateful to Penny David, Natasha Martyn-Johns and Emma Tait for their insight and care in editing the text and to Janet James for making the design appear simple. Frances Kelly and Vivien James steered the book through critical stages with kindness and determination.

The owners and keepers of Arts and Crafts gardens, without whom this book would not have been possible, deserve special thanks. I owe it to Peter Herbert to put on record that Gravetye Manor's hospitality does indeed achieve perfection. Anne Ellis at The Hill House shared her scholarly research into the interior garden with me and Paul Nichols introduced me to individuals who knew Hidcote before its National Trust years. Jean-Paul Marix-Evans kindly shared his extensive knowledge of great Tangley Manor with me. I must thank the Baron and Baroness of Earlshall, David Usher, Lady Clark, Stephen King, Edward Hollamby, Lois Marshall, Stephen Biddulph, Edward Bosley, Penny and Gerry Reading, M.J. Allen, and Jack Percival. Finally, I should like to thank Patrick Taylor for reminding me of Sir Robert Lorimer's importance as a garden designer, and John Brandon-Jones and Maurice Howard, both of whom extended my understanding of Arts and Crafts, although we seldom talked of gardens.

Introduction

Arts and Crafts is generally defined as a reforming movement in architecture and design that evolved out of the writings and practice of John Ruskin and William Morris. It began to emerge as a recognizable style in the 1880s, flourished in the 1890s, achieved its most brilliant effects in the decade around the turn of the century, and was terminated by the First World War. Although there is an appealing completeness about this historical assessment, it presupposes an emphasis on the articulation of a separate style with a definite beginning and end. The facts are less convenient. Taking the design of Red House, William Morris's home, as its starting point in 1859 and the War as the final blow to an already diminishing momentum, the movement has a life-span of fifty-five years – too long to be interpreted as a self-contained artistic proposition. In its own time, the term 'Arts and Crafts' signified a general association of like-minded artists, designers, manufacturers and crafts people, who met through the Art Workers' Guild and other regional associations, and exhibited together under the auspices of the Arts and Crafts Exhibition Society, which gave the movement its name and a public identity from 1888. Arts and Crafts was never restricted to an exclusive artistic membership in the way that the Pre-Raphaelite Brotherhood was, nor was it defined by a written manifesto.

The Arts and Crafts movement rejected 'style' as an artificial imposition (thus confounding historians). Nevertheless its designs are distinguished by an insistence on modesty and simplicity, on traditional craft methods and finishes passed down over generations from master to apprentice, and on the inherent qualities of natural materials simply worked. It evolved independently in Britain and America. Although Arts and Crafts is specifically associated with the design of country houses, garden suburbs, furniture, domestic objects and graphics, its fascination as a movement lies in its extension beyond the physical limits of design. The Arts and Crafts house and its garden signified a range of ideas and exploratory interests that coursed through the progressive elements of its culture. It was often indicative of a striving for purity and innocence; an investigation into spirituality, into ancient and cosmic symbols and Oriental religions; and a quest for profound meaning in a century of radical changes.

In its formative years the Arts and Crafts movement coexisted with the Aesthetic movement. The Aesthetic vogue for Oriental porcelain and 'the love of art for art's sake' advocated by Walter Pater in the 1870s can be differentiated from the wholesome 'cottage-style' furnishings and plain oak furniture hand-made to Arts and Crafts designs of the 1880s and 1890s; there are too many ideals, stylistic associations and even key personalities belonging to both movements, however, to draw a clean dividing line between them. The importance of creative collaboration between artists and designers, an insistence on simplicity, and an underlying belief that the quality of life could be enhanced or undermined by architecture and interior decoration were fundamental to both movements.

Both the Aesthetic and the Arts and Crafts movements presented women with new domestic opportunities that led them to a degree of artistic independence and ultimately, in some cases, to professional status. The perception of women in the 1870s as creatures of refined sensibility with particular responsibilities for the domestic realm, perpetuated through handbooks advising the lady amateur on all matters of interior design, expanded to include a physical and professional assertiveness through the Arts and Crafts garden. The Arts and Crafts house provided a progressive environment in which liberal ideas and alternative doctrines were *de rigueur*. As healthy pursuits like cycling and tennis became fashionable, the attractions of gardening took women out of the house and eventually into the domain of paid employment. By the turn of the century gardening expertise was one recognized route to professional credibility for women.

There is a clear relationship between the women's suffrage movement and the Arts and Crafts garden that deserves further research. It is no coincidence that a meeting of women horticultural students at Gertrude Jekyll's house was disrupted by the police on suspicion of subversive activities, nor that the garden ornament workshop founded by Mary Watts at Compton for the training of village craftswomen became a centre for local suffrage meetings. A study of the evolution of the Arts and Crafts garden brings to the forefront nineteenth-century women whose influence has been trivialized or marginalized in more general studies. Kate Greenaway's images of childhood innocence and their effect on fashion were essential factors in distilling artistic ideas and giving them a popular identity. On a more concrete level Gertrude Jekyll's passion for building, and her architectural influence merit particular emphasis.

The ideals of the Arts and Crafts movement and the social and economic conditions in which it was nurtured coexisted in a state of tension. Arts and Crafts houses, interiors and gardens catered very specifically for the artistic aspirations and preoccupations of the fashionable middle classes. They were designed and built on the proceeds of industrial and financial achievement, but they deliberately sought to reinstate and revitalize the rural crafts and traditions that industrialization had undermined. Ironically many Arts and Crafts gardens were designed for successful industrialists or entrepreneurs intent on achieving a cottage in the country to escape the squalor of urban life. A substantial proportion of the money that was spent terracing acres of countryside, building garden walls and pergolas and paying armies of gardeners was new money, or new money filtered down through a generation or two. Some of the most influential figures in garden design, too, were the children of middle-class families whose fortunes were founded on investments in industry. Although they reacted against mass-production and the consequent devaluation of tradition and craftsmanship, their livelihoods were dependent upon the commercial benefits of industry.

As people distanced themselves from natural forces by living in urban conurbations and by manufacturing or importing (rather than breeding or growing) the products on which their wealth and survival were based, their relationship with nature became more complex. This physical distancing coincided with vehement philosophical and theological debate as scientific and technological advances challenged religious doctrines and brought into focus an understanding of evolution that, for many, set the laws of nature in direct opposition to areas that had previously been accepted as the law of God. Nineteenth-century paintings, literature and music abound with reassuring references to pastoral scenes. Nature, like Erda the Goddess of Earth in Wagner's

Ring (first performed as a cycle in 1876), became associated with ancient, regenerative and prophetic powers, or loaded with rationalist implications.

The wealthy industrialists who commissioned houses with Arts and Crafts gardens in the country, and the philanthropists who sponsored the design of garden suburbs and garden cities, sought to reinstate the ideal of man and nature living together in harmony, either on a personal or on a collective basis. Their architects strove to devise an organic architecture, inspired by nature and reflecting the landscape's contours and materials. Local conditions of site, soil and climate were identified and endorsed as fundamental considerations in the design of the house and its garden. As a consequence, the Arts and Crafts garden enjoyed a very broad stylistic range. The gardens of Greene and Greene in California were very different in appearance, in planting and in visual references from the gardens of Gertrude Jekyll and Edwin Lutyens in Surrey, because they responded to different climatic and vernacular conditions. The aspirations of their owners, the artistic doctrines of their designers and the relationship between planting and architecture, however, were remarkably similar.

Broader national and political issues had a bearing on the development of the Arts and Crafts garden. Expansions in trade and industry coincided with national and commercial empire building, and the export and exhibition of Japanese prints and artefacts, in particular, had a profound influence on design in North America and Europe. Japan had been closed to the Western world for more than two hundred years until the revolution in 1848 opened the way to trading and diplomatic relations. Fine Japanese prints were discovered by painters in Paris when they were used as packing around ceramics from China in 1856 and when, two years later, Japan signed a commercial treaty with Britain and America, the sudden rush of Japanese exports into Europe and into America informed progressive new artistic directions as well as creating superficial fashions for blue and white ceramics and Oriental silks. Impressionist painting in France, the Aesthetic movement in England and the architecture of Frank Lloyd Wright and Greene and Greene in America all owe a debt to the clear, simple outlines and startling compositions of Japanese art. Japanese influences were expressed quite literally in the Oriental tea-houses and gardens that enjoyed a revival in English Arts and Crafts gardens. They inspired Monet's water garden at Giverny. Their effect was most extensive, however, in America, where the exhibition of the Ho-o-den pavilion at the Chicago World's Columbian Exhibition in 1893 introduced a generation of architects and garden designers to hand-crafted construction, to the contemplative integration of landscape and architecture and to new concepts of symbolism in landscape and design.

International exhibitions brought artists and designers into direct contact with each other's work, as well as promoting international trade. As the barriers to trade and communication between countries diminished, however, there was a compensatory emphasis on national characteristics and differences. A sense of national history, even of local history, was added to the factors contributing to the Arts and Crafts garden. In Barcelona Gaudí's roof gardens, devoid of plants but erupting, nevertheless, with organic energy, evoked the mythical figures of St George and the Dragon that symbolized Catalan nationalism and reflected the mountain formation outside the city. American gardens responded to colonial and indigenous garden traditions: in southern California

Left: *Monet's water garden at Giverny translated the influence of Japanese art into a subject for Impressionist painting.*

Irving Gill explored and adapted Hispanic traditions in the design of his houses and gardens; where history presented the garden designer with a relentless trail of pioneers, the scale and grandeur of the great American plains became a focus and inspiration for garden design. English gardens drew on medieval and Tudor traditions as representing a golden age in British history, and in doing so they endorsed and refined an existing taste for Tennyson's Arthurian tales and for Pre-Raphaelite paintings.

The Arts and Crafts garden varied in scale as well as character. At its most ambitious it inspired the grandiose formal layout and topiary elephants of the Moghul Garden in New Delhi, designed by Lutyens in 1917. It reached its zenith in the country estates of between ten and twenty acres, where house and garden were laid out as a single entity and the garden was arranged as a series of outdoor rooms, each with a specific function and a character of its own. The principle of a house connected to the landscape, where the lines and materials of the building spread like surface roots into the walls and pathways of the garden, and where the sharp divisions between interior and exterior space were exploded in open-air living rooms that projected like decks over the landscape, was immensely attractive to designers, gardeners and clients alike at the end of the nineteenth century. Besides being scaled up in an expression of imperial splendour, it could equally be distilled down to its essential elements for the small terraced town-house plots of Baillie Scott, or the semi-detached and detached houses of the garden suburb.

The Arts and Crafts movement presented its gardeners with a rich and versatile set of rules and references that offered an escape from the pressures of nineteenth-century modern life. Healthy fresh air and physical exercise, a renewed connection with the forces of nature and the promise that gardening, cottage-style, was easy enough for amateurs were all put up as enticements. The owners of Arts and Crafts gardens, however, unlike most gardeners today, could abandon the border fork at the slightest twinge of backache. Gardening was seldom allowed to interfere with the equally serious ritual of tea-time, and any task that proved to be tiring or dull could be left to the steady and reliable back-up of the gardening staff. Working up a sweat or turning over the compost would have been quite out of the question.

Then, as now, the gardener was inspired and informed by a proliferation of gardening books and magazines. Just as gardeners today are seduced and encouraged by colour photographs, late nineteenth-century gardeners were inspired by watercolours of ancient topiary rising above a haze of annual and perennial flowers, and of thatched cottages half-concealed behind a profusion of hollyhocks and roses. Artists and gardeners cheated here and there, not just by the addition of strategically placed potted flowers plunged into the border, but by painting flowers in bloom together that in reality would have flowered several weeks apart. The Arts and Crafts garden was a mixture of truth and illusion, of nostalgia and regeneration. It was inspired by contemporary painting, and in equal measure the most romantic gardens were painted to hang in the Royal Academy, or illustrate the pages of picture books.

The Arts and Crafts garden combined rational, 'man-made' structures with abundant, 'natural' planting. It resolved the interface between architecture and nature, between control and the unknown. It was a place of reassurance and rest, often incorporating factors which remained constant through time – traditional walls and gateways. It established a backdrop to the seasons' changes and withstood the erosion of time. It harnessed and exhibited the ideals of its period, but it also harboured a space for fantasy and imagination away from the insistent demands of a reforming age in which everything from politics to education was scrutinized and reorganized in the interests of progress.

Chapter One

Origins

The Arts and Crafts garden established the foundations of modern gardening practice. In England elaborate Victorian planting schemes with brightly coloured annuals arranged in geometric designs were rejected. The celebration of exotic plants, collected on plant-hunting expeditions to the farthest corners of the earth and cosseted in specially designed glasshouses, was set aside. In their place the Arts and Crafts garden revived the studied restraint and timeless English quality that were epitomized by perceptions of the Tudor garden, combining strong architectural structures, box-edged beds and the division of the garden into a sequence of separate compartments, with an abundance of natural planting. Tall hedges and walls

Right: *Holes and crevices for planting were built into the walls at Hestercombe*

divided the garden into a series of outdoor rooms and straight brick or stone paths defined long deep borders filled with herbaceous perennials. The plan was ordered into formal vistas with tanks or sundials forming the focus of an axis, but within this orderly layout there were unexpected and often mysterious enclosures: a sunken garden, or a simple seat, half-concealed within a rose-covered arbour. Topiary birds and animals introduced an element of wit and evidence of painstaking attention to detail; artistically designed steps accentuated the organization of a sloping site into a series of level terraces.

Within this sharply defined and orderly structure the plants were given free rein. They were allowed to scramble over arches and pergolas, to spill across the outlines of pathways and to burst out of the joints of stone retaining walls. Relatively common trees, shrubs and flowers were used, often natives or hardy exotics from similar habitats, and the gardener entered into a partnership with (rather than a dictatorship over) nature. Old roses, medieval flowers like pinks, and flowers with unruly habits like verbascum and foxgloves – which the Victorian gardener would have weeded out – became fashionable for their unsophisticated simplicity. Annuals were allowed to self-seed in their appropriated places, and where nature would not oblige, the crevices between rockery stones and the earth joints of retaining walls were crammed with rock plants such as creeping gypsophila and cerastium (snow-in-summer), or covered from above with trails of rambling roses.

The Arts and Crafts garden was far more than a superficial fashion in design. It was charged with intellectual and visual jokes, provocations and subtleties, most of which have faded or been obscured by time. Garden design does not evolve in a cultural vacuum. It relates to contemporary values and aspirations, to the paintings, music and literature of its time, as well as its architecture. The Arts and Crafts garden evolved as part of a comprehensive movement away from the ostentation and vulgarity of Victorian taste and it represented a deliberate rejection of the social values and oppressive conditions of the Victorian era. Arts and Crafts gardens had a shock value in their own time: they were the gardening equivalent of bra-burning, and they enjoyed a youthful ebullience and an effrontery that can be appreciated today only by an effort of imagination and by looking at the discipline and conventions of the Victorian gardens they replaced.

The great Victorian gardens had been founded on two factors. The first of these, essential to any ambitious garden design, was wealth. Vast new fortunes made in manufacturing, finance or trade were channelled into building new country houses and laying out their estates, or restyling the faces and gardens of old ones. The second essential factor was a brazenly acquisitive attitude to historical style. Eighteenth-century gardens that had contrived to look natural in the Picturesque tradition were far too esoteric for ambitious Victorian patrons, and authentic seventeenth-century topiary and knot gardens were too dull. In their place imposing new mansions borrowed and bastardized every conceivable style, demonstrating a marked preference for the more grandiose and elaborate ones. Their gardens were inspired by Tudor, Stuart and Rennaissance designs. They copied French, Italian and Dutch motifs, as well as exotic styles from the Orient. Notions of heritage and appropriateness were disregarded by the Victorian gardener. They interfered with an impulse to display the resources, if not always the good taste, of the client on a grand scale.

LEFT: *The bog garden at Great Tangley Manor defies Victorian conventions of order and formality.*

Colour and pattern were essential elements in the design of the Victorian garden, just as a profusion of colour and pattern overwhelmed the Victorian interior and dazzled the artistic sensibilities of its occupants into abeyance. The planting of brightly coloured annuals into shaped beds to form patterns in sharply defined areas of colour (known as 'carpet bedding' or 'bedding out') became a salient feature of the Victorian garden. Loathed by the Arts and Crafts gardener, it was to most Victorians a celebration of the latest achievements in horticulture: by importing exotic and novel plants, then 'improving' their performance through hybridization, flowers could be manufactured in astonishing quantities and exhibited together in glorious and inventive new forms. It is no coincidence that parks and public gardens, often established as benevolent gestures by wealthy Victorian patrons, proliferated in the nineteenth century and it is in these gardens that bedding out survives at its most resplendent today, as a chest-swelling display of municipal extravagance.

The Victorians were compulsive collectors, importing treasures and curiosities from all over the world. They celebrated the exotic as a vehicle for fantasy and curiosity, yet at the same time they pursued stringent collecting policies with scientific rigour and tenacity. The Victorian garden reflected a broader social context, in which the expansion of the British Empire and political domination over foreign subjects abroad were fervid and lucrative concerns. The study of botany flourished in the nineteenth century as nature was subjected to increasingly refined scientific and intellectual investigation. The physiology of plants was analysed and explained, plants were organized into families and specimens were recorded in exquisitely detailed watercolour paintings. The scale and intensity of explorations in the laboratory were matched by a zeal for plant-hunting expeditions that took collectors into the mountains, swamps and deserts of previously uncharted territory. Often their expeditions were financed by acquisitive patrons. Seeds and specimens were meticulously packaged and despatched to gardens and nurserymen at home, where they were catalogued and propagated and then planted in grandiose gardens on country estates.

Victorian gardens and glasshouses became showcases for exotic new specimens. In the first decades of the century a succession of hardy new plants were introduced from the Himalayas, North and South America and China. Rhododendrons made such an impression when they were first imported from the Himalayas that huge areas of gardens were redesigned to display their different varieties. Arboretums and pinetums were laid out so as to accommodate collections of specimen trees, and huge conservatories and glasshouses, like those at Kew, were built to house tender exotics. Faced with this unprecedented range of high-performance plants, it is hardly surprising that Victorian gardeners abandoned their native species in order to indulge in a fascination for the rich colours and intricate shapes of acers and azaleas, or the sheer novelty of the coniferous monkey-puzzle tree.

Biddulph Grange in Staffordshire, designed from 1846 onwards by its owner, James Bateman, was a perfect expression of the Victorian gardener's instinct for horticultural adventure and imperialism. The garden was designed as a miniature world tour. Bateman financed ambitious plant-hunting expeditions and he designed his fifteen-acre garden as a series of theatrical settings. These included an Egyptian Court with stone sphinxes and yews clipped into obelisks, an arboretum with an avenue of some of the first wellingtonias to be planted in England, and a Chinese garden with its own temple and ornamental bridge across a pond of water-lilies. The dark tunnels, massive rock-work and brightly coloured sculpture and buildings brought a quality of melodrama as well as an attempt at geographical scene-setting to the planting at Biddulph. The extraordinary reduction of each country's history and culture into a few symbolic buildings, however, told more about contemporary Victorian attitudes than about the natural habitats of their new plants.

If gardens exhibit the character and aspirations of their owners, then Biddulph Grange was designed to display the worldly sophistication of James Bateman and his daring and connoisseurship as a collector of rare and exotic species. Bateman's fortune, inherited from his father, had originated in the coal-mining industry. The English aristocracy would have spurned him as *nouveau riche* unless he had had marriageable daughters whose wealth might have rejuvenated a title and the sort of centuries-old, crumbling country seat that so many rich industrialists sought to emulate in their new country houses. He was typical of his generation in compensating for the newness of his fortune with a prestigious old (Oxford) education; his ambition to join the gentry by commissioning a country house was tempered by a learned specialization in cultivating orchids – the quintessence of gentlemanly behaviour.

The ambitious intentions, the exotic species grouped together and the sense of scale and extravagance at Biddulph were typical of the great Victorian estate garden. Biddulph was typical, too, in its dependence on immense glasshouses, both at the working core of the garden and as more elaborate structures attached to the house where artificial climatic conditions could simulate the natural habitats of tender exotics. It boasted an orangery, a camellia-house, a conservatory corridor and a fernery in addition to the more functional heated glasshouses where flowers and fruit for the house were grown, where the propagation and overwintering of Bateman's extensive collection was attended to by a team of expert gardeners, and where thousands of tender and half-hardy plants were prepared for a succession of bedding schemes that had to be changed two or three times a year. Gardens like Linden Towers in Menlo Park, California, designed in 1876 by Rudolf Ulrich, boasted pathways lined with a mosaic effect of hundreds of thousands of succulent plants, pandering to the prevailing fashion for finely detailed and brightly coloured pattern. Victorian fabrics, wallpapers, ceramics and metalwork could all be patterned very cheaply by machine, but in the garden, quite self-consciously, the intricate patterns of labour-intensive bedding-out schemes were evidence of considerable expense and extravagance.

While Victorian horticulturists were demonstrating the extent to which nature could be disciplined, analysed and mass-produced under man's supreme control, Victorian scientists were grappling with evidence that it was natural forces rather than divine intervention that had shaped the Earth and everything on it. Man might play God with nature, but nature was spreading tendrils into God's domain. Religion was of paramount importance to Victorian culture. In many families, Sundays were devoted entirely to church-going and to reading the Bible. The Holy Scriptures were learnt verbatim. When geologists suggested, very tentatively, that the Creation could not have been completed in seven days they initiated a chain of scientific and rational debate that was to shake the very foundations of Victorian society. According to the scriptures, God had revealed the events of Genesis directly to Moses. If the scientific facts of geology contradicted the gospel truth of Genesis (and geological evidence offered tangible proof that the Earth had evolved over a period of more than seven days), then the absolute authority of the Bible was called into question and a host of other rational doubts leapt into the gap between scientific discovery and religious dogma.

The Origin of Species by Charles Darwin became a best-seller when it was published as a book in 1859. Its detractors condemned it as a blasphemous heresy and for many the idea that humans were related to animals was dangerous, contemptible or laughable. No theory of evolution could compete with the story of Adam and Eve, with its inherent notions of misogyny and its moral conclusion, irresistible to the Victorian sensibility, that a life of comfort and plenty could never be enjoyed by women who defied instructions and consorted with serpents. For progressive and rational thinkers, however, Darwin's findings represented a release from doubt. They provided conclusive evidence that the teachings of the Bible were not to be read literally, and this, far from undermining the validity of Christian teaching, made it compatible with contemporary life and ideology.

The omnipotence of nature and the principle that mankind was integrated within a supreme natural order inevitably led progressive Victorians to consider their environment in a new light. From the eighteenth century wild nature and the beauty of uncultivated landscape had been regarded as a sublime expression of God's bounty and benevolence. New religions were founded, such as Theism (in 1871), which recognized nature as a direct expression of God's munificence and suggested that by making a reverent study of nature, man was in direct communion with God himself. The illustrator Kate Greenaway, although not renowned for the profundity of her ideas, summed it up in a letter to John Ruskin written in September 1898:

> 'How is it that I have got to think the caring for Nature and Art of all kinds a *real* religion? I never can, never shall see it is more religious to sit in a hot church trying to listen to a commonplace sermon than looking at a beautiful sky, or the waves coming in.'[1]

To these new radicals, the Victorian method of gardening, which divorced plants from their natural habitat and subjected them to artificial conditions and regimes, was not only ostentatious and vulgar, it was tantamount to heresy.

One of the most influential critics on the side of the radicals in the second half of the nineteenth century was John Ruskin (1819–1900). He articulated a growing concern that factory employment and urban conditions had robbed the worker not only of his self-esteem, but of the dignity of labour as a form of spiritual expression. Ruskin formulated a theory by which architecture could be judged by its dependence on natural form, and ornament was only acceptable when it was clearly derived from natural sources. Ruskin criticized the terraced houses spreading in 'gloomy rows of formalized minuteness' around Victorian cities in gardening terms:

> 'not merely with the careless disgust of an offended eye, not merely with sorrow for a desecrated landscape, but with a painful foreboding that the roots of our national greatness must be deeply cankered'.[2]

He struck at the heart of Victorian aspirations when he pointed to domestic architecture as evidence that 'every man's aim is to be in some more elevated sphere than his natural one', concluding:

> 'When men do not love their hearths, nor reverence their thresholds, it is a sign that they have dishonoured both ... Our God is a house-hold God, as well as a heavenly one; He has an altar in every man's dwelling.'[3]

Ruskin was a passionate and persuasive writer. The idea of a domestic God, and of house building as a form of devotional offering, was both inventive and effective. He was equally specific on the subject of garden making. The Victorian formal bed represented 'an assembly of unfortunate beings, pampered and bloated above their natural size, stewed and heated into diseased growth'.[4] A more reverent study of nature would reveal 'the real purpose and operation of flowers' and expose the insensitivity of reducing their beauty to a 'meretricious glare'. Instead of organizing their gardens into brightly coloured patterns Ruskin implored his readers to take inspiration from the drifts of colour and irregular clusters of nature's planting:

'bluish purple is the only flower colour which Nature ever uses in masses of distant effect; this, however, she does in the case of most heathers, with the Rhododendron ferrugineum, and, less extensively, with the colder colour of the wood hyacinth.'

He was sensitive to the virtues of wild flowers, recommending that

'on the turf, the wild violet and pansy should be sown by chance, so that they may grow in undulations of colour, and should be relieved by a few primroses. All dahlias, tulips, ranunculi, and, in general, what are called florist's flowers, should be avoided like garlic.'[5]

Ruskin's books on art and architecture influenced a generation of designers. As a young art student, Gertrude Jekyll (1843–1932) was inspired by his analysis of Turner's painterly use of colour. William Morris (1834–96) read Ruskin's *The Stones of Venice* and *The Seven Lamps of Architecture* out loud to his circle of fellow Oxford undergraduates, recalling later, when his own Kelmscott Press reprinted Ruskin's chapter 'The Nature of Gothic' in 1892: 'it seemed to point a new road on which the world should travel.'[6]

Ruskin pointed a new way forward for patrons as well as designers. He tested their consciences when he compared the lies and deceptions of ostentatious building with malicious deceit, treachery and 'the glistening and softly spoken lie'. He sympathized with their frustrations: 'Modern builders are capable of little; and don't even do the little they can.' He promised them a voice in posterity if they would plant forests to give shade to future generations and raise buildings for their children to enjoy:

'God has lent us the earth for our life ... It belongs as much to those who come after us, and whose names are already written in the book of creation, as to us; and we have no right, by anything that we do or neglect, to involve them in unnecessary penalties, or deprive them of benefits which it was in our power to bequeath.'[7]

For designers like William Morris, and for many patrons of Arts and Crafts gardens whose fortunes had been founded a generation or two earlier on investment in mining industries, or factory buildings that had ravaged the natural landscape, Ruskin's high moral tone assuaged a sensitive layer, barely beneath the surface, of Victorian guilt. By subscribing to his aphorisms, like sitting through an especially fiery sermon, they might in some way atone for the sins of their fathers. Ruskin's call to build well, but to build modestly, in a spirit of 'honourable, proud, peaceful self-possession' coincided with an economic shift in demand for country properties. During the first three-quarters of the nineteenth century in England, and after the end of the Civil War in 1865 in North America, the ideal of a country house had represented a means not only of displaying wealth, but also of gaining admission into polite society. A 'country place' had been designed to rival (or at least to impress) more established country seats in scale and grandeur. Now, towards the end of the nineteenth century, a demand for more modest 'country cottages' began to gather momentum.

The reason for this was partly financial. Until the 1880s the country mansion, set in a working estate of about a thousand acres of farm land, had been a sound financial as well as a social investment. The successful entrepreneur, having made his pile in the city, might retire to a convenient country estate and manage his business affairs from there. With good fortune he could live the life of a gentleman, marry his daughters to the sons of the neighbouring lords, and still make a reasonable return on his investment in the land. Until the agricultural depression, a working estate could generate a substantial income. In Britain, however, from the beginning of the 1880s, the combination of a series of disastrous harvests and the introduction of cheap imported beef, bacon and corn undermined the viability of the working estate and as a consequence the number of prestigious commissions for country houses with extravagant Victorian gardens, which had risen during the first seven decades of the century, fell into sharp decline.

The country cottage, by comparison, was a modest proposition. It was championed by the 'artistic' middle classes, often people with comfortable (although seldom excessive) private incomes, successful artists, writers or entrepreneurs who had founded businesses that had flourished in a period of economic growth. Their fortunes would not stretch to great estates, but the ideal of a cottage in the country, away from the rigours of urban life, appealed to a philosophical desire to live in harmony with nature, as well as to a more moderate budget. The railways made it possible to commute from cottage to city, and areas of spectacular natural beauty could be reached at weekends and holidays within a few hours by train.

The image of the white-painted cottage with its garden of rambling roses, hollyhocks and sunflowers was no less laden with nostalgic associations than that of the country estate. For the city dweller it represented a life of honest simplicity where the pace of work was driven by the season's changes and where the hardships of poor harvests or extreme weather conditions were shared by a tightly knit community of individuals labouring together. For the idealist, prepared to edit a few economic facts, the benefits of rural life and the health-giving properties of fresh air, open space and working the land compared favourably with the treadmill existence of industrial life and labour where appalling conditions were endorsed in the pursuit of profit and competition. The idealized

ABOVE: *Helen Allingham's paintings nurtured and endorsed a Victorian nostalgia for the idealized country cottage.*

country cottage was a symbol, too, of historic continuity. It represented a balanced social system and a way of life that had remained unchanged for centuries. It had a comforting quality in a period when the threat of industrial unrest and the prospect of revolution kept the middle classes awake at night. There was a purity that was associated with the rural countryside and its communities of cottage dwellers that, provided it was preserved and protected against industrialization, could somehow be used as a weight in the balance to compensate for urban squalor and degradation.

The modern country cottage of the 1890s and early 1900s was no longer the domain of the traditional peasant worker. It was requisitioned by the affluent middle classes. As the great estates sold off tracts of land and farmhouses that were no longer viable for agricultural purposes, new buyers reorganized the land into their gardens and refurbished the estate buildings, or demolished them and commissioned improved and enlarged 'country cottages' in their place. *Country Life* summarized the 'real want of the age' in 1899:

'Prolonged town life is becoming more and more intolerable every year, and men of moderate means, who had long yearned for country houses on a small scale, are beginning to realise their desires. Sometimes they are men with families who are content to make the little country house their home, and to keep mere chambers in London for use when business calls them to London, or to some great provincial centre, for the working week. More often, perhaps, they are men who, after taking their families for years to poky and remote and expensive seaside lodgings, have discovered at last that it is cheaper, healthier, and infinitely more enjoyable to possess themselves of an accessible house to which they may resort for holiday or semi-holiday purposes.'[8]

The country cottage was not to be confused with 'a home for a labourer or an artisan'. If an old manor house or farmhouse 'which will bear conversion' could be found it was generally doubled in size. If not, then readers were encouraged to commission a new cottage.

A 'cottage' large enough for a family with six or seven children and the household's servants would be classified as a substantial house by today's standards, with at least five or six bedrooms. However, it was distinguished from the suburban 'villa' (the very name of which, according to *Country Life*, was 'suggestive of unheard-of atrocities in architecture on the fringes of provincial towns') by its artistic simplicity. Commuters and 'men of moderate means' could play miniature farms (*Country Life* recommended a Jersey cow or two and some poultry for the grounds) and enjoy the liberation of peasant life. The ideal of a traditional cottage surrounded by an orchard, with a garden crammed with old-fashioned flowers and wholesome vegetables, could be modified and enlarged to meet modern domestic requirements. It could be adapted as a model for modest suburban plots or incorporated into the planting of more ambitious garden designs. This rural domesticity, however, was designed with a sting in its tail. It was a deliberate slap in the face for parents' and grandparents' generations who had gone to such lengths to improve themselves and to differentiate their own elaborate houses and gardens from those of the labouring classes.

The cottage as an icon transcended all the imperfections of real cottages and their gardens. This combination of Romantic idealism with the resources and practical determination to transform reality was an essential element of the Arts and Crafts movement. The need to romanticize history, mythology and the rural idyll was as clearly expressed in the literature and music of the period as in its architecture and garden design. The nineteenth century nurtured the musical talents of Tchaikovsky, Dvořák, Richard Strauss and Elgar. William Morris rationalized the prevailing taste for medieval images in both art and literature on the grounds that they described for modern patrons

'what they have thought has happened to the world before their time, or what they deem they have seen with the eyes of the body or the soul: and the imaginings thus represented are always beautiful indeed, but oftenest stirring to men's passions and aspirations, and not seldom sorrowful or even terrible.'9

The scientific rigour and rational tenacity of the period could be suspended in the arts. Historical and mythological fantasies invited credibility with the sheer force of their detail, and this relationship between lovingly crafted detail and romantic fantasy recurs in the Arts and Crafts garden. *Ophelia* by John Everett Millais was painted with such realism that she might have been floating down the stream at the bottom of the garden. The illusion that allowed viewers to believe they could reach into the water and pick out the poppies and daisies that had escaped her grasp also enabled them to bridge the gap between the legend and contemporary life.

Fictional images in children's illustrated books are as revealing of the nineteenth-century consciousness as the paintings of Millais and Rossetti, and as relevant to an appreciation of Arts and Crafts gardens. The moral inconsistencies of the age gave rise to a degree of anarchy that, although suppressed with ferocity and determination, found its way into middle-class houses through the nursery door. *Alice's Adventures in Wonderland* by Lewis Carroll was published with illustrations by John Tenniel in 1865, followed by *Through the Looking-Glass* seven years later. Once through the looking-glass, Alice was able to talk to flowers who talked back to her. She threatened to pick the daisies when they shouted, and when she said, quite reasonably, that she had never before been in a garden where the flowers could talk, she was advised by the Tiger-lily: 'In most gardens ... they make the beds too soft – so that the flowers are always asleep.'

Lewis Carroll invented a parallel world for Alice in which parlour games were turned upside down and their pieces and playing cards given an astonishing independence. Creatures from the wild, the deep and the land of legends mimicked or ridiculed human patterns of behaviour and Alice managed to be both imperious and apparently quite incapable of controlling her destiny at the same time. Anarchy was circumscribed in *Alice*, just as sexual desire was sanctified in the paintings of the Pre-Raphaelites, because it was set within the surreal, disconnected world of dreams. Until Sigmund Freud (1856–1939) pointed out the uncomfortable relationship between the conscious and subconscious mind in 1900, dream images provided an ostensibly innocent framework for fantasies and passions that were otherwise socially taboo. Even after Freud the garden continued to be a fertile ground for fantasy and illusion.

Brer Rabbit and his English counterpart, Peter Rabbit, brought country ways and a note of gentle anarchy to the moral education of urban children in the 1890s. When Brer Rabbit was first published in 1896 the tales were already part of black American folklore, having been passed down, in story-telling tradition, from generation to generation. The Peter Rabbit stories were new, laying claim to a determination to preserve and animate the ideal of a rural England peppered with cottage gardens and

ABOVE: *'Ophelia', John Everett Millais, 1851–2.*

woody glades. Peter lacked Brer Rabbit's ruthlessness, his sense of humour and his ability to turn any situation to his own advantage. He was terrified when his adventures in Mr McGregor's vegetable patch brought him face to face with its owner, but his relationship with the real cottage garden, rather than an imaginary one, is complex and revealing. To nineteenth-century children and parents alike, the world of Peter Rabbit represented a world untouched by industry where every creature had its place, safe within a natural system of order and balance. At the

LEFT: *Peter Rabbit appreciating the cottage garden ideal of Mr McGregor's vegetable patch.*

same time, Peter's creator, Beatrix Potter, was actively involved in preserving the real natural system in her revitalization of rural farming traditions.

Fairy-tales and nursery rhymes illustrated by Kate Greenaway, Randolph Caldecott and Walter Crane in the 1870s and 1880s propagated new fantasy images in which make-believe characters animated aesthetic interiors and old-fashioned gardens. Kate Greenaway dresses were made up and marketed (although not by her), and her stylized gardens and sparsely decorated interiors popularized progressive design ideas and shaped the taste of the artistic middle classes. From the 1860s the ideal of the simple life could be bought over the counter in the form of Morris & Co. products and over the next two decades both Morris and Greenaway became household names, which were synonymous with enlightened (and achievable) ideas. Morris's airy chintzes and the clear colours and fluid lines of his designs, patterned with common hedgerow birds and flowers, heralded a release from Victorian controls and restrictions. This liberation was accompanied, quite literally, by a loosening of stays. The Aesthetes who ordered their wallpapers from Morris & Co. discarded their bustles and tightly laced corsets in favour of the loosely draped, flowing gowns made out of the 'Art Fabrics' that Liberty of London sold in its new department store. Liberty's 'Artistic Silks' made less than ideal gardening clothes, although they were perfect for drifting languidly about the borders after tea. The foundation of the Rational Dress Society in 1881, however, and the Hygienic Wearing Apparel Exhibition the following year, encouraged women to adopt 'a style of dress based upon considerations of health, comfort, and beauty' and when *The Science of Dress* by Mrs Ada Ballin was published in 1885 it became a best-seller.

Women were urged to take a more active part in styling their homes and gardens, and for the first time, in Arts and Crafts gardens, it became fashionable for middle-class women to take up their border forks and develop practical as well as creative gardening skills. As early as the 1840s Jane Loudon had instructed ladies in the art of gardening through her book *Gardening for Ladies, and Ladies' Companion to the Flower Garden*, published in England and North America. From the 1870s a plethora of gardening books and magazines were published to introduce the amateur, and in particular the lady amateur, to the refined art of gardening. The ladies in question were not the duchesses of the great country estates, who could consult their head gardeners if horticultural expertise was required, nor were they the peasant women and factory workers whose poverty, lack of education and long arduous working hours precluded the reading of any books. They were the wives and daughters of wealthy Victorian industrialists and entrepreneurs. They had both time and resources at their disposal, and in an age when nursing and teaching were the only careers that respectable women were encouraged to follow (and then only under certain circumstances), garden design and garden making came to represent an essential release for physical and creative energy.

The options available to progressive young women in the second half of the nineteenth century are polarized in the figures of Gertrude Jekyll (1843–1932) and Jane Morris (1839–1914). These two women were almost exact contemporaries and each achieved a degree of fame, even notoriety, in her own right. Both Jekyll and Morris played an important part in shaping and promoting the Arts and Crafts garden, and their achievements were envied and to some degree emulated by other women of the period and by successive generations. They were very different, however, in the ideals they represented and in what they achieved.

Jane Morris was born Jane Burden, the daughter of an Oxfordshire stable hand. Her extraordinary beauty attracted the attention of the Pre-Raphaelite painter Dante Gabriel Rossetti, and when she was eighteen she was introduced to William Morris as a model. They were married two years later. She became the Pre-Raphaelite muse representing an ideal of beauty that was intense, mysterious and perceived to be medieval. Certainly her appearance was very different from the modest ideals of Victorian beauty – the diminutive figures, tightly corseted, with curtains of hair pulled down over the forehead and knotted away out of sight. Jane Morris was a tall, striking woman, with masses of thick hair, grey introspective eyes and a full sensuous mouth. As the wife of William Morris and the muse of Rossetti, who was her lover, she achieved a remarkable status. The exploitation of her beauty enabled her to defy social conventions, firstly by marrying outside her social sphere and then by taking lovers, although this status was acquired at a cost of absolute dependency. She was portrayed as the personification of latent sexuality, representing an element of savage nature that fascinated and at the same time terrified Victorians. Rossetti painted her as Proserpine framed by tendrils of ivy; the foliage in the paintings, crisply in focus, symbolized her virtues and supplied the mythological (and thus respectable) context for her smouldering sexuality.

Jane Morris's beauty was closely associated with natural forces. Pre-Raphaelite paintings were vividly descriptive in their juxtaposition of nature with feminine beauty. The wild garden and its mistress were celebrated as provocative, mysterious, unfettered by convention. Yet among her contemporaries Jane Morris, and descriptions of her gardens in Kent and Oxfordshire, may have represented a different kind of role model. She did not engage in active pursuits; she was a pale and languid figure, confined by some unspecified, presumably feminine, complaint to her

ABOVE: *Jane Morris as Prosperine, painted by Dante Gabriel Rossetti, 1874.*

couch for much of the time; and her gardens, like her artistic drawing-rooms, were devised as settings for her iridescent beauty. Old-fashioned gardens were designed and nurtured so that she might drift wistfully through them, and because these gardens were widely known in artistic circles and sometimes painted, they were influential. Pre-Raphaelite paintings became fashionable among wealthy middle-class patrons because they appealed to a romantic, even a sexually charged, nostalgia for an age before industrialization. Arts and Crafts gardens evolved in response to the same middle-class fantasies, the same complex and culturally loaded attitudes to nature and history. Like their painted counterparts, they incorporated finely crafted detail, wild nature and Romantic fantasy. They were cultivated as a form of escapism.

Gertrude Jekyll was the antithesis of Jane Morris. She was practical, energetic, articulate and plain. When William Nicholson came to paint her portrait he was left with her old gardening boots, while she, too busy to be immortalized in paint, got on with the business of running a garden. Jekyll was a beacon for every practical and motivated woman in an age when paid employment, for a married woman of means, was socially unacceptable. She belonged to the artistic middle classes that Jane Morris joined by her marriage, but Jekyll could claim 'armorial' status and her childhood had been cushioned by wealth; moreover she benefited from the stimulus of exceptionally progressive and educated parents. She was given a professional training as a painter at the School of Art attached to the South Kensington Museum, and she moved in the same social circles as John Ruskin, Florence Nightingale and George Eliot. Jekyll was only four years younger than Jane Morris and the two women shared a keen interest in embroidery. It is tempting to imagine that they may have met when Jekyll visited William Morris at Red Lion Square in 1869, but while William Morris and Gertrude Jekyll shared an enthusiasm for practical investigation into traditional crafts, a painter's eye for design and an energetic determination to restore and preserve the old barns and farmhouses of rural England, it is more difficult to imagine common ground between Jekyll and Jane Morris.

Jekyll was to provide the linchpin in the styling of the Arts and Crafts garden. In addition to her genius as a designer she established, both in practice and in principle, a role for women as garden makers and designers. She gentrified gardening into an aesthetic art and her work as a writer for *The Garden* magazine from 1875, and from the 1890s as an author of gardening books, encouraged women to take an active role in the garden, both as professional designers and as amateur practitioners. Jekyll was as influential in North America as in England. She inspired American women in their pursuit of careers as garden writers and as professional garden designers. As Mac Griswold has pointed out, in America: 'Every single book written after the turn of the century pays homage to English garden designer and writer Gertrude Jekyll.'[10]

Men as well as women were encouraged to become involved in the physical business of gardening towards the end of the nineteenth century, as outdoor pursuits – the healthy constitutional or the highly fashionable bicycle ride – became increasingly popular. The modern country cottage was invariably equipped with a tennis lawn or a bowling green in addition to the tea lawn and the flower garden. In its most complete form the Arts and Crafts garden could accommodate the enthusiastic amateur, the aspiring professional and the garden aesthete with a refined appreciation of artistic planting principles. It was laid out with the modest dignity and sense of place that Ruskin had implored his followers to adopt. The cottage-style planting of native annuals and old-fashioned flowers was revived and mixed with a discerning selection of the hardier imports that had been introduced by Victorian horticulturists. In its provision of sheltered terraces and scented arbours, and in the orientation of house and garden to maximize a spectacular view, it encouraged a quasi-religious contemplation of nature. The organization of the garden into a sequence of outdoor rooms, of secluded and open spaces, made it equally perfect as a quiet space in which to read Gertrude Jekyll's latest book, and as a meeting place for the newly established garden clubs that, in North America and England, were to provide amateur women gardeners with a national forum for their gardening ambitions and achievements.

Footnotes

1 Letter from Kate Greenaway to John Ruskin, 16 September 1898, quoted in M.H. Spielmann and G.S. Layard, *Kate Greenaway*, Benjamin Blom, New York/London, 1905; reissued 1968, pp.234–5.
2 John Ruskin, *The Seven Lamps of Architecture,* first published by George Allen, London, 1908 edition, p.327.
3 Ibid., p.329.
4 John Ruskin, 'The Poetry of Architecture', *The Architectural Magazine*, 1837–8; reprinted in E.T. Cook and A. Wedderbury, *The Works of Ruskin,* 1903, Vol.1, pp.156–7.
5 Ibid., p.157.
6 William Morris, introduction to Kelmscott Press edition of 'The Nature of Gothic', 1892.
7 John Ruskin, *The Seven Lamps of Architecture*, 1908 edition, p.337.
8 'Houses for people with hobbies. Walnut-Tree Farm, Castlemorten.', *Country Life*, 28 October 1899, p.525.
9 William Morris, 'Some hints on pattern-designing. A lecture delivered at the Working Men's College, London, on December 10, 1881.', *Lectures on Art and Industry,* p.176
10 Mac Griswold and Eleanor Weller, *The Golden Age of American Gardens*, Abrams, New York, 1991, p.17.

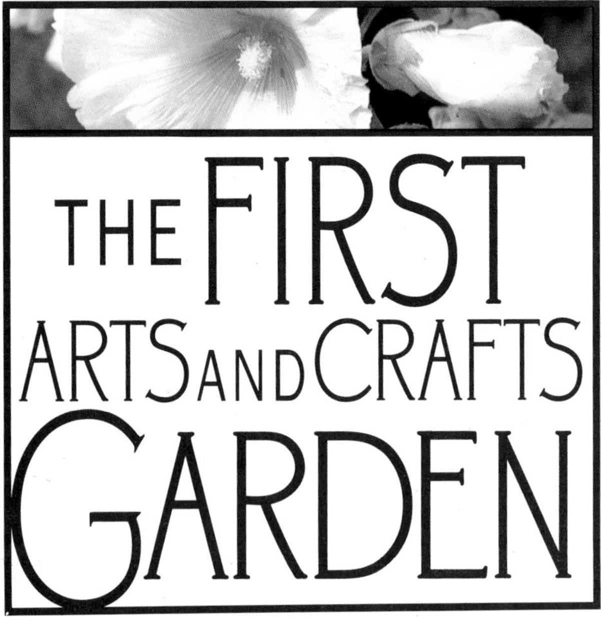

CHAPTER TWO

THE FIRST ARTS AND CRAFTS GARDEN

William Morris is famous for an extraordinary range of talents and achievements. He was an artist-craftsman whose decorating company, Morris & Co., was one of the most fashionable and influential design businesses in England in the last quarter of the nineteenth century. Many of his designs for wallpapers and fabrics are still in production today. His practical philosophy that the artist should be a maker – that it was through the physical process of dyeing or weaving fabric, or of typesetting print, that the designer could evolve a complete understanding of his art – has become ensconced in design education. Morris was a pioneering socialist, a passionate conservationist and one of the most highly regarded

RIGHT: *Red House and its garden set in an old Kent orchard, designed for William Morris by Philip Webb in 1859.*

poets of his generation. It is hardly surprising, given this brilliance and diversity, that his importance as a garden maker has been overshadowed. His influence in creating and promoting a new simplicity in garden design, nevertheless, went hand in hand with the reforming Morris & Co. interiors that swept through the fashionable households of Britain.

The first Arts and Crafts garden was made as part of a private manifesto, before the term 'Arts and Crafts' had ever been coined. It was designed in 1859 by Morris with his friend and former colleague Philip Webb as part of Red House, which was to be the country home of Morris and his new bride. Webb (1831–1915) was to become one of the most revered and influential architects of the Arts and Crafts movement. When Morris first met him he was the senior clerk in the architectural office of G.E. Street, where Morris had articled himself, straight from Oxford at the age of twenty-one, as a young apprentice to train to become an architect. Webb was given the task of supervising Morris's work and later in a letter he gave a graphic description of Morris having laid claim to him 'in the chase of his early life' just as though he had branded him, like a sheep, with the letter M.[1]

Morris and Webb were very different in character. Where Morris was brimming with physical energy and enthusiasm (Webb remembered him striding around the office, 'thumping his head resounding blows with both fists and muttering over some silly snatch of rhyme'),[2] Webb was introverted, intensely intellectual in his approach to architecture and vehemently opposed to any form of self-promotion. Morris's appreciation of architecture was intuitive, whereas Webb's was meticulously researched and considered. Morris had already abandoned a vocation for the Church by the time he met Webb and was soon to give up architecture to train as a painter under the influence of Rossetti. Webb, on the other hand, committed his entire career to a resolute pursuit of architecture. As opposites, the two men were perfectly complementary and they shared a profound admiration for Gothic architecture.

Morris was twenty-five when he invited Webb to design Red House at Bexleyheath on the edge of Kent; the commission enabled Webb to leave Street's office and set up in independent practice. The house and its garden were first envisaged during a bachelors' boating holiday in France in the summer of 1858, a few months after Morris's engagement to be married, and for both Morris and Webb Red House represented a chance to take a visionary ideal and build it. For Webb it was a long-awaited opportunity to focus and express his carefully formulated architectural ideals. For Morris there was a liberal dose of defiance mixed in with the idealism that conceived Red House. He was the eldest son of a wealthy middle-class family. His father had died while he was a schoolboy, leaving the family, in his own words, 'very well off, rich in fact' and there would have been considerable pressure on him to make a good marriage and conform to the social conventions of his parents' generation. By proposing to the daughter of a stable hand he struck a sharp blow to his mother's best intentions, and by rejecting the extravagant mansion style of his family home to commission an artistic cottage in the country where he and his friends could live in Bohemian simplicity, he dealt her another.

Red House established the foundations of the Arts and Crafts movement. When Morris commissioned it he was still undecided about the course of his career; as the critic Hermann Muthesius noted in 1904:

'Building this house was immensely important to him for through it he discovered his true mission in life. As he set about furnishing the interior according to his ideas, he found that ... he had to create every element afresh and he began to see ever more clearly that his life's work must be to re-organise the domestic interior.'[3]

Morris called on his friends the painters Edward Burne-Jones and Dante Gabriel Rossetti, as well as Philip Webb, to help him furnish and decorate the house. Georgiana Burne-Jones, the wife of the painter, later recalled the weekends in the country, when time spent painting, embroidering or decorating the house was interspersed with excursions into the countryside and games of bowls played on the lawn:

'O the joy of those Saturdays to Mondays at Red House, the getting out at Abbey Wood Station ... and then the scrambling swinging drive of three miles or so to the house; and the beautiful roomy place where we seemed to be coming home ... it was a country place then and we were met with this fresh air full of sweet smells.'4

The site for the Red House was an existing orchard, amid 'the rose-hung lanes of woody Kent'. It was not the Morrises' only home; they retained apartments in Bloomsbury. By the turn of the century, however, it was recognized throughout Europe as the first modern country cottage 'to claim artistic and individual quality'.[5] It established a set of principles that were to cut a swathe through Victorian ostentation. Hermann Muthesius, describing the English Arts and Crafts movement to his fellow Germans, was intensely enthusiastic about it: 'It is the first private house of the new artistic culture, the first house to be conceived and built as a unified whole inside and out, the very first example in the history of the modern house.'[6] The two factors, according to Muthesius, that made it 'highly important in the history of art' were the 'revolutionary' interiors, designed by Morris and his friends, and the fact that the house, its garden and its interiors were designed as a single entity.

The house and its garden were planned together and it is probable that Morris influenced Webb's decisions while the plans and elevations were being drawn up. The architect W.R. Lethaby, who knew both men, wrote in his biography of Webb that 'the early work of Webb and Morris was so interwoven that we cannot tell in some instances where the work of one man began and the work of another finished.' Plant names were pencilled on to Webb's elevation drawings of April 1859: white jasmine and roses were to be grown between the dining-room windows, which faced west in defiance of the English convention that 'the only sunlight that is welcome in the dining-room is that of the morning sun at breakfast', and their scent would have drifted up to the drawing-room bay windows on the floor above. Farther along, passion-flowers were planned around the pantry window. Red House wraps around its garden, partially enclosing it within an L-shaped plan, and a succession of projecting bays, gable ends and deep sheltering roofs give the building a craggy organic quality as though it has evolved out of the landscape. 'The only thing you saw from a distance', according to a contemporary writer, 'was an immense red-tiled, steep and high roof.' The hand-made clay roof tiles, together with the red brick of the walls, which gave the house its name, were directly related to the heavy clay soil of the site, although Red House is not built of local bricks and tiles (they were probably made in Berkshire).

Both Webb and Morris were preoccupied with the idea of interlocking the house with its landscape, using local materials and vernacular building traditions. Morris's biographer Fiona MacCarthy asserts that 'Morris had a sense of place so acute as to be almost a disability. Places clung to him.'[7] Webb's architectural practice was founded on a determination to preserve and regenerate the craftsmanship and traditions of English building. For each commission he would trawl the local villages, seeking out the tumbledown cottages and centuries-old farmhouses and churches. He would sit down with the old masons and persuade them to tell him all they knew about the old way of building: the structural traits; the quarries, brick kilns and forest sources for local materials; and the decorative flourishes that distinguished one craftsman's work from another. Then he would lock himself away in his office and make a series of drawings that would itemize every detail of a new building. The local traditions were preserved and revitalized, giving the new building a sense of place and of history, but they were worked into a rational composition that was a unique blend of historical observation and contemporary innovation.

Red House has a rough-edged idealism. It sparkles with a bright, sharp determination to forge a new harmony between man and nature, and to bring art into every detail of domestic life. The house and its garden were inseparable ideologically, as a fusion of art and nature. In addition to the artistic and philosophical principles implicit in designing the house and its garden as a single entity was the fact that the house and its garden were to be *used* as a single entity. The clear divisions between house and garden that prevailed in traditional Victorian houses were chiselled away at Red House and in their place the idea of the garden as an idyllic outdoor extension to the house – a place where the artistic spirit could draw inspiration from wild nature – began to emerge. Georgiana Burne-Jones remembered the house as a place where city routines and conventions were abandoned. The women wore medieval-style gowns in rich 'art colours' without the restrictive and artificial shaping of Victorian underwear. Georgiana's more conventional sister Agnes complained that the Red House doors were too narrow for her to pass through wearing her crinolines.[8]

In the mornings the women would sit upstairs in the drawing-room bay, looking out over the orchard while they worked at their wood engraving and embroidery. On fine days they might work, sheltered from the wind, at the red-painted table in The Pilgrim's Rest, a south-facing porch named by Morris in homage to the course of the Chaucerian route of the Canterbury pilgrims through Bexleyheath. In the afternoons they would take a map of Kent and go out exploring. This seems tame enough by today's standards, but the locals of Bexleyheath regarded the artistic community at Red House, with their wild hair and peculiar clothes, out for a jaunt in the Morris's cart festooned with brightly coloured hangings, with a mixture of horror and amusement. May Morris recalled that the locals looked upon them as though 'they were the advance guard of a travelling show' and one local autocrat spread the story that she 'had heard, and felt sure it must be true, that Mrs Morris had been in a circus; no one could ride and manage a horse so beautifully but a performer.'[9]

The garden at Red House is an enigmatic mixture of known facts and reasoned probabilities. We know that Morris's expertise as a practical gardener was considered exceptional in his own time:

Right: *The L-shape plan of the house shelters a well court, originally enclosed by trellis covered with roses.*

'Morris's knowledge of architecture was so entirely a part of himself that he never seemed to think about it as anything peculiar. But in his knowledge of gardening, he did, and did with reason pride himself ... of flowers and vegetables and fruit trees he knew all the ways and capabilities.'[10]

The garden was laid out and planted while Red House was being constructed, so that they literally grew up together. There are no separate planting plans for the garden (although elements of the garden appear on the plans and elevations for the house). There are clear indications, however, that it was Morris, rather than Webb, who defined the shape and character of the garden. Morris had already described his ideal of a medieval garden in his *Story of an Unknown Church* published in 1856:

'At the edge of the lawn, near the round arches, were a great many sunflowers that were all in blossom on that autumn day; and up many of the pillars of the cloister crept passion-flowers and roses ... in the garden were trellises covered over with roses, and convolvulus, and the great leaved fiery nasturtium.'[11]

When the garden at Red House was described it was Morris's 'ideals of gardening', his fondness for 'roses and trellises, hollyhocks, great spires of pink, orange, red and white, with their soft, downy leaves' and his passion for 'many sunflowers' that were listed.[12] No mention was made of Webb's favourite flowers. Webb's later practice, nevertheless, and his drawings for the garden fence and gate, suggest that he was closely involved in planning the garden.

There was a formal garden on the north side of the house, described by W.R. Lethaby as 'the first of the modern square-plot and trained hedge type, which is now well known'.[13] Within the large square, as Georgiana Burne-Jones described, were 'four little square gardens making a big square together, each of the smaller squares having a wattle fence round it, with roses growing thickly'. A series of openings led from one garden to the next. According to a contemporary who knew the garden in 1863, it was 'divided into many squares, hedged by sweetbriar or wild rose, each enclosure with its own particular show of flowers'. The model of a medieval garden, divided into a sequence of semi-enclosed spaces, was consistent with the medievalism of a brotherhood of artists, living and working together in harmony with nature. The unusual effect was described as 'vividly picturesque and uniquely original'.[14]

The orchard, characteristic of the Kent landscape, that had covered the site before Morris arrived was retained over the main area of the garden so that there would be blossom in spring, fruit in the autumn and 'orchard walks amid gnarled old fruit-trees'. The trees were widely spaced, arranged in long parallel lines, giving the garden a simple structure with straight gravel paths and long grass walks between flower beds bordered by lavender and rosemary.[15] On the west side of the house there was a lawn where Morris and his

RIGHT: *Hollyhocks growing in 'great spires of pink, orange, red and white, with their soft downy leaves' were among Morris's favourite flowers.*

friends played bowls and from within the garden the friends could look out across the open fields and orchards of Kent. The boundary on to Red House Lane, however, was defined by a high red-brick wall, partly to protect the friends from the gaze of curious passers-by, but also to draw a line between Morris's home-made Utopia and the rest of the world.

The combination of a formal structure, derived from medieval sources, and the orchard areas, adapted into a garden setting and filled with the old-fashioned fruit trees and flowers of a half-imagined rural England, established the ground rules for the Arts and Crafts garden more than a decade before William Robinson published *The Wild Garden,* and thirty years before Gertrude Jekyll defined the style in her writing and her garden designs. In the summer the garden was filled with the scent of lilies and in the autumn there was a profusion of the sunflowers that were soon to become a symbol of the Aesthetic movement, lovingly described by Edward Burne-Jones: 'Do you know what faces they have – how they peep and peer, and look arch and winning, or bold and a little insolent sometimes? Have you ever noticed their back-hair, how beautifully curled it is?'[16] The garden became an inspiration for paintings, drawings and decorative designs; Georgiana recalled how one morning Edward Burne-Jones arrived at breakfast with a drawing of a poppy that he had made at dawn. William Morris's notebooks from the Red House years are peppered with studies of simple flowers and foliage that must surely have been taken from the garden and the plants he had chosen for his garden began to appear in his designs for wallpapers and fabrics.

A well court was originally framed by a wooden trellis facing south and east and covered with climbing roses. A long run of trellis connected the court to the enclosed gardens at the front of the house, contributing to the intrigue of a sequence of scented and half-mysterious outdoor spaces. Morris's first wallpaper design, 'Trellis', designed in 1862 as the garden grew to maturity, was inspired by the well court. Lethaby recalled that 'The idea was probably taken from the hedges of roses on wattlework at the Red House and that it was Webb who drew the birds on to the design. Within a few years the jasmine and honeysuckle that covered the walls of the house had inspired designs for fabrics and wallpapers. Morris was inspired by medieval manuscripts and embroideries, however, as well as by flowers in his garden. The design for his 'Daisy' paper was prompted by a Froissart manuscript in the British Museum, and one wonders how much of his planting and the wooden structures (which have disappeared) were also a response to medieval sources. For Morris the model of wild nature, encouraged and structured by the designer, was a vital source of inspiration whether he was writing poetry or weaving a carpet. His affection for cottage-garden flowers, massed together, and his preference for a clear, uncomplicated framework were translated into the design of embroidered hangings for Red House and later, when he lectured on pattern designing, he advised his fellow craftsmen: 'I must have unmistakable suggestions of gardens and fields, and strange trees, boughs and tendrils, or I can't do with your pattern.' He urged his audience to remember that when designing for embroidery, 'we are gardening with silk and gold-thread.'[17]

The principle of painters, designers, craftsmen and decorators working together, established at Red House in a spirit of spontaneity and friendship, was to become one of the ideals of the Arts and Crafts movement. The experience of decorating and furnishing the house gave

Above: *Morris's first wallpaper pattern 'Trellis' of 1862 was inspired by the rose trellises at Red House. Philip Webb drew the birds onto the design.*

Morris and his friends the confidence to found the decorating firm of Morris, Marshall, Faulkner and Co. (which became Morris & Co. in 1875). As Aymer Vallance put it: 'what he began by doing then on a small scale, was destined to engage him from that time forward for the remainder of his life.'[18] The daisies and lilies in the Red House garden, together with the blend of precision and naïve simplicity that Morris adapted from Jacobean embroideries and manuscripts, were used as ingenuous motifs in a concerted attack on the 'horrors' of Victorian domestic design:

> 'the crochet antimacassars upon horse-hair sofas; the wax flowers under glass shades; the monstrosities in stamped brass and gilded stucco; chairs, tables, and other furniture hideous with veneer and curly distortions; the would-be naturalistic vegetable-patterned carpets with false shadows and misplaced perspective; and all the despicable legion of mean shams and vulgarities which have been exposed.'[19]

Morris remained at Red House for nearly six years. His two daughters Jenny and May were born there and there were plans to build separate living quarters for the Burne-Joneses, so that the youthful ideal of a brotherhood of artists living and working together in the countryside could be secured as a tangible fact for the future. Eventually, financial difficulties meant that the dream had to be relinquished. The extension was never built, Red House was sold and the Morrises moved back to London. The garden at Red House, nevertheless, and its intricate relationship with the house, remained a fundamental influence on the Arts and Crafts movement. It was important because it took a medieval ideal and translated it into garden design. It was liberated and artistic in its planting, rediscovering the charm and simplicity of old English flowers. At the same time, it revived elements of English Tudor garden planning at a time when there was a growing interest in Gothic architecture but little understanding of the structure and planting of historic gardens.

There were no direct links between the principal rooms at Red House and its garden. The French windows and sunny verandas that connected later Arts and Crafts drawing-rooms with their terraces would have been alien to Webb's Gothic sensibility. The two porches, facing north at the front of the house and south over the well court at the rear, offered sheltered, intimate spaces at the interface between inside and out, but they were more akin to parish-church porches than to garden rooms. The idea of a house wrapping around its garden, however, and of fragrant climbers designed from the outset to scramble over the building's walls, set Red House apart. Morris's definition of a garden that crystallized around the tranquillity and nostalgia of an old Kent orchard and his choice of semi-wild shrubs and flowers, extracted from the stanzas of English poetry rather than the lists of fashionable garden plants, was both creative and provocative.

Although Morris's stay at Red House was relatively short-lived, its importance as a model of innovative and enlightened design continued long after his departure. The house was subsequently owned by Charles Holme, who became editor of the influential art and design magazine *The Studio* and it must have been visited by many of the writers and artists who featured in the magazine. The garden was maintained without significant alterations, partly because it was easy to manage, but also because it represented a coherent part of an entire philosophy. Morris, Burne-Jones and Rossetti went on to make other country gardens in Oxfordshire and Sussex. The lilies, fruit trees and wild flowers of Red House were perpetuated in the stained-glass windows and tapestries of Morris

& Co. They detailed the foregrounds of Burne-Jones's painted medieval legends and Rossetti's portraits of Jane Morris. Perhaps most importantly, printed on the fabrics and wallpapers manufactured by Morris & Co., they entered the homes of the fashion-conscious middle classes. It was only a matter of time before the vogue for simple indigenous flowers and medieval principles spread to the middle-class garden.

RIGHT: *The west face of Red House with its projecting drawing-room bay, viewed from the orchard.*

Footnotes

1 Letter from Philip Webb to May Morris, 7 July 1898, British Museum.
2 W.R. Lethaby, *Philip Webb and his Work*, Oxford University Press, 1935.
3 Hermann Muthesius, *Das Englische Haus*, first published by Wasmuth, Berlin, 1904–5; translated into English by Crosby Lockwood Staples, 1979, p.17.
4 Georgiana Burne-Jones, *Memorials of Edward Burne-Jones*, 2 vols., Macmillan & Co., London, 1904.
5 Hermann Muthesius, op. cit, p.124.
6 Ibid, p.17.
7 Fiona MacCarthy, *William Morris, A Life for Our Time*, Faber and Faber, London, 1994, p.viii.
8 Ibid., p.164.
9 Laura Hain Friswell, *In the Sixties and Seventies*, Hutchinson & Co., London, 1906, p.269.
10 J.W. Mackail, *The Life of William Morris,* Longmans, London, 1899, p.143.
11 William Morris, 'Story of an Unknown Church', *Oxford and Cambridge Magazine*, 1856. Also published in *Works* (1910–14), Vol.i, p.151. It is interesting that in Morris's perception the medieval garden was stocked with exotics.
12 W.R. Lethaby, *Philip Webb and his Work*, Oxford University Press, 1935, p.28.
13 Ibid, p.28
14 Quoted in Aymer Vallance, *William Morris. His art, his writings and his public life.,* George Bell and Sons, London, 1897, p.49.
15 A photograph of the garden, captioned 'orginally laid out by William Morris', was published in *The Studio*, Vol. 21, 1901, p.35.
16 Georgiana Burne Jones, op. cit.
17 William Morris, 'Some hints on pattern-designing. A lecture delivered at the Working Men's College, London, on December 10, 1881.' *Lectures on Art and Industry,* pp.195-7.
18 Aymer Vallance, op. cit, p.55.
19 Ibid, p.55.

CHAPTER THREE

OLD-FASHIONED GARDENS

The architectural lineage for the Arts and Crafts garden can be traced with clarity. The basis for an Arts and Crafts style of planting, however, and the formation of a receptive market for the movement had more to do with fashion and the influence of famous personalities – artists, actresses and writers – than with erudite architectural theories. The remains of seventeenth-century and earlier gardens were 'discovered' and studied by painters. They became part of an imaginative re-creation of the ancient garden and a vocabulary of images evolved that owed as much to contemporary taste and desires as to historical analysis. Sometimes, as at Hardwick Hall, an old-fashioned garden was reinvented as the setting for a period

RIGHT: *The seventeenth-century plan and topiary bones of Brickwall, romantically planted with more ephemeral annuals and perennials. Painted by George Samuel Elgood in 1911.*

George S. Elgood

building. The idea of the old-fashioned garden was never defined or prescribed, however. The box standards in Kate Greenaway's book illustrations were old-fashioned, as were the briar roses that she admired in the paintings of Edward Burne-Jones. In the 1860s old-fashioned gardens were the domain of an artistic elite associated with the Aesthetic movement. They established and popularized a romantic approach to planting that was later adapted, within an architectural framework, in the Arts and Crafts garden.

Oscar Wilde epitomized in a single gesture (and a single outfit) the position of the Aesthetic movement in England when he walked the length of Regent Street in London wearing a green velvet suit and carrying a lily in worshipful reverence for the actress Ellen Terry. Aesthetes were delicate, artistic people. The men were dandies and the women affected the medieval-style gowns and intensely wistful expressions that they admired in the paintings of Dante Gabriel Rossetti and Burne-Jones. They were celebrated, and at the same time parodied, in Gilbert and Sullivan's *Patience*, first produced in 1881, and they frequented the pages of *Punch* in the satirical cartoons of George du Maurier. They were irrelevant to the history of garden design as practical gardeners – they would have found themselves quite unable to look at a garden spade, still less pick one up. Their importance lay in their ability, as influential clients, to translate painted and literary gardens into real ones.

At the 'greenery-yallery, Grosvenor Gallery' in Bond Street Aesthetes would gather on opening nights to catch a glimpse of William and Jane Morris, or in the hope that they might overhear a snatch of conversation between the American painter James McNeill Whistler (1834–1903) and his fashionable architect Edward Godwin (1833–86). If the Aesthetic movement had any heart at all it was on display at the Grosvenor Gallery, founded in 1877 to counterbalance the Royal Academy's failure to give adequate exposure to the most important paintings of the day (according to the Aesthetes), those of the Pre-Raphaelites. Aesthetes were hungry for 'cultchah', but they relied upon the guidance of fashionable artists and progressive entrepreneurs to show them exactly how and where they might purchase it. They shopped at Liberty in Regent Street, ordered their interiors from Morris & Co., adored the popular actress Sarah Bernhardt (and restyled their hair in imitation of her hazy fringe), and collected blue and white porcelain from Japan with passionate determination. One of du Maurier's sharpest cartoons depicts a young couple enraptured by a blue and white teapot, announcing their solemn intention to 'live up to it', and the leading lady in a popular play of the period expressed the same sentiment to the delight of the audience: 'There is so much to be learned from a tea-pot.'[1]

Artistic ideas quickly progressed from painting to the theatre, from the theatre to the high street, and from the high street to the Aesthetic house and garden. The main arbiters of taste all knew one another, and many of them were close friends or arch rivals. One of the most influential and socially sought-after painters of the 1870s was the American James McNeill Whistler who, arriving in London from Paris, introduced the cult of the Japanese print to British artistic circles. He became a friend of Arthur Liberty, whose Regent Street store, established in 1875, sold some of the most exotic Japanese treasures to be found in London. When D'Oyly Carte began preparations for the production of Gilbert and Sullivan's new opera, *The Mikado*, in 1885, Liberty was commissioned to supply the fabrics for the costumes and the stage sets, and its buyers were despatched to Japan to make a detailed study of the patterns and materials of traditional Japanese dress. It was only a matter of months before Liberty was advertising its 'Art Fabrics' made up into kimonos and sketched on to characters from *The Mikado* and Ellen Terry was dressing her children fashionably in miniature silk kimonos.

If the Aesthete's personal wardrobe was of paramount importance, the artistic condition of his or her house and garden was only marginally less portentous as a subject for soulful introspection or audacious display. Just as the soft flowing gowns of the women in Pre-Raphaelite paintings and the theatrical Japanese costumes of *The Mikado* had a profound influence on the wardrobes of progressive young women, the painted gardens of Rossetti, Burne-Jones and other Victorian artists became the inspiration for old-fashioned gardens, artistically dishevelled and suggestive of half-forgotten, half-imagined, medieval origins. Painting and poetry were closely linked in the mid-nineteenth century. Paintings often depicted specific scenes from Tennyson and the fashion for Arthurian tales in literature stimulated visual responses to the poetic evocations of romantic old English gardens. Often Victorian painters depicted their medieval scenes against a backdrop of wild flowers and forests, but as early as 1854 Arthur Hughes had painted his *Fair Rosamund* in a garden of old roses and herbaceous perennials massed within the confines of low box-hedged borders.

The quest for a poetic English garden untouched by the vulgarity and worldly display of Victorian design coincided with a determination among architects that the tumbledown cottages and barns of rural England should be recorded and preserved; that the traditional old building methods and materials that had gone into making them should be revitalized and properly understood as the craft of building; and that the simple lines and wholesome domesticity of these buildings should be celebrated in a revival of English domestic architecture that would expose and disgrace the shams and excesses of Victorian building. One of the earliest and most enthusiastic experts on rural domestic architecture was George Devey, who restored the Tudor and Jacobean house of Brickwall in East Sussex in the mid-nineteenth century. Little more than a decade later Rossetti, while exploring the Sussex countryside, found the remains of its seventeenth-century garden and was so enchanted by it that he arranged to have it photographed. Rossetti used photography to record his models, and so the fact that he went to the trouble of having photographs made of the garden at Brickwall suggests that he intended to use it as a source either for his paintings or for designing his own gardens.

Fortunately for Rossetti, Brickwall had suffered a century of neglect. Its owners, the Frewen family, preferred their estates in Yorkshire and Leicestershire and from the mid-eighteenth century Brickwall was retained, like an old treasure in the attic, as a rather fusty and unfashionable adjunct to the family's more prestigious effects. It had escaped the Victorian passions for exotic species and orderly and brightly coloured beds, just as it had been spared the eighteenth-century enthusiasm for the Picturesque that had devastated knot and topiary gardens throughout Britain. When Rossetti found it the garden at Brickwall had been tidied up and set in order by Devey, but its seventeenth-century bones and the last vestiges of its fine topiary were still in evidence. He might have seen it as a sleeping beauty: romantically abandoned, a little wild and overgrown in places, and shimmering with the possibility of redemption. Barely beneath the surface the lines of a formal structure were clearly in evidence: there were topiary cones and pyramids, long straight paths passing beneath arches of yew, and the spaces were separated by long yew hedges and pleached beech. There was a walled garden and a bowling green. Although Brickwall was not medieval it was the nearest thing to an ancient garden that a Victorian painter could hope to find.

One of the most impressive things about the garden was its evident longevity. Topiary cannot be shaped in a season and the original yew topiary at Brickwall was among the earliest in Britain. John Evelyn claimed to have introduced the fashion for yew, writing in 1676 that it should be substituted for cypress

'whether in hedges or pyramids, conic spires, bowls, or what other shapes; adorning the parks or larger avenues with their lofty tops, thirty feet high, and braving all the effects of the most rigid winter which cypress cannot weather.'

The house and garden at Brickwall were refurbished a few years later, in 1685, after Thomas Frewen was rewarded for services to James II. Although much of the seventeenth-century yew topiary may well have been replaced before Rossetti's arrival, the pieces that remained would have had a ponderous grandeur. Their scale alone would have testified to the age of the garden and, by implication, to the fact that the family's history and its association with royalty could be traced back over two centuries.

Brickwall was celebrated as a rare example of a Tudor and Jacobean timber-framed house still set within the sympathetic framework of a formal seventeenth-century garden. As the aesthetic middle classes moved in increasing numbers to newly commissioned 'Olde English' houses in the country, with half-timbered gables and towering Tudor-style chimneys, the garden at Brickwall became a model for the period element in their gardens. It revived the old controversy over topiary (even Evelyn, having introduced yew, had argued that 'everyone who has the least pretension to taste must always prefer a tree in its natural growth to those monstrous figures'). Like the Japanese models for *The Mikado,* it established a degree of historical authenticity so that the first garden historians, purists who wanted evidence and accuracy in the reconstruction of a period garden, could study its topiary forms and measure the simple geometric elements of its formal plan. For Aesthetes, however, for whom historical accuracy was always less important than style, Brickwall was at its most perfect in a slightly dilapidated state.

The delicate balance between order and chaos – the ideal of a historical structure half-concealed beneath layers of wayward growth – appealed to the Aesthetic sensibility far more than the prospect of restoring the crisp straight paths of Brickwall, or of trimming its box-bordered beds meticulously back into shape. Aesthetes wanted old-fashioned gardens with a dash of medievalism mixed in. They wanted topiary beasts and rampant roses. They wanted a garden that looked as though it had been around for a century or two, that could be left to look after itself, and most of all they wanted it straight away. After his visit to Brickwall Rossetti found an old topiary armchair in a Sussex cottage garden. Unable to transport the entire garden back to his house in Chelsea (this was before the wonders of the Chelsea Flower Show), Rossetti consoled himself with buying the armchair on its own. He had its ancient roots dug up and the whole chair carted to Cheyne Walk in London – where shortly after it was planted it began to die.

ABOVE: *Lady Louisa Egerton's 'old-fashioned' garden, invented to complement the Elizabethan Hardwick Hall. Painted by George Samuel Elgood in 1897.*

Hardwick Hall in Derbyshire is one of the finest Elizabethan buildings in Britain. In the mid-nineteenth century, however, the garden had kept pace with prevailing fashions, so that the fine stone front of the house looked out over a brightly coloured bedding scheme. Hardwick had been built for a woman, 'Bess of Hardwick', the Countess of Shrewsbury, and there was a tradition that the lady of the manor should determine the nature of the garden. The parterre was laid out in 1832, to the instructions of Lady Blanche Howard, patterned around Bess of Hardwick's monogram. The remainder of the eight-acre garden was rearranged just over thirty years later by Lady Louisa Egerton. Lady Louisa was ahead of fashion. She used the surviving Elizabethan walled enclosure together with the flat topography of the grounds around the house to design an old-fashioned garden so convincing that Sir Reginald Blomfield and Inigo Thomas in *The Formal Garden in England* mistook it for an original less than twenty-five years after it was laid out.

The garden was described in the *Journal of Horticulture* when its new hedges were beginning to fill out in 1875:

'It is divided into four parts by avenues of Yew and Hornbeam hedges running north and south and east and west, the grass walks between them being 20 feet wide and in excellent condition. The first part contains the croquet ground, surrounded by fine evergreens and conifers ... The second part, which is in close proximity to the house, is a fruit orchard, and Apples, Pears, and Plums are well presented. The third is chiefly taken up with Filberts and other fruit trees; the fourth is entirely devoted to vegetables.'

The idea of dividing a garden into separate enclosures and treating each one differently was essentially medieval. Lady Louisa's design was exceptional because she gave equal weight to the croquet lawn on one side and the vegetable patch on the other. Within the formal structure over half the garden was given over to producing fruit, nuts and vegetables, and the flowers and vegetables were mixed in together, in cottage-garden style.

The formality of Lady Louisa's garden increased as the hedges grew taller. They were shaped into niches to frame life-size lead figures, giving the garden a classical aspect, and the separate rectangles were connected through arched openings. Viewed from the grass walks or the *rond-point* at their intersection, the garden was an emphatically classical statement. Around the Elizabethan perimeter walls, however, deep borders were densely planted with herbaceous perennials, and rambling roses and clematis scrambled over the old stone walls with an exuberance that contradicted the orderly structure. The combination was so successful that it satisfied classicists and Romantics alike, ensuring the survival of the garden in this form (it is now owned by the National Trust). Blomfield wrote enthusiastically about the fine lead statues, each representing a muse. The Edwardian artist George Samuel Elgood captured the formal and the romantic elements of Hardwick in two separate paintings that convey the grand scale as well as the dual nature of the garden, and Hardwick is particularly important to the development of the Arts and Crafts garden because of its largess. It combined an Aesthetic pleasure in formal structures and abundant planting with an aristocratic talent for planning on a grand scale. The old-fashioned garden came of age at Hardwick Hall, gathering respectability as well as grandeur, without altogether relinquishing its Bohemian origins.

If Lady Louisa groomed the old-fashioned garden to a refined gentility, Kate Greenaway styled it with a 'Katish' twist into an essential fashion accessory. Greenaway (1846–1901) was one of the most popular and influential artists of her generation. Her earliest recorded childhood memories were of idyllic rural life in Rolleston, Nottinghamshire, where she was 'put out to nurse' for a year or two when her mother was suddenly taken ill. Her biography, written in 1905 in sugary-sweet style, glosses over any painful aspects of this experience and Greenaway's own recollections admit only to 'the happiness inspired by the flowers, with which she struck up friendships that were to last

ABOVE: *From Kate Greenaway's 'Under the Window' 1878.*

to her life's end.'[2] Greenaway had a gift for focusing on details and disregarding everything she did not want to see. It was the wild flowers of the hedgerow and simple cottage flowers that she remembered from her childhood:

'There was the snapdragon, which opened and shut its mouth as she chose to pinch it. This she "loved"; but the pink moss rose, which grew by the dairy window, she "revered". It grew with the gooseberry bushes, the plum tree, and the laburnum in the little three-cornered garden near the road.'

She christened the toadflax 'yellow dragon's-mouth' and the cranesbill 'my little blue flower'. In later years, when she became a professional author and illustrator her intense delight in simple native flowers continued undiminished.

Her first picture books – nursery books, old-fashioned fairy-tales and rhymes – were published in 1871. Because the tales had been passed down from generation to generation, in story-telling tradition, it was fitting that the pictures, too, should have a quality of not quite belonging to any specific period. Greenaway invented a world of childhood peopled by earnest little girls in large bonnets or mop caps and Regency dresses tied with wide sashes. They played quaint little games. Even when they were naughty they were endearing and it is almost impossible to imagine them really making a noise. It was a world that Aesthetic young parents wanted to believe in so much that they set about re-creating it in real life. The tightly fitting velvet suits in which conventional Victorian children were dressed were discarded in favour of the 'frocks and aprons, hats and breeches, funnily neat and prim, in the style of 1800, adding beauty and comfort to natural grace' that Greenaway had devised for her illustrations. As her Christmas cards and books spread across Europe to America her influence on children's dress and behaviour increased:

'for a time she dressed the children of two continents ... An Englishman visiting Jules Breton, in the painter's country-house in Normandy, found all the children in Greenaway costumes; for they alone, declared Breton, fitted children and sunshine'.

Greenaway's influence on garden style was hardly less pervasive. The cottage gardens she remembered from her childhood were popularized in her picture books. The 'gaudiest of the gaudy' nasturtiums planted against bright blue palings that she had 'loved and admired ... beyond words' in her Aunt Thorne's garden (although she had disapproved of the slovenly state of Aunt Thorne's house) were painted into a picture of Cinderella fetching her pumpkin, 'for the delight of thousands'. On the cover of her *Marigold Garden*, published in 1885, three little girls clasping bunches of marigolds hung over a simple wooden gate with the bough of a tree overhead; behind them the order of the garden was indicated by two clipped cones of box or yew. Greenaway's gardens were not true-to-life cottage gardens. Like her children, they were deliberately composed and restrained by a degree of formality. They were often very small, which was part of their appeal, contained within neatly clipped high hedges, with a fruit tree and a few flowers, perfectly positioned. She knew the leading Aesthetic figures of the day and their work, and to some extent her painted gardens were an astute observation of current Aesthetic preoccupations and perhaps of the gardens of some of her artist friends. Her images were never cluttered as real cottage gardens would be. They were concerned with the precise presentation of a very few beautiful things, brought together in a deceptively simple composition. Like the dresses, her gardens made specific period references. Their clarity and charm, however, were essentially 'Katish' inventions.

The importance of Greenaway's influence in artistic circles and in popularizing progressive design has been trivialized, partly because her medium, children's book illustration, is easily disregarded, and partly because she was a woman working in a world of Victorian men. Her friendship with John Ruskin is evidence of her relative importance among Victorian painters, although the success of the relationship was dependent upon her playing the child to Ruskin's patriarchal authority. The friendship developed through their correspondence, which started in January 1880; they did not meet until almost three years later. In March 1884 he wrote to her from Brantwood, his retreat in the Lake District, seeking to influence her love of flowers and describing his own order of preferences:

'I think flowers in *my* order of liking would come nearly like this, Wild rose, Alpine rose, Alpine gentian, White Lily, Purple Flag, Purple convolvulus, Carnation – all the tribe, Pansy, all the tribe, Thistle – all the tribe, Daisy and Hyacinth, Snowdrop and Crocus'.

Wood anemones, apple, almond, hawthorn and cherry blossom were given a 'separate queendom'.

A few months later he suggested that they should do a book on botany together: 'you do the plates and I the text – a hand-book of field botany', but the next year he wrote to tell her they had been pre-empted by 'a perfect primrose of a clergyman'. He encouraged her to take her art more seriously and in July 1884 he wrote:

'it is so *very* joyful news to me that you like doing trees and see them all leaves and are going to do feet and ankles and be so good. There's no saying what wonderful things you may do, all in an instant, when once you've fought your way through the strait gate. And you will have the joy of delighting many more people beside me; and of doing more good than any English artist ever yet did.'

In numerous letters he suggested that the little girls she drew for him should be naked, so that her understanding of anatomy would be improved, but Greenaway declined. She was his confidante in times of depression and she sent him exquisitely illustrated letters, telling how her work was progressing and describing the paintings by Rossetti and Burne-Jones in the latest London exhibitions.

When Greenaway discussed contemporary painting she was always attentive to the details of flowers and foliage: 'I always look with envy at the May-tree Burne-Jones painted in *Merlin and Vivien.*' She described the water-lilies in J.W. Waterhouse's *Hylas and the Water Nymphs* and the campanulas and nasturtiums in Millais's *The Huguenots*. She believed Millais's *Ophelia* to be 'the greatest picture of modern times' and, searching for a definition of 'what art really is', she concluded:

'It's what Burne-Jones does when he twists those roses all about his people in the *Briar Rose*. They don't often grow like that, but they could, and its a great comfort to like such things, at least I find it so.'

Kate Greenaway did not see herself as a feminist. In 1897 she wrote with dismay to her friend Miss Violet Dickinson of the 'strong-minded women' who were going to exhibit in an 'Exhibition of Lady Artists':

'oh what a worm they would think me if I dared write and say my true views, that having been always fairly and justly treated by those odious men that I would far rather exhibit

Above: *'The Briar Wood', Edward Burne-Jones, 1869.*

my things with them and take my true place, which must be lower than so many of theirs. For I fear we can only *hope* to do – what men can do. It is sad but I fear it is so. They *have* more ability.'

Greenaway had a formidable reputation in Europe, where her work was widely imitated and often mistaken for that of a man:

'Kate Greenaway is known on the Continent of Europe along with the very few English artists whose names are familiar to the foreign public – with those of Millais, Leighton, Burne-Jones, Watts, and Walter Crane – being recognised as the great domestic artist'.

A Dutch admirer once sent her a photograph of a good-looking young man with a black moustache, believing it to be a portrait of her, and asked her to autograph it. Greenaway was amused by the incident and wrote back to explain his mistake: 'he feared I was laughing at him, as Kate is a man's name – in Holland.'

Greenaway was successful financially, as well as artistically, and the royalties from her books enabled her to commission one of the most fashionable and highly respected architects of the Aesthetic movement, Richard Norman Shaw (1831–1912), to design a house for her at 39 Frognal in Hampstead, London. When the house was completed, in 1885, Hampstead was almost a country place, surrounded by open fields, although it was rapidly being colonized by artists, writers and designers. An early perspective drawing of the house emphasized its rural qualities, with a flock of sheep trundling along the road towards the front gate. Childish figures loitered in the road outside and Greenaway herself could be seen on the second-floor balcony, pointing out the splendours of the landscape. The house itself was a fine example of Shaw's 'Queen

Anne' style, prettily tile-hung with generous bay windows and prominent chimneys. It was set back from the road within a walled garden, and Greenaway's brother recalled how she used to work in the mornings and spend summer afternoons in the garden 'seeing to her flowers'. The garden was maintained with a vestige of romantic wildness. Greenaway wrote to a friend less than a year after she moved in:

'I've had a deep disappointment to-day. Some one told me of a nice old gardener who wanted a little more work. I thought he would just do for us so I wrote, and when he called, instead of the old man there stood a gorgeous young one in a gorgeous white tie. My heart sank. – He began:
"Path wants gravelling,
Grass wants seeding,
Roses want pruning,
Trees want cutting,
Everything wants rolling,
Everything wants nailing up."
A nice idea! my cherished garden made the exact facsimile of every one in Frognal. I found myself composing the note that should dismiss him later on. Nothing should induce me to consent to such desecration.'

Later she boasted of the size and variety of her weeds, claiming 'our garden has forgotten that it is a garden and is trying to be a field again'. She had a great affection for 'fine tall fresh green thistles and docks spreading out their leaves in lovely curves' reminding her of the docks she used to play with as a child, weighing out their seeds as pretend tea. She told Ruskin that once a plant was in the ground it had to stay there and look after itself: there was to be no digging it up 'to see after its root, or go to another spot for change of air – perseverance does it!' Again in a letter to Ruskin she described her Hampstead garden at its best in June:

'It is very fresh and flowery at this moment. The rain has brought out the flowers. There are roses, white peonies, purple irises, large herbaceous poppies, lupins, syringa, marigolds, foxgloves, delphiniums, and campanulas, and day lilies, and many others. It is the garden's best moment.'

Greenaway's painted gardens and Shaw's Queen Anne houses appealed to the same set of aesthetic, affluent middle-class clients. The artist and the architect both exploited a nostalgia for (and a willingness to invent) a bygone age of grace and enlightenment. Shaw's red-brick houses and Greenaway's simply dressed figures had an air of the country. They side-stepped the dilemmas of scale, convenience, poverty and historical accuracy that the real countryside presented. Historically, the countryside had been the domain of feudal landlords and peasant farmers. Shaw and Greenaway skilfully extracted the most picturesque attributes of both parties to reinvent a rural England of fresh clean cottages and quaint old-fashioned ways that was perfectly adaptable to the simple pleasures of middle-class aesthetic town life.

In 1876 Shaw had begun work on the design of a village of town houses at Bedford Park, which soon acquired a reputation as the artistic quarter of London. They were designed with old-fashioned oriel windows, shady porches and white wooden railings enclosing first-floor balconies. By 1876 the 'many sunflowers' that William Morris had first described in his *Story of an Unknown Church* had come to symbolize the Aesthetic movement. They were modelled into the brickwork of the houses at Bedford Park and planted in profusion in their gardens. The houses were set back behind trim little front gardens, and they differed from their more conventional terraced contemporaries in having generous back gardens in place of the usual yard. The interlocking of house and garden that was later to distinguish the fully fledged Arts and Crafts garden was still undeveloped at Bedford Park, although the garden was gathering momentum as a setting for afternoon tea and for select garden parties. A gardening society vied with the Park's tennis club, amateur dramatic society, musical society, the Ladies' Discussion Society and the Conversazione Club.

Few amateur gardeners achieved the clipped simplicity of Greenaway's painted gardens. However, they were encouraged to believe that the artistic way was not to employ a professional gardener for so small a plot, but to cultivate instead a more Bohemian approach to gardening. In doing so they became consumers of new gardening magazines and books, invariably bringing a knowledge of painted gardens and a keen eye for fashion to a dedicated readership of *The Wild Garden.*

Footnotes

1 Line from *The Colonel*, written by F.C. Burnard, who was editor of *Punch.*

2 M.H. Spielmann and G.S. Layard, *Kate Greenaway*, Benjamin Blom, New York; first published 1905, reissued 1968. This biography is the source for all later quotations in this chapter concerning Greenaway and her correspondence with Ruskin.

CHAPTER FOUR

WILD GARDENING

One of the most pernicious attacks on the Victorian manner of gardening was delivered by an ambitious and fiercely determined young gardener from Ireland, William Robinson, who was thirty-two when he first published *The Wild Garden* in 1870. Unlike many of his detractors, he had already developed a formidable practical knowledge of plants and gardening methods as a gardener's boy and worked his way up through the profession. Robinson was unconventional and irascible in his approach. If he disliked a plant or a popular gardening practice he shot it down with words: 'A not infrequent feature is the ugly, formless pool that no skill can make tolerable. Made without any pretence of grace of outline, it

RIGHT: *Densely planted borders at Gravetye Manor show William Robinson's daring use of colour.*

LEFT: *The garden structures and furniture at Gravetye reflect a taste for simplicity and tradition in architectural matters.*

is a disfigurement, sometimes a danger.' His strong condemnations, delivered like rattles of gunfire, often spontaneously in otherwise uneventful passages of writing, were undoubtedly part of his popular appeal. However, if they brought him an avid readership they also made him powerful horticultural enemies. In retrospect his reckless verbal assaults have caused garden historians to cast him in the role of villain or hypocrite, at the expense of a more objective appraisal of his work.

Robinson was born in County Down in 1838. When he was about ten his father, a land agent, eloped to

America with the wife of one of his clients, leaving the family 'on the mercies of relations'. It was necessary for Robinson to earn his living as soon as possible, and gardening was one of the few crafts in which a boy could learn a trade and earn a small salary at the same time. A profession like architecture, or a craft like cabinet-making, would have required a down-payment of anything up to £500 for a five-year pupillage, and although this would have included the provision of food and lodgings, there would have been no salary until the training was complete; for poorer families the costs were prohibitive.

Robinson began work as a gardener's boy at Curraghmore, and then became an apprentice gardener at Glasnevin, the National Botanic Garden in Dublin, where he gained a comprehensive horticultural training. By the time he was twenty-one he had secured a position as foreman in a large garden in Ballykilcavan and this was the scene for the first fictional black spot on his reputation. There is a story, only part true, that Robinson was in charge of a range of greenhouses: 'We can imagine the number of tender and rare plants that furnished them, after the fashion of Chatsworth, and the numerous seedlings and cuttings they harboured' as one historian has evoked the scene. According to the tale, Robinson left his job in a fit of temper after a violent disagreement with the head gardener:

> 'that night, as the thermometer, always watched by Robinson so carefully, fell first to freezing and then below, he went to the stokehole and drew out the fires. Then after walking round the houses and opening all the windows, he set out for Dublin, arriving there early on the following morning.'[1]

Robinson's biographer Mea Allan has established that the gardens at Ballykilcavan never held such elaborate greenhouse collections and that although 'there was a dispute and some damage was done', the tale of vandalism is a malicious exaggeration.[2] Both Robinson's confrontational style and his uncompromising doctrines made him an irresistible challenge to critics and there is still a tendency to focus on the minor inconsistencies – the stakes to his carnations – rather than on the achievements of his remarkable career. All accounts agree, however, that Robinson left Ballykilcavan on foot for Dublin and then, armed with a letter of recommendation from his previous employer, Dr David Moore at Glasnevin, he travelled to England and presented himself to the Royal Botanic Society's garden in Regent's Park. In later years he recalled his arrival in London and the prevailing taste for 'false and hideous' flower gardens,

> 'made up of a few kinds of flowers which people were proud to put out in thousands and tens of thousands ... I saw the flower-gardener meanly trying to rival the tile or wallpaper men, and throwing aside with contempt all the lovely things that through their height or form did not conform to this idea'.[3]

He was given a job at the Botanic Gardens in Regent's Park, not in the greenhouses (which he detested for the rest of his life), but in charge of the hardy herbaceous borders:

> 'there was at the time a small garden of British plants, which had to be kept up, and this led me into the varied country round London, from the orchid-flecked meadows of Bucks to the tumbled down undercliffs on the Essex coast, untroubled by the plough; and so I began to get an idea (which should be taught to every boy at school) that there was (for gardens even) much beauty in our native flowers and trees'.[4]

Robinson was a passionate and persuasive writer. He made up for his rudimentary education by teaching himself botany and his specialist expertise in native British plants earned him a place in the prestigious Linnean Society in 1866. Soon afterwards he gave up his work at the Botanic Gardens in order to write full time, first of all as horticultural correspondent to *The Times* and for smaller gardening magazines, then, from 1871, as the founder of the influential weekly magazine *The Garden*.

Robinson's importance as an innovator has been challenged by recent historians and it is true that native British plants had been championed by earlier, less charismatic garden writers. His ability to take a controversial stance and popularize it, however, was incomparable. *The Garden* was the most widely read gardening magazine of its day, eagerly awaited every week by middle-class amateur gardeners and professionals alike. It combined the most up-to-date horticultural news with sound practical advice and Robinson spiced it with criticisms of his rivals' books; Sir Reginald Blomfield and J.D. Sedding were regularly used for target practice and they, in turn, sniped back.

Robinson's interest in wild flowers and their natural habitats paralleled that of his intellectual and artist elders. He put into practice the gardening philosophy that Ruskin had initiated in the 1830s, and that both Ruskin and Morris continued to apply to their own gardens. He was interested in contemporary painting, sharing Greenaway's admiration for Millais's *Ophelia* and Ruskin's appreciation of Turner's painterly use of colour. With Ruskin, however, his intellectual debt was balanced by a lively dialogue about gardening as well as fine art. They corresponded on the differences between the wild lilies of Italy and the orange ones that Ruskin could grow in his greenhouse, and we know that in 1885 Robinson sent irises to Ruskin. There is a story that at one of their meetings Robinson bemoaned the fact that in warmer countries the fruit of an orchard was always more beautiful than the blossom until Ruskin exclaimed: 'Give me the flower and spare me the stomach-ache!'[5] Robinson's passion for sunflowers, hollyhocks, honeysuckle and foxgloves was akin to that of Morris and Ruskin. The salient difference between them was that Robinson had developed his love of wild flowers as a practical gardener rather than through a romantic longing for a utopian age, and it was to practical gardeners that he sought to appeal.

In *The Wild Garden* Robinson launched a campaign to reinstate indigenous shrubs, bulbs and perennials: 'The passion for the exotic is so universal that our own finest plants are never planted'. There were chapters on 'The Garden of British Wild Flowers', on 'Wild gardening on walls, rocks or ruins' and on wild roses. Robinson encouraged gardeners to study the wild flowers of hedgerow and meadow, and to follow nature's method of planting in irregular drifts. It would be a mistake to assume from its title that *The Wild Garden* was concerned only with wild flowers and the creation of meadow gardens or woody glades. Only the most progressive Aesthetes were ready to take wild

Right: *Michaelmas daisies, seldom planted in Victorian gardens, provide drifts of colour at the end of the summer.*

gardening to these extremes in the 1870s. Robinson explained in his preface that he was not proposing 'a garden run wild, or sowing annuals in a muddle', nor was he insistent that only flowers and shrubs native to the British countryside should be used. The main thrust of the book was a vehement opposition to all that was 'mechanical and strait-laced' in gardening, and in particular to the practice of tearing up the garden twice a year, 'to effect what is called spring and summer "bedding"'. He set out to prove that hardy plants, both native and 'from the northern and temperate regions', could provide a richer and less labour-intensive display, and to persuade his readers that a garden that changed with the seasons, with a sequence of different focuses as the months progressed, was more interesting and rewarding than one that offered just two relatively static and artificial effects.

For the thoroughly modern young Aesthetes in Britain and North America who were decorating their dining-rooms with William Morris wallpaper, Robinson's theories represented the simple old 'country way' of planting that was the perfect compliment to their fashionable cottage-style homes. *The Wild Garden* was intended for the substantial country estate, with meadows and woodland around its perimeter. However, it must have been read by many aspiring gardeners with far more modest plots because it went through numerous editions and it is still in print today. For the benefit of armchair gardeners the 1881 edition was illustrated by one of the most distinguished garden painters of the period, Alfred Parsons, and, then as now, gardeners were able to draw on it as a source book for inspiration, adapting the parts that best suited their personal taste and the conditions of their site and soil.

Robinson's popularity made him rich. In *The Garden* he gave his public a balanced diet of what he thought would be good for them together with what they really wanted. There were articles on when to weed, how to keep cats out of town gardens, the habits of aphids and their relationship with ants, and the mysteries of miniature mushroom beds: 'We have heard of a Belgian cook who grew them in his old shoes, and assuredly they can be grown very well in four or six inch pots, pans, boxes, or even in a cracked tea-pot.' Articles on carpet bedding were set alongside more edifying pieces. By 1878 Gertrude Jekyll had already made her publishing debut with the first of many articles to appear in the magazine, and it was to Jekyll that Robinson handed over the editorial responsibility for *The Garden* in 1900. A collection of the best articles, substantiated by a 'cyclopaedia' of plants, was published in book form in 1883 as *The English Flower Garden,* consolidating Robinson's success and going through fifteen editions in his lifetime. Like *The Wild Garden,* it is still widely read and in print today.

Although Robinson's success was founded on his skill as a garden writer and editor, he never lost the practical, down-to-earth approach of his early years as a gardener; nor did he lose his progressive edge as prosperity and middle age set in. In 1883 he delighted in redesigning the gardens to Shrubland Park in Suffolk, an elaborate mansion with a formal layout by Sir Charles Barry, whose work Robinson despised. The scroll-shaped formal beds cut into the lawn and planted with brightly coloured annuals were carefully filled in and the coloured stones that decorated the parterre were removed. In their place Robinson laid out a simple lawn with wide mixed borders of roses and perennials, and Barry's architecture was at least partially concealed behind clematis and wisterias. In *The English Flower Garden* he had noted:

'among the unfortunate attempts of certain architects who designed gardens to get rid of the gardener and his troublesome plants were instructions that no climbers were to be allowed on walls'.

At Shrubland he took his revenge.

In 1885, at the age of forty-seven, Robinson bought a superb Elizabethan stone mansion house, Gravetye Manor, in West Hoathly, Sussex, set within its own estate. He lived there for the remainder of his long life, changing and developing the garden and compulsively acquiring tracts of land for the estate until it swelled to almost a thousand acres. It was in the gardens at Gravetye that Robinson made his most convincing practical testimony to wild gardening. *Gravetye Manor, or Twenty Years' Work Around An Old Manor House*, published in 1911, is a detailed personal record of the transformation of the grounds from an ungainly Victorian compromise into a working model of the rural countryside that Ruskin and his followers had evoked and eulogized in their writings. Robinson was still working full-time as an editor in Southampton Street, London, and it is a measure of his dynamism that he commuted on the seven o'clock train to Victoria every morning yet still had the energy after a day's work to throw his papers into a waiting carriage at Three Bridges station then make the last few miles of the journey home on foot across the fields. The evolution of his own garden, and the practical experiments and trials there, were not only a release from the business and editorial pressures of managing *The Garden*, they inspired and regenerated his writing.

Robinson's first priority at Gravetye was to clear away the obtrusive Victorian landscaping and to reinstate, as far as was possible, the natural land levels. The wellingtonias that crowded in on the house were chopped down in the first months of 1885 'as being at once ugly and unsuited to the climate'. Thirty men were set to work removing an immense grass terrace on the south side, and within months Robinson had 'determined to do away with the old kitchen garden, which was right against the house and had a poor effect'. The older apple trees were retained but not the 'many iron trellises'. A rock garden 'of the ghastly order' in front of the east wing was instantly condemned because it 'consisted of stones and small

ABOVE: *The garden porch at Gravetye where nature almost obliterates the architecture of the house.*

rocks, stuck in promiscuously, with great Ash pollards (sawn in lengths) reared on end amongst them, the effect being hideous'. It was replaced by a simple sloping bank, with stone steps at the west end connecting the two levels; the upper level was designated a 'Playground' where village children were allowed to come and play. Each part of the garden had to be pegged out on the ground as it was designed. Robinson believed that a paper plan could be made after a garden had been laid out, but that it was 'useless theory' beforehand. Every change in the topography of the land, even slight changes in soil type, had to be accommodated. Although a photographic record of the developing garden was kept, the only surviving plan was made for publication in a *Country Life* article in 1912 and it is limited to the areas closest to the house.

Flowers and trees for the new garden were sent by gardening friends from all over the world. Edouard André (responsible for the suburban parks and squares of Paris, and befriended by Robinson during his visit to the 1867 International Exhibition) sent a case of 400

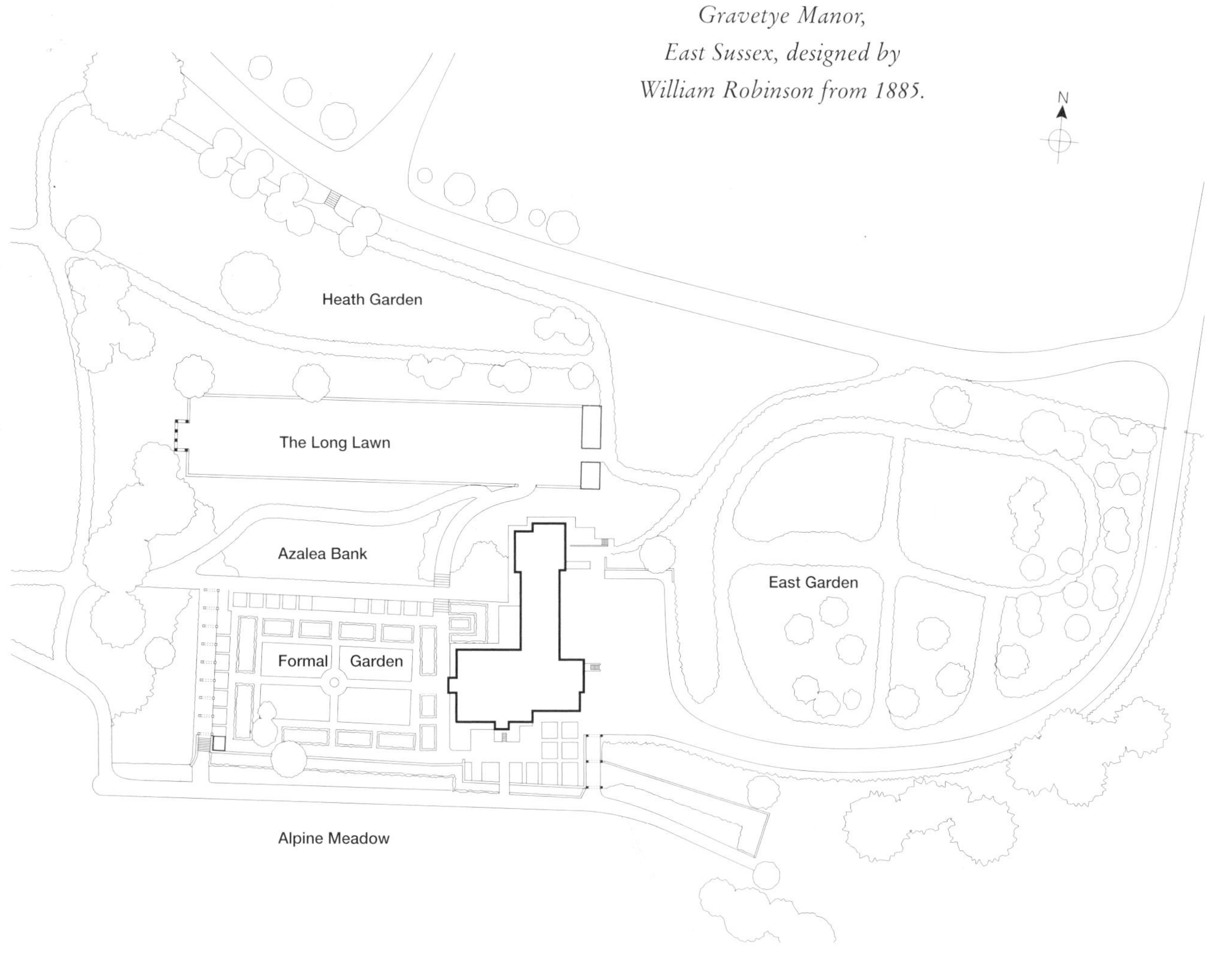

Below: *Garden plan of Gravetye Manor, East Sussex, designed by William Robinson from 1885.*

autumn-flowering cyclamen, white moccasin flowers (the orchid *Cypripedium acaule*) arrived from friends in Philadelphia and white wood lilies (trilliums) from Pittsburgh. Robinson was keen to try out new flowers in his garden, as well as to establish a natural habitat for old favourites. In 1887 he wrote to George Nicholson, the curator at Kew:

'I should like to grow any new promising flowering shrubs of the hardier sort on my rather loamy cool soil. You know all that is good in that way & I am sure would be willing to help me with the names of some likely kinds. It might interest you to see them grown on a very different soil to yours. I am not seeking rarities or curiosities at all but beautiful things likely to add to the charm of our gardens & to be worth figuring from a gardener's point of view.'[6]

Thirty-two small plants were sent in response, followed a few months later by 'a set of young trees'.

If any vestiges of a Tudor garden had survived at Gravetye when Robinson took it on, he would have had them out without compunction; he loathed topiary, describing it as 'Vegetable Sculpture'. In the preface to *Gravetye Manor* he wrote with characteristic dogmatism: 'Nothing is more miserable for the gardener, or uglier in the landscape, than a garden laid out with clipped Yews.' He confessed to having used a yew hedge at Gravetye to make an 'emphatic division' between two flower beds on different levels:

'One day, Mr Mark Fisher, the landscape painter, was sketching the flower garden, and this Yew hedge formed the extreme end of the picture. He said to me, "Why don't you give me a free line there instead of a hard, black one?" The remark struck me very much. Next Autumn I took away the hedge of Yews and planted the noble rose Bouquet d'Or, mixed with the claret-coloured Clematis, and both have formed a charming dividing line for years. The lesson I never forgot; we abolished the shears and clipped no more.'[7]

ABOVE: *Robinson thrived on breaking rules, mixing formal and accidental effects in planting schemes which evolved with the seasons.*

Nevertheless, the garden retained a clear structure. It was terraced, with more formal areas close to the house on one side and a generous oval fruit and vegetable garden, contained within a stepped stone wall, conveniently close to the kitchen. There was a formal garden but Robinson would not have seen this as contradicting his passion for wild gardening. He believed (like Monet) that a clear geometric framework of rectangular beds divided by brick or stone paths was appropriate close to the house in a country estate. Initially he designed a simple lawn up against the west side of the house, informally edged with his favourite 'tufted pansies': native heartsease crossed with alpine horned pansies to make blue, lilac, white and yellow flowers, which were smaller and simpler than the elaborately patterned 'florists' pansies'. In 1902, however, the lawn was taken up and in its place Robinson planted a rose garden. It is tempting to imagine old shrub roses and ramblers undermining the strict geometry of the plan, in keeping with the general conception of Robinson as a champion of wild and old-fashioned flowers with unruly habits. There was much more to Robinson than wild gardening, however, and the rosary was a fine example of his enthusiasm for Tea roses: 'I wished to gratify my own taste for these things, and at the same time do something to make them better known.' Tea roses, at the turn of the century, were generally overlooked in favour of the Hybrid Perpetual. At Gravetye each separate species was given its own bed and they were underplanted with violas, saxifrage, pinks and thyme. In among the roses there were beds filled with alstroemerias and with forget-me-nots as companions to clematis on tripods.

Robinson has been branded a hypocrite for abandoning the rambling roses of the English cottage garden in favour of the cultivated glamour of a Hybrid Tea.[8] This was not the case. Even in *The Wild Garden* he had written that there was a place in his garden for both wild and cultivated roses:

'It will not do to put Wild Roses in the flower-garden, where we want choice cultivated flowers; but there are ways in which any Wild Rose we bring or gather might be delightfully used; i.e. in the shrubbery, and in forming fences ... let no one suppose I wish them to take the place of our lovely Tea Roses in the flower-garden. There are, at least in my own garden, places for both.'[9]

The view that wild and formal gardening are mutually exclusive is a late twentieth-century misconception, Robinson's garden was designed on a scale that could incorporate both. A massive oak pergola, clothed with white wisteria, connected the rose gardens with a gazebo that looked out over the alpine meadow, and again Robinson was true to his written word:

'The finest of hardy climbers, the Wisteria is much more frequently and rightly planted in France than in our gardens ... It should be, in addition to its use on walls and houses, made into bold, covered ways and bowers and trained up trees.'

Below the house a 'beautifully clothed old wall' was carefully retained and a vast south-facing border planted with hardy shrubs and perennials at its foot. In other parts of the garden Michaelmas daises, which Robinson called 'starworts', were planted in drifts for autumn colour. They were hardly seen in Victorian gardens and the effect of them massed together at the end of the summer when traditional bedding schemes were ready for the compost heap must have swayed the resolve of some of Robinson's more conservative visitors. He seldom stuck to a colour scheme, preferring to plant in bold groups, often using colonies of smaller plants like violas running between the

Right: *Festoons of white wisteria cover the pergola at the west end of the formal garden.*

clumps to bind a bed together. Vast mixed borders were planted with an eclectic choice of plants that included foxgloves, verbascum and tender, evergreen shrubs like carpenteria and melianthus. Where plants spread or seeded themselves they were allowed (within reasonable limits) to remain, so that the fine stonework of steps was half-concealed beneath red valerian, and cracks in the York stone paving sprouted feverfew. Changes in level were skilfully manipulated so that the garden unfolded gradually and the traces of formality disappeared farther away from the house, where Robinson planted an alpine meadow with naturalized drifts of spring bulbs followed by meadow flowers.

The acres of land at Gravetye were gradually refined into an idealized rural landscape. Robinson composed the grounds much as an artist might organize the composition of a painting. He opened up the view to a picturesque collection of old farm buildings which previous owners of the Manor had screened from the house with tall trees. In English aristocratic tradition he invited artists to stay for long periods on the estate, providing accommodation as a form of patronage, and in return they made scores of paintings of the gardens and grounds beyond, which were exhibited together in London. His own photographs, too, are composed in the landscape tradition, occasionally peopled by the village children picking blackberries or resting by a stile. Every year on his birthday the village children came to dance around the maypole in a celebration of country ways. His birthday was in July, so the traditional May Day festivities were always a little late, but the children were given tea on the lawn and one of the gardeners had the task of 'keeping the little varmin out of the flower beds'. In his own way Robinson was creating a responsible role for the wealthy middle classes, combining the best traditions of benevolence and conservation, associated with manorial obligations, with the industrious vigour and clear-sighted determination of the successful businessman. Farther away from the house he planted woodlands, surely as a response to Ruskin's appeal that future generations should be provided for, and although he delighted in exotic trees, they were mixed with native species.

Gravetye was Robinson's home for fifty years. He was always hospitable and the gardens were visited by some of the most influential figures in gardening as well as by potential patrons of wild gardens. He used to tease lady visitors by stopping, halfway through a tour of the garden, to bend down and peer between his legs. This, he claimed, was the best position for looking at the landscape in general and plants in particular; he attempted to persuade his guests to try it for themselves – not least, one suspects, to see whether they would take up the challenge and lift up their long skirts. He remained a bachelor throughout his life. At the age of seventy-two Robinson lost the use of his legs, but he continued gardening undeterred in a caterpillar-tracked motor vehicle. When he was ninety-five he replanned one of the old orchards and planted a new one. He died two years later in 1935.

LEFT: *The gazebo which looks out across the alpine meadow, viewed from the azalea bank. Robinson allowed the natural contours of Gravetye, steeply sloping from north to south, to determine the garden's design.*

The gardens grew completely wild over the next two decades, so that when the present owner, Peter Herbert, bought Gravetye in 1958 the stone paths of the formal garden were so overgrown with coarse grasses and weeds that they had disappeared entirely. Gradually the garden's structure was reinstated, the paths and steps were cleared and restored, the summerhouse was repaired and the pergola rebuilt. Robinson's photographs, together with the detailed record of his planting in *Gravetye Manor*, provided the most exacting documentation for every decision in the restoration of the garden, and his old gardener from the 1930s was consulted on gardening methods and planting. A decision was made, very early on, that newly available plants should be used in addition to Robinsonian ones: 'Robinson was a pioneer, and think of the plants we would have missed out on.'[10] The Elizabethan mansion became a country-house hotel and the gardens continue to attract and enchant visitors from all over the world. More than a century after they were first laid out they remain a model of natural planting and one of the most convincing testaments to Robinson's reforming convictions.

The success of *The Wild Garden* and *The Garden* magazine was indicative of a boom in gardening publications. As the dense inner cities overflowed into leafy suburbs, and terraced and semi-detached houses were built with their own front and rear gardens in place of the tiny yards of city houses, Robinson's writings were taken up by a generation of amateurs who found themselves with a garden to keep for the first time. His style was deliberately accessible; he was not interested in discoursing in Latin (insisting that every plant should have an English name) or in propounding academic theories. He had very little time for the pontifications of architect garden designers, who he believed should restrict themselves to making buildings and leave gardening matters, about which he claimed they generally knew very little, to the professional gardener. His practical and straightforward approach made gardening sound easy, and the ideal of wild gardening, reviving the use of hardy native perennials and annuals, must have encouraged even the most tentative would-be gardeners to believe that if nature could do it all by herself in the fields and hedgerows, then a little artful intervention here and there, with Robinson for reference, could make something stylish of the new back garden.

Robinson was at least as widely read in America as in Britain. On both sides of the Atlantic his work was open to interpretation by gardeners. At its most extreme it provided a basic tenet for Charles Fletcher Lummis's meadow garden at El Alisal in Highland Park, southern California. Lummis was so committed to the principle of enhancing the existing sense of place in a garden – its *genius loci* – that his own garden was cultivated as a meadow of wild flowers:

> 'On my own little place there are, today, at least forty million wild blossoms by calculation. Short of the wandering and unconventional foot-paths, which are almost choked with the urgent plant life beside them, you cannot step anywhere without trampling flowers – maybe ten to a step, as a minimum.'[11]

Lummis brought theology and nationalism together in gardening, describing the California poppies, California wild oats, Spanish lily and owl clover of his garden as 'The Carpet of God's Country'.

The principle of relinquishing control over nature, of nurturing a harmonious partnership with the landscape and its indigenous history in order to draw closer to God and to achieve a sense of belonging within a continuously changing pattern, offered solace as well as encouragement to a generation who believed that modern life was out of step with the teaching of Christianity. In addition, the ideals of taking the existing landscape as a reference point for the garden, and of planting native species, both of which became seminal to the Arts and Crafts movement, encouraged American garden designers to devise a specifically American garden style and so break away from the prevailing trend of importing English garden design into America, irrespective of incompatibilities in climate and location. The conversion took some time. As late as the 1930s the employment of an English or Scottish gardener on an American estate garden was still considered an indication of status: 'There is a new swank! Greater and more crushing at a dinner party than wearing a new rope of pearls is it to say: "My Kew gardener has just arrived."'[12]

In many instances estate gardens, built with the vast fortunes of families like Ford, Kellogg, Rockefeller and Vanderbilt, set out to emulate (if not to outstrip) the great gardens of Europe's cultural heritage. Just as American architects were trained at the Ecole des Beaux-Arts in Paris – hardly a hotbed of innovation in the late nineteenth century – the rules of garden design were drawn from the writings of John Claudius Loudon and even from Humphry Repton's eighteenth-century publications and practice. Andrew Jackson Downing, writing in the mid-nineteenth century, was the first American to translate European landscape theories into terms that were specifically appropriate to American topography, climate and lifestyle. It was not until the 1890s, however, that American designers cast off the influence of their European forebears. First in the shaping of national parks and then in estate gardens they took up the challenge of interpreting the great American plains. By incorporating the dramatic range of plants, some semi-tropical, that would flourish in their climates and by responding to the land and its people they produced a design style that was uniquely their own.

Footnotes

1 Miles Hadfield, *Pioneers in Gardening,* Routledge & Kegan Paul, London, 1955, p.216.
2 Mea Allan, *William Robinson 1838–1935*, Faber and Faber, London, 1982, p.23.
3 William Robinson, *The English Flower Garden*, John Murray, London,1898, 6th edition.
4 Ibid.
5 Geoffrey Taylor, *Some Nineteenth Century Gardeners,* Skeffington, 1951, p.86.
6 Quoted in Mea Allan, op.cit., p.152.
7 William Robinson, *Gravetye Manor, or Twenty Years' Work Around An Old Manor House*, 1911, facsimile published by Sagapress, New York, 1995.
8 See Patricia Morison, 'Voice of the revolution', *Gardens Illustrated*, April/May 1995, pp.70–6.
9 William Robinson, *The Wild Garden,* John Murray, London, 1884, 4th edition, pp.120–4.
10 Peter Herbert in conversation with the author, 26 June 1995.
11 Charles Fletcher Lummis, 'The Carpet of God's Country', *Out West 22*, 1905.
12 Quoted in Mac Griswold and Eleanor Weller, *The Golden Age of American Gardens*, Abrams, New York, 1991, p.18, from the writings of Marion Cran.

CHAPTER FIVE

THE ARCHITECTURAL TREATMENT OF GARDENS

The integration of house and garden, and of architectural structure with natural planting, was fundamental to the Arts and Crafts garden. The principle of equality between architects and gardeners, however, and the relative qualifications of each to practise 'the art of garden design' were as often an area of combat as of harmonious collaboration in the 1880s and 1890s. Architects have always played a part in directing the course of garden history. Historically they had the double advantage of being entrusted with both the budget for a building and the confidence of the client in artistic matters, and invariably they were several rungs higher on the social ladder than most gardeners could hope to climb. A few landscape

RIGHT: *The lake in autumn, Great Tangley Manor.*

gardeners like Humphry Repton and Joseph Paxton managed to turn the tables, training in gardening and the study of botany then, once the right connections were secured, adding architecture to their repertory as 'an inseparable and indispensable auxiliary' to the art of gardening. In the main, however, it was the architect who determined the structural outlines of an estate – whether it should be formal or picturesque – and the landscape gardener was employed to work out the details of how this was to be achieved.

There was a clear division of responsibility. As late as 1864 architects were advised in *The Gentleman's House*, a handbook by Robert Kerr listing every element to be considered in the design of the country estate, that the ornamental grounds were 'of course the domain of the landscape-gardener alone. He may form them on whatever quarter he deems advisable and in whatever manner.' According to Kerr, the architect should be aware of all the necessary ingredients that the landscape gardener might employ: 'The Fountain, Basin, and Fish-pond; Dipping-well and Grotto; Arbour, Bower, Summer-house, and Seat; Statuary, Sun-dial, and Vases; Terrace-walls and Screen-wall; Lake, Stream, and Pool; Bridge and Boat-house; Avenue and Shrubbery-walk; Archery-ground and Bowling-green'. But he was advised to consider these 'as the last class of the many and varied considerations affecting the plan of a Gentleman's House'.

By the last decade of the nineteenth century progressive young architects were beginning to see things very differently. A quiet revolution in the design of country houses was changing the very ethos of country life. Whereas previously the successful Victorian architect could secure a commission by working up a few sketches while dressing for dinner, presenting them to his host during dessert, and then getting the office clerks to work up the details, the new progressives took a more earnest view of the roles and responsibilities of the architect. Just as William Robinson had rejected the vulgarity and the artificial imposition of Victorian carpet bedding, Arts and Crafts architects repudiated the practice of dressing a building up in any architectural style that suited the fancy of the client, regardless of its purpose. They saw the architect's role as encompassing the design of everything for the house, including the position and style of the garden furniture and the structure of the pergola.

Like Robinson they were inspired by the writings of Ruskin. They wanted an architecture that would respond to the native conditions of its country, which would draw on cottage traditions and at the same time be appropriate to the demands and conditions of modern life. They set out to reinvent the homestead, to promote honesty and restraint in place of ostentatious display, and to reinstate fine craftsmanship and good traditional materials as an antidote to the 'gimcrack ornament' and thin veneers of the jerry builder. In their written philosophies and in their buildings there is an element of naïvety and nostalgia, a desire to return to a state of innocence, to focus on the daisies while factory chimneys belched out smoke and the lives of child labourers were gobbled up. The rural utopia invented by the Arts and Crafts movement was as artificial as Kate Greenaway's essence of childhood. However, it was redeemed by the ideal that architecture and the

RIGHT: Prunus *overhanging the lake. Webb's timber bridge leading across the moat to the library extension can be seen in the background.*

domestic environment could have a psychological effect on the way people thought, as well as physically changing the way in which they lived and worked.

The evolution of the Arts and Crafts movement was a gradual process rather than a sudden revelation; it coexisted with the formal view of architecture promoted in Kerr's handbook and later championed by Sir Reginald Blomfield. The practice of artists and craftsmen working together to design the house, its garden and everything for the interior had been established at Red House in 1859. For William Morris artistic collaboration was a conscious revival of medieval traditions, breaking down the hierarchy that separated the crafts and putting art back into objects for everyday life. His philosophy inspired young designers training in established architectural firms to make designs for fabrics and wallpapers, furniture and metalwork, in addition to designing buildings. From 1877 there were two very different contexts in which the latest work of Morris and Webb could be studied in detail. Morris & Co. products were immaculately displayed in the Oxford Street shop, tactfully referred to as 'the establishment' by those too delicate to concede that Morris might be both poet and shopkeeper with equal conviction. Morris and Webb themselves, however, could be found every week at meetings of 'Anti-Scrape', the name given to the Society for the Protection of Ancient Buildings (SPAB), which they founded in March 1877.

The 'Anti-Scrape' committee met every Thursday at five o'clock, above Morris's shop in the early months but later at 26 Queen's Square. Reports of 'cases in progress' were considered, with accounts of visits to buildings in danger, and Morris and Webb would talk passionately and authoritatively, recommending a course of action for each case. As SPAB promoted a better understanding of historic buildings, very gradually an appreciation of the historic landscapes and gardens that surrounded them began to evolve. In its first annual report the Society condemned the 'destruction and falsification' of ancient monuments, which it believed were under threat not only from urban development but also from the prospect of being 'skinned alive' by insensitive or inept restoration. It declared the Society's principal aim to be 'guarding the life and soul of these monuments, so to speak, and not their bodies merely'. In addition, it set out to impress upon the public 'the duty of preserving jealously the very gifts that our fore-fathers left us, and not merely their sites and names'. For Morris, Webb and the group of younger architects who formed the core of the committee, old buildings represented much more than an architectural heritage. The desecration of ancient monuments was a paradigm for the destruction of rural England, its traditional values and customs:

> 'The England that we love is the England of old towns, tilled fields, little rivers, farms, churches, and cottages. If by violently marring the fair country and vulgarising the shy old buildings we obtain so much less to love, what shall it profit? Without an England to love we cannot remain stout of heart and enduring. Civilization cannot be had merely as a word – it rests on foundations.'[1]

William Morris was vocal and energetic in his opinions, while Philip Webb conveyed 'a most potent quality of silent influence'.[2] Webb believed most passionately in the craft of building:

> 'Building is an art of doing. The architect cannot learn all the ways of workmanship, or may not master even one craft, but actual doing is necessary at the foundation to give direction to the mind.'

A paper architect, according to Webb, was almost as absurd as a paper athlete. His instinct for good materials well laid was matched by a 'deep religious love for England' that was neither sentimental nor patriotic. According to his biographer W.R. Lethaby, land for Webb was

> 'not merely "nature", it was the land that had been laboured over by the generations of men; buildings were not "architecture", they were builded history and poetry. Art was not "taste" but human spirit made visible.'[3]

Webb believed that the root of architecture was in the land. Before any new building was designed he paced over the site until it relinquished its full possibilities, offering up 'particular suggestions'. Even the English weather was a source of constant delight: 'there is no bad weather,' he is quoted as saying, 'only different kinds of good weather.'

W.R. Lethaby recalled that after the weekly SPAB meetings Webb and the younger architects would go across the Strand to Gatti's for a simple meal: 'Here talk flowed.' Webb's integrity, his detailed knowledge of the practicalities of building and his interest in every element of the house 'from the plan to the cupboards and sinks' served as an awe-inspiring model for younger architects, and his ability to weave nature and architecture together revived the quest for an organic architecture. There can be no doubt that Webb was committed to garden design as an integral and essential part of the architect's responsibility. At one of his houses, Rounton, the client designed the garden himself after the house was finished and then wrote inviting Webb to come and see the result. He wrote back: 'I will do my best to forget that I ever did any work for you.' The garden was ploughed up and begun again under Webb's superintendence.

Webb's involvement in the design of new gardens at Great Tangley Manor, near Wonersh in Surrey, is one of the rare instances when *Country Life* magazine recorded his work, giving us an insight into his carefully resolved integration of new work with an ancient structure. Three articles on Great Tangley Manor, published between 1898 (when the magazine was only a year old) and 1905, offer guidance on restoration to 'other owners of beautiful old houses', casting the new owner of an ancient manor house in the role of enlightened saviour rather than interloper.[4] *Country Life* flattered its readers. It nurtured their aspirations by encouraging them to be generous and far-sighted in their patronage, and it rewarded good practice in the form of complimentary articles. Great Tangley Manor, it was claimed, would appeal to *Country Life* readers for its English picturesqueness, its location in rural Surrey, and as an example of an ancient building restored with taste and skill.

From its earliest issues *Country Life*'s tone and content were carefully pitched. It focused on the activities of the aristocracy, but at the same time its articles were carefully constructed to accommodate (and to educate) the social and cultural aspirations of a more general magazine-buying public. Aristocratic traditions were skilfully reconciled with the requirements of the newly rich modern patron. In the first article on Great Tangley Manor there is a general discussion of 'evidences of decay in the shires – deserted mansions, ruined gateways, weed-grown moats, and other marks of the changed condition of modern times'. An image is conjured up of the farmer's wife more or less squatting in the mansion of the forgotten lord: 'She has bedaubed the oaken wainscot with whitewash, clothes from the washing are hung on the rail of the minstrel's gallery, and broad sheets of

Left: *Wisteria growing across a loophole in the ancient stone wall bounding the forecourt to Great Tangley Manor.*

glass fill the place of beautiful latticed panes'. Although Great Tangley Manor was not named specifically as a case in point, its use as a farm for almost a century was noted and its transformation by a new owner, Mr Wickham Flower, from a working farm to a country retreat was recommended:

'It was no small achievement to regenerate Great Tangley Manor from its recent uses, and to replace its surroundings of kitchen gardens, stables, cow-sheds, piggeries, and barns, by the beautiful and wholly appropriate pleasure grounds which now adorn it. ... May the example of Mr. Flower be the inspiration of many.'

Wickham Flower was a London solicitor and an experienced Arts and Crafts client. In 1875, a decade before the purchase of Great Tangley, he had commissioned Richard Norman Shaw to design Swan House for him in Chelsea. The furnishings and decorations were supplied by Morris & Co. in 1881. Great Tangley Manor, a small fifteenth-century manor house with a half-timbered Elizabethan front, was purchased early in 1885 as a country place.[5] Flower described it as 'a little white house, bending with age as if it would fall forward, held together with a framework of rings and panels of dark oak'. The prospect of a garden was equally important:

'What I had specially wanted to find and what I had been on the lookout for for years, was a garden in the open country, far removed from building or town, and here exactly was what I wanted, a garden absolutely without a flower.'[6]

Wickham Flower was a founder member of SPAB. He would have benefited from Webb's understanding of ancient buildings before the purchase of Great Tangley, and Morris & Co. was later to furnish Webb's extension to the building. Although *Country Life* gives scant attention to the restoration of the house, other sources show that the main structure had survived in good order and the principal tasks in 1885 were to clear away the farmyard debris and to reinstate an appropriate garden setting around the house. The original moat, choked with earth and rubbish, overgrown with brambles and partially infilled so that farm wagons could drive right up to the house, was systematically cleared and its treasures of sixteenth-century glass and pottery, a Roman coin and a wooden ball (which *Country Life* supposed to have been part of a set of bowls) were recorded. Within the moated enclosure, beneath ground level, the remains of an earlier structure on the site were discovered and carefully preserved.[7]

While the excavation of the moat was in progress, the remainder of the garden (between six and seven acres) was laid out. Although *Country Life* is specific about the number of labourers employed (eighteen) and the duration of the work (six months), it is irritatingly vague about the identity of the designer. The plan of the garden evolved out of the inherent qualities of the land; the labourers were given their instructions only week by week:

'no formal plan has been laid down, and no written direction given. Great Tangley gardens have thus a delightfully spontaneous character, but their features have been dictated by good judgement and experienced taste.'

The question of whose taste is left hanging. The architectural elements closest to the house were certainly Webb's, and in the last of the three articles the gardener, Mr Whiteman, was recorded as being the client's faithful friend as well as his gardener. It is probable that Whiteman was responsible for the planting and that there was a degree of collaboration over the planning of the garden.

Within the moat the house was enclosed by a walled courtyard: 'The enclosing walls are very old, the parts on the southern and eastern sides being of the time of Queen Elizabeth.' They are of the local Bargate stone, with loopholes accentuated with brick dressings, which *Country Life* suggested might have been for purposes of defence in lawless times. Where the cart track had been driven right up to the house the wall had been partially demolished (one *Country Life* article suggested this was where the drawbridge had been), and the only surviving planting was a rough orchard and a cabbage ground. Webb's task was to design an approach to the house, across the moat, which would repair the existing structure and establish a garden setting for the building appropriate to its antiquity. There was no question of exploiting the gap in the wall and driving a new path straight to the front door, or of replacing the missing wall with a modern imitation. Instead Webb designed a timber screen (now demolished), which completed the sense of enclosure within the courtyard, while retaining the view of the front of the house from beyond the moat. The new work placed no structural load on the old walls, and the clear disparity between the screen and the original structure allowed the perspicacious viewer to imagine the completion of the structure in Bargate stone, and at the same time to appreciate the historical and structural implications of its partial demolition.

Webb designed a covered way to bridge the moat and create an approach, along the outside of the courtyard, which would be emphatic enough to announce the entrance to the manor, without compromising the intimate scale and delicacy of the house. The timber frame and red-tile roof of the covered way corresponded to the courtyard screen, while making a contemporary comment on the materials of the main house. No intrusion was permitted into the seclusion of the courtyard, which became a court garden, so that this small walled area in front of the house retains an atmosphere of secrecy. The ancient walls were planted with white and yellow jasmine, wisteria and guelder roses trained as climbers. Where an old vine growing across the front of the house had survived, it was retained.[8] Peonies and roses were named among the plants in the herbaceous borders in front of the walls, among great bushes of rosemary 'for remembrance' and myrtle, which symbolized everlasting love.

RIGHT: *A pleached lime walk makes a witty play on the timber frame of Great Tangley Manor. Philip Webb designed a timber screen with tiled roof (now lost) to replace the demolished area of garden wall so that the timber frame of the Elizabethan house was interpreted in modern materials in the garden wall and then mirrored in the vertical lime trunks and branches beyond.*

An old mulberry tree, perhaps a survivor from the rough orchard, cast a canopy of shade over a simple lawn at the centre of the court garden. *Country Life* listed a host of spring flowers, either naturalized in the grass or in the borders, including *Iris pumila*, fritillaries, hepaticas and yellow and grey tulips:

'Daffodils are there, but only those of choicest and most beautiful kinds. In the early spring days of February and March the deep purple and orange flowers of *Iris reticulata* bloom profusely, and sometimes they may be seen to great advantage rising over a carpet of pure snow.'

Webb was not initially consulted about the planting of this court garden. The final scheme replaced an earlier design that he described in a letter to his friend the painter George Boyce in September 1885:

'I have been down to see Tangley Manor and found that the pleasure garden maker has been dancing a "pas d'orticulture" there, playing da gooseberry there in fact and something must be done to remove ... some of his miserable handiwork.'[9]

The 'pleasure garden maker', whether Flower or Whiteman, had peppered the front lawn with trees and shrubs and made a focal point of a single standard box raised on a brick plinth. The response to his disapproval must have been rapid, because Webb was able to write to Boyce again in November this time noting that 'the garden arrangements are being made somewhat more decent in appearance.'[10]

Beyond the court garden a 'little garden, girt about with yew hedges, on every side' reiterated the ideal of a Tudor garden. It was planted with lilies and irises, delicate blue larkspurs and Japanese anemones. Webb designed a second timber bridge across the moat, leading to the more expansive (and at the end of the century more modern) areas of the garden. There was a clear dialogue between the planting and structure of the enclosed gardens and the open areas farther from the house. Across the moat an alley of pleached limes, running parallel to Webb's screen, made an organic play on its rhythm of open and closed spaces that was surely intentional.

Country Life was at pains to encourage its readers to plan for the future in their garden designs. When the new orchard at Great Tangley was ten years old the practice employed there of pruning away lower branches so that the ground below could be carpeted with alpine strawberries and buttercups was eulogized. The rapid growth of the yew hedges was especially observed, too:

'Remember, as you note the yew hedge parting the lawn from the meadows, that although it stands 10ft. high now, it is the result of trees which were but 18in. high when they were planted in the winter of 1884, only fourteen years ago, after all.'

The bog garden was described as one of the most successful of its kind in the country and its construction and planting were given in detail as a guideline for comparable schemes: finely chopped peat was mixed with the soil for moisture retention, and although the sandy soil gave good drainage the area for the bog garden was below the level of the lake so that it

Right: *Webb's timber bridge linking the library wing with the garden beyond the moat.*

could be flooded when necessary[11]. It was planted with

'the beautiful Cypripedium spectabile and others of its kind, orchids of many varieties, Spiraea [now Filipendula] venusta and palmata, rose-coloured and deep crimson day lilies, fulvous and yellow, wood lilies and Canadian lilies, yellow musk and white ranunculus, fair maids of France, calthas of deepest and most brilliant yellow, golden iris, Christmas roses, and a score of things besides'.

William Robinson was cited as an influence on the planting of the adjoining heath garden, and there would certainly have been a close connection between the heath garden at Gravetye and the one at Great Tangley, but if *Country Life* was correct in its assertion that the entire garden at Great Tangley was laid out over the winter of 1884/5, then it predates Gravetye by a few months.[12] It seems more probable (although there is no evidence for this) that after the initial laying out of the grounds the planting at Great Tangley Manor evolved as a gradual process, and that Mr Whiteman and William Robinson were well aware of each other's work. Gertrude Jekyll, whose home at Munstead was only a short drive away, was also familiar with Great Tangley. She had known the old manor as a child, and it is possible that she was the author of one of the *Country Life* articles. In *Some English Gardens*, published in 1904, she described the planting around the margins of the small lake as a paradise for flower lovers with masses of water irises, water-lilies and groups of arum lilies rising from the water. The lake was fed naturally by a stream, and its water, in turn, fed the moat. Both Jekyll and Robinson would have approved of the pergola walk beside the lake, covered with vines and 'approached by borders of old-fashioned and fragrant flowers – pinks, sweet Williams, and Canterbury bells'. There were lavender

Left: *The pergola walk beside the lake at Great Tangley.*

hedges, drifts of Michaelmas daisies and in the vegetable garden a broad border of perennials planted to provide a succession of flowers from spring through the summer and autumn until December.

Great Tangley Manor was one of the most progressive gardens of the 1880s. It combined a learned and sensitive approach to a historic building with an adventurous and emphatically natural attitude to landscape design and planting. The use of hardy plants massed together and of annuals that were allowed to self-seed responded to the writings of William Robinson, and anticipated the completion of Jekyll's garden at Munstead Wood. The gardens represented an intriguing collaboration between the client, the gardener and the architect that is almost as tantalizing as the juxtaposition of Philip Webb's name against those of William Robinson and Gertrude Jekyll. Regrettably *Country Life* was not specific about the influence of the personalities involved in the shaping of Great Tangley Manor. It is known, however, that Wickham Flower's ambitions to extend the old house ultimately forced Philip Webb into retreat. In 1893 Webb agreed, reluctantly, to add an extension to the Tudor house to accommodate a library and sitting-room, with extra bedrooms above. There may have been an element of bowing to the inevitable – that if he didn't design the new wing, somebody else would. *Country Life* observed:

> 'it was done in such a way that it assumed no effect of competition with the timbered front. It is perfectly in harmony, but gives the impression of voluntarily effacing itself in order to enhance the value of the older work.'

Webb himself was more critical, describing the extension as 'my architectural mess', and writing in September 1894 that 'we have now done all the mischief contemplated at present and I hope I shall not be called upon to do any more.'[13] He was adamant that no further additions could be made without serious loss to the character of the original building. Less than five years later Wickham Flower insisted on a new music-room and still more bedrooms, and the design was given to a younger architect.[14] *Country Life* offered a gentle reprimand: 'there can be little doubt that it overloads the old house, and takes away much of its charm.'

If Webb represented the most serious and conscientious influence on architects of the Arts and Crafts movement, his exact contemporary Richard Norman Shaw played an equally important role in shaping the movement with a very different interpretation of English architectural traditions. When Webb left G.E. Street's office in order to design Red House for Morris, Shaw took his place. In 1863 he had set up what was to become one of the most successful country-house practices in England. Although Shaw followed Webb's progress and admired his work, describing him as 'a very able man indeed, but with a strong liking for the ugly', his own buildings contradicted Webb's rational and restrained approach. They were extravagant and flippant in their free handling of historical motifs, and at the same time reminiscent of all the things the public liked best about their architectural heritage. Shaw was impervious to the moral undertones of Arts and Crafts. When discussing an 'extra' on a house for a portrait painter, he quipped: 'Oh, he can paint another nose.'[15] He was seldom inhibited by the honest expression of structure. When it was pointed out to him on one occasion that he had designed a massive fireplace on the first floor of a building with nothing underneath to hold it up, he is reputed to have said: 'That's nothing to worry about.

I have found that a six by three steel beam will hold almost anything up.'[16]

It was in Shaw's London office that some of the most innovative designers of the 1890s were trained. He was unusual in allowing his clerks to design minor details, rather than restricting them to making the necessary copies of drawings and press-copying correspondence. G.E. Street, he recalled, 'would not let us design a keyhole'. When a clerk completed his apprenticeship Shaw would sometimes secure a 'setting-up' commission to get him started in his own practice, and it was five young architects from Shaw's practice who established one of the most influential societies at the core of the Arts and Crafts movement. The Art Workers' Guild was founded in 1884 by W.R. Lethaby, E.S. Prior, Ernest Newton, Gerald Horsely and Mervyn Macartney. Shaw advised them: 'The Architects of this generation must make the future for themselves and knock at the door of Art until they were admitted.' The Art Workers' Guild was formed to promote 'the Unity of all the Aesthetic Arts'; to break down the traditional barriers between painting, sculpture, craft and architecture; and to establish a return to honest simplicity in design.

The Guild, it was claimed, was not a school, nor a club, nor a debating society. According to its second master, J.D. Sedding (1838–91): 'A mere club does not to my mind represent a force that communicates an electric shock to the thick hide of the Art Philistine of the present day.'[17] It was a combination of school, club and society: a meeting place where artists of different specializations could discuss their work, and a focus for solidarity. At each meeting a different artist would give a paper, often illustrated by examples of his own work, and this was followed by vigorous discussion. The talks were technically detailed and they embraced a wide range of subjects. In the 1880s there were papers on book illustration, needlework, pattern designing, Holbein and the architectural use of coloured marble. The Guild facilitated collaboration, giving rise to several commissions where an architect would design a house incorporating panels for sculpture or embroidered hangings to be designed and executed by one of his fellow Guild members. There was a tendency too, however, for architects to absorb the specialist skills and technical expertise of their Arts and Crafts colleagues, and to design everything for the house themselves: furniture, sculptural reliefs, light fittings, clocks and even clothes for the client to wear. To these multi-talented designers no specialist expertise, no lifetime's work of practical application, was sacrosanct. Architecture was the mother of all the arts, and when architecture embraced nature in a new and meaningful relationship the gardener was either sucked into the partnership or publicly castigated for his artistic inadequacies.

In spite of the Guild's claims for unity in the arts, a vitriolic dispute developed in the early 1890s between the art of the architect and the craft of the gardener. Gardeners lined up behind the articulate and outspoken William Robinson while architects took the side of the opinionated and bombastic Sir Reginald Blomfield (1856–1942), and insults were exchanged across the apparently 'dainty' and refined pages of gardening books. Ironically, the seeds of the conflict were sown in a paper given at the Art Workers' Guild by J.D. Sedding in May 1889 on 'The Architectural Treatment of Gardens'. Further contributions were given by Mervyn Macartney, Halsey Ricardo, John Belcher, Somers Clarke and Sir Reginald Blomfield, and in 1891 Sedding's paper formed the basis of a book, *Garden-Craft Old and New*.

Sedding was a practical gardener. According to the Reverend Russell, who wrote the preface to *Garden-Craft*, every evening he commuted home to West Wickham by train, kissed his wife and children,

'and then supposing there was light and the weather fine, his coat was off and he fell to work at once with spade or trowel in his garden, absorbed in his plants and flowers.'

After supper and prayers, when the rest of his family had gone to bed, Sedding 'would settle himself in his little study and write, write, write, until past midnight'. Yet for all his practical enthusiasm, Sedding claimed garden design to be an art, and therefore within the remit of the architect rather than the landscape designer: 'It is not so much at what he finds in the landscape gardener's creations that the architect demurs, but at what he misses.' Although he conceded that some knowledge of plants was necessary to garden design, it was the structure of the garden, its mysterious or picturesque qualities, that really interested him. The gardener's craft was largely ignored, and gardeners, not qualifying as 'art workers' and therefore prohibited from joining the Guild, depended on William Robinson and the horticultural press to come to their defence.

Sedding was a vehement defender of English traditions in garden design. He eulogized the genius of Repton, adding to his vocabulary of English picturesque the discipline and nostalgic charm of the Tudor garden. He defended the art of topiary: 'I have no more scruple in using the scissors upon tree or shrub, where trimness is desirable, than I have in mowing the turf of the lawn.' One of the illustrations in *Garden-Craft Old and New* was a drawing by W.R. Lethaby of a formal garden enclosed by tall yew hedges, crowned by topiary obelisks with peacocks perched on their pinnacles. Like William Morris, Philip Webb and Richard Norman Shaw, Sedding had been apprenticed in G. E. Street's office and he shared their passion for English landscape and architectural traditions. There was some common ground between his view of garden craft and that of Robinson, and the two men were exact contemporaries. Although Sedding insisted upon symmetry close to the house, like Robinson, he believed that the garden should become more natural towards its boundaries:

'the symmetry should break away by easy stages from the dressed to the undressed parts, and so on to the open country, beginning with wilder effects upon the country boundaries of the place.'

Sedding's commitment to garden design was important because of his influence on younger members of the Art Workers' Guild and his former architectural pupils, who included Ernest Barnsley and Ernest Gimson. Like Morris and Webb he wanted to revive the old-fashioned garden as a return to the simplicity and harmony with nature of a pre-industrial culture: 'The old-fashioned garden ... represents one of the pleasures of England, one of the charms of that quiet beautiful life of bygone times.' His old-fashioned garden was structured by the architect, however, and he criticized William Robinson, condemning one of his designs for a town garden published in *The English Flower Garden*: 'No wonder he does not fear Nature's revenge, where is so little Art to destroy!'[18] Sedding died just a few months before the publication of *Garden-Craft Old and New*, so that if Robinson had composed an acrimonious review of the book, good taste restrained him from printing it, and he contented himself with a dismissal of Sedding's 'Art drivel'. The next year, however, Sedding's position was taken up by another member of the Art Workers' Guild, the British bulldog figure of Sir Reginald Blomfield. In his book *The Formal Garden in England* he championed the architect as supreme garden designer and accused the natural or wild gardener of fraudulent hypocrisy.

Like Robinson, Blomfield abhorred the Victorian garden with its brightly coloured carpet bedding. Where Robinson proposed a new style of gardening, however, combining the best new hardy plants with old-fashioned and wild flowers, laid out from a gardener's perspective so that each plant could be grown under both optimum and relatively natural conditions, Blomfield insisted upon a return to first principles, a step backwards into history. He argued that in the seventeenth century

> 'garden design took its place in the great art of architecture, with the result of that well-ordered harmony which was characteristic of the house and garden in England down to the middle of the eighteenth century.'

The nineteenth century, he claimed, had offered only

> 'a habit of specialising which may sometimes arrive at technical excellence, but which has assuredly lost us the architectural sense. It is the absence of this sense which is the most glaring fault of modern design, and it is shown most conspicuously in the work of the modern landscape gardener.'

The landscape gardener was not the only culprit, according to Blomfield, for the deterioration in design standards. He warned of the 'dangerous fascination' for garden writers 'with a turn for pretty sentiment rather than for exact habits of thought'. The amateur, he warned, 'should be on his guard against abstract rules and recipes. What looks well in one place may look very ill in another, and when the copy is based on a print or a drawing ill understood, the result is probably disastrous.'[19]

The garden, according to Blomfield, was not a question of horticulture at all, but of design:

> 'The question at issue is a very simple one. Is the garden to be considered in relation to the house, and as an integral part of a design which depends for its success on the combined effect of house and garden; or is the house to be ignored in dealing with the garden?'

He focused his argument on the current preoccupation with uniting architecture and nature: 'The object of formal gardening is to bring the two into harmony, to make the house grow out of its surroundings, and to prevent its being an excrescence on the face of nature.' Blomfield believed that architecture could not resemble anything in nature, 'unless you are content with a mud-hut and cover it with grass'. It was up to the architect, therefore, to control and modify nature in order to bring it into harmony with the house: 'The harmony arrived at is not any trick of imitation, but an affair of a dominant idea which stamps its impress on house and grounds alike.'

Blomfield's dictatorial view of architecture and its supremacy over horticulture was one of the principal tenets of the classical revival, which displaced the Arts and Crafts movement in the first years of the twentieth century. His premise that the architect need know nothing of horticulture in order to design a garden was fundamentally opposed to Arts and Crafts principles. It denies the ideals that William Morris had personified, that a practical knowledge of craftsmanship and materials was essential to good design. Blomfield wrote that the horticulturist and the gardener were indispensable, but that their contributions were subservient to the designs of the architect:

'they stand in the same relation to the designer as the artist's colourman does to the painter, or perhaps it would be fairer to say, as the builder and his workmen stand to the architect.'

Just as the architect need not concern himself with the process for manufacturing bricks, he argued, 'so in the garden the designer need not know the best method of planting every flower or shrub included in his design; the gardener should see to that.' Blomfield personified the age of the British Empire, of Victorian arrogance and expansion. In the preface to the third edition of *The Formal Garden in England* he recognized that the first two editions of his book had precipitated 'a somewhat acrid controversy' between architects and landscape gardeners. He also gave a succinct summary of the dispute: 'The gardeners said the architects knew nothing about gardening, and the architects said the gardeners knew nothing about design, and there was a good deal of truth on both parts.'

The Formal Garden undoubtedly played an important part in shaping the Arts and Crafts garden. It defined, verbally and with superb illustrations by Inigo Thomas, the formal aspects of the old English garden. The walled gardens of Haddon Hall in Derbyshire and Edzell Castle in Forfarshire, as well as Brickwall, were considered and the differences between old English and Italian gardens were described. Ambitious formal layouts of gardens like Rycott in Oxford were illustrated and plans were drawn for knots. The chapter on garden architecture was beautifully illustrated with old stone gateways, dovecotes and pavilions that were to inspire the architecture of Arts and Crafts gardens for the next twenty years.

Blomfield's ideal of shaping nature to the architect's cause was more conservative than the commitment to nature's materials, celebrated through architecture, that some of his contemporaries were writing about at the same time. In 1889 the architect Edward Prior had lectured ardently on 'the velvet thatch, the soft warm tile, the silver splashed lead, the hoary roughness of stone ... how charmingly these lie in the lap of the countryside.' There was a determination among many members of the Art Workers' Guild to follow Philip Webb's example and evolve an architecture that, through deep sheltering roofs, craggy forms and local materials, would achieve a harmony with nature that would be more radical than anything Blomfield could conceive. By generating a controversy over the role of the architect versus the gardener in garden design, both Blomfield and William Robinson prepared the ground for the Arts and Crafts architect. Although in theory Blomfield's arguments for the artistic pre-eminence of the architect contradicted the Arts and Crafts spirit of collaboration, they were irresistible to the vanity of even the most progressive architect.

The revival of the old English formal garden structure was to be the backbone of the Arts and Crafts garden. The architect's involvement in designing the garden as a seamless continuation of the plan of the house promoted an identity for the garden as an outdoor extension to the living-rooms, which accommodated changes in country-house lifestyle, as well as creating patterns and repetitions between the gardens and the interiors of the house. Robinson's vigorous promotion of naturalizing plants, and of using a wide range of hardy perennials, made gardening less labour-intensive and more accessible to the enthusiastic amateur. There are clear similarities between his writings on gardening and Philip Webb's building philosophy, and the two men knew and appreciated each other's work. On paper William Robinson and Sir Reginald Blomfield were diametrically opposed to one another. In the flesh, however, they were less antagonistic. Robinson invited Blomfield to be his guest at Gravetye Manor, and while in public they admitted to no compromise, in private they must both have recognized that their legacy to garden design was a joint affair: it was the wild or natural method of planting contained within the structure of the formal garden that defined the Arts and Crafts garden.

Footnotes

1 W.R. Lethaby, *Philip Webb and his Work*, Oxford University Press, 1935, p.156.
2 Ibid., p.125.
3 Ibid., p.128.
4 These three articles, from which subsequent quotations are made, appear in *Country Life* for 30 July 1898, pp.144–7; pp.109–12; 6 August 1898, and 21 January 1905, pp.90–9.
5 The date 1582 inscribed over the door refers to the front of the building only.
6 Wickham Flower's description of Great Tangley is in the archaeological collection of Surrey Local Studies Collection. It is quoted in an unpublished manuscript, *Journal of an Ancient Manor*, in the possession of J-P Marix Evans.
7 J-P Marix Evans has kindly pointed out to me that Wickham Flower's father had been a keen amateur archaeologist, so that the methodical thoroughness with which the moat was cleared could be attributed either to the client's involvement or that of his architect.
8 Anon., 'Great Tangley Manor Surrey, the country house of Mr. Wickham Flower.', *Country Life,* 6 August 1898, p.146.
9 Webb's letters to George Boyce are in the British Library. They are quoted in *Journal of an Ancient Manor*, an unpublished manuscript in the possession of J-P Marix Evans.
10 Ibid.
11 According to *Country Life* it could be flooded from the moat, but this was not the case. A sluice gate from the lake is still in place, while the water level in the moat was at a lower level.
12 This issue of *Country Life* of 30 July 1898 was inaccurate on the date for Webb's library extension by four years. It is known that Great Tangley was conveyed to a colleague of Flower's on 27 January 1885 and presumed that it was conveyed to Flower more or less immediately. Unless he began work on the garden before the purchase was complete, therefore, the date of 1884/5 seems too early.
13 Letter from Philip Webb to George Boyce, September 1894, British Library.
14 The architect was Webb's assistant, George Jack.
15 W. R. Lethaby, *Philip Webb and his Work*, Oxford University Press, 1935, p.76.
16 This story was relayed to me by John Brandon-Jones.
17 Quoted in H. J. L. J Masse, *The Art Workers' Guild 1884–1934*, Art Workers' Guild, London, 1935.
18 J.D. Sedding, *Garden-Craft Old and New*, Kegan Paul, 1891, p.129.
19 Reginald Blomfield and F. Inigo Thomas, *The Formal Garden in England*, Preface to 3rd edition, Macmillan, London, 1901, pp. vii-viii.

Chapter Six

The Influence of a Single Woman: Gertrude Jekyll

'The name of Gertrude Jekyll will not be found linked with the beginnings of the Arts and Crafts Movement. Just as Morris's name is unavoidable, so hers is invisible, though she would seem to have been just as talented.'[1]

Jane Brown has suggested that Jekyll's amateur status, together with the delicate issue of her being a lady of independent means, dwarfed her reputation in the recording of design history. In the quality and diversity of her own work, however, and in her collaboration with architects, Jekyll personified the Arts and Crafts movement. Although she was not eligible to join the Art Workers' Guild (women were excluded), she contradicted the Guild's dismissal of gardeners for

RIGHT: *Munstead Wood, designed by Lutyens with Jekyll's collaboration in 1893–7, viewed from the north-west with Jekyll's borders leading away from the house.*

their lack of artistic training, and at the same time confounded the prejudices of gardeners against artists and architects for their lack of practical experience. She had both artistic training and practical experience. Although she was one of the most knowledgeable and practical garden designers of any period, she warded off the prejudices of both camps by emphasizing her status as an amateur. She numbered some of the most influential designers and clients of the day among her friends, and her network of connections and acquaintances was extensive. Through her work as a writer she inspired and instructed gardeners in England and North America, from the absolute beginner with a pocket-handkerchief plot to the experienced professional with a string of substantial commissions. She was neither condescending nor dogmatic in her writing. Her clear and well-founded opinions were worded with a mixture of poetry and reason; they were practical and specific enough to inspire action, and at the same time so lilting and persuasive that they could be read purely for pleasure. Unlike Blomfield and Robinson, Jekyll was seldom confrontational. She earned others' respect without demanding conformity, and this was an inherent part of her success.

Jekyll was born in London in 1843, the fourth surviving child of a progressive upper-middle-class family. When she was four and a half the family moved to a mansion house close to Bramley village in Surrey, so she grew up with the freedom of a large old garden and, later, the village lanes to wander through and explore. She was an energetic and feisty child. In *Children and Gardens* she recalled the expeditions with her brothers into Bramley Park 'to go up trees, and to play cricket, and take wasps' nests after dark, and do dreadful things with gunpowder'.[2] Her father was a retired captain in the Grenadier Guards with a keen interest in science and the arts. Gertrude and her brothers were encouraged to help him with his electrical experiments and to make things in the workshop, which she later described as 'a kind of heaven of varied delights after the fixed restriction of the schoolroom hours'. She gathered a rudimentary understanding of mechanics and learnt to work with specialist tools skilfully:

'an early acquaintance with tools and materials and mechanism is a valuable possession in anyone's life ... I have always taken much pleasure in working and seeing things grow under my hand, so I feel that the mechanical part has become much easier because of the ever-busy workshop at home.'[3]

Even as a child there must have been a seriousness of purpose about Gertrude Jekyll. Many of her adult philosophies stemmed from a deep intuitive knowledge of country ways that was gathered in childhood. There was nothing patronizing or nostalgic in her observation of what she later described as 'the true old country people, some of whose womenkind have hardly ever been more than ten miles from home; people who still retain the speech and ways of thought and plain simple dress of the early part of the century'. Her thorough understanding of their crafts and the seasonal patterns of their tasks was based on the keen interest and familiarity that a child could achieve, escaping to the kitchens or the old cottages of the village where adults of her privileged background would have been ill at ease. Throughout her life the barriers of sex, class and professional or social propriety that strait-jacketed her contemporaries dissolved in the face of Jekyll's intelligence and determination, so that she could write of James

Furlonger, the carter she photographed for *Home and Garden:* 'All my life I can remember my old friend with the donkey-cart, in intimate association with the lanes near my home.' She described his work trimming overgrown hedges and keeping the lanes clear, and his grief when his old white donkey had to be shot after twenty-seven years of service. Jekyll's interest was factual and affectionate, but never sentimental. The account ended with a description of how she bought the donkey's pelt, 'and now my friends take it for the skin of a polar bear, for it is almost white, and the mass of soft hair is nearly three inches deep.'

Soon after the family moved to Bramley, Jekyll was given her own patch of garden between the shrubbery and the field, some distance away from the house with its formal bedding schemes. There was a ditch where ferns grew alongside a thornless climbing rose, 'Blush Boursault', with pink flowers that she later recalled with great affection. At first, not knowing the names of flowers, like Kate Greenaway she invented her own names for them 'and greeted them as friends on her daily wanderings'. One wonders to what extent this idea of the little girl befriending flowers was a Victorian convention. Jekyll's relationship with plants, however, was exceptionally and unusually intimate, as she later described:

> 'If you will take any flower you please, and look it over and turn it about and smell it and feel it and try to find out all its little secrets, not of flower only, but of leaf, bud and stem as well, you will discover many wonderful things. This is how to make friends with plants, and very good friends you will find them to the end of your lives. I had got to know them as friends long before I could find out what their names were.'[4]

Jekyll enjoyed the flowers in her garden but she was interested in building too. She made a hut for herself between the laurels: 'I did not know anything about building then, so it was simply made of supple willow stems bent over and tied, with other sticks of willow and hazel wattled in.' Having read about walls made of wattle and clay, she dug up the clay soil in a swampy part of the garden. This had to be given up after 'one or two of my little barrowfuls and making a great mess of myself, so that I was not very well received in the schoolroom.' She made herself a stool out of old bits of board, and had to learn to sit very carefully to 'avoid a collapse'. Typically, when she was recalling the construction, she was still thinking how she might make it stable: 'If I had only known about putting in a bit on edge underneath, and nailing it through the top and at the ends, it would have been firm.'[5]

She was fortunate in having liberal parents, who nurtured and encouraged her individuality and gave her the benefit of a formal education at home, without attempting to mould her into a marriageable asset. Her father fondly described her as 'my oddity' and when it transpired that she was bright and creative as well as enterprising, with a resolute desire to train as an artist, she was enrolled for a two-year course at the School of Art in South Kensington. In the autumn of 1863, when her art-school training was complete, Jekyll accompanied Charles Newton and his wife Mary, her father's friends, on a study tour of Greece. Newton was Keeper of Greek and Roman Antiquities at the British Museum and there are drawings of Jekyll diligently sketching throughout the tour. On her return to England she continued to study paintings in the great national collections and to set herself professional standards in her own work.

In 1865 she visited Ruskin for the first time, and her diaries recorded many subsequent visits. Like all progressive artists of her generation she had copies of

The Seven Lamps of Architecture and *The Stones of Venice*, well thumbed and annotated, in her library. She was aware of the commands in *The Stones of Venice* to seek beauty in natural forms, to revere the 'savage' and soulful expressions of the simple labourer, and to abolish the slavery of man to the machine by returning to the dignity and spiritual expression of craftsmanship. Jekyll infiltrated the nerve centre of the dawning Arts and Crafts movement. She visited William Morris at Red Lion Square, and met Rossetti and Burne-Jones. We do not know whether or not she met Philip Webb, who was far less likely to be found at society gatherings than his fellow partners of Morris, Marshall, Faulkner and Co., but they had numerous mutual friends and acquaintances – not least William Robinson and Edwin Lutyens – so they would certainly have been informed of each other's work.

Through the 1860s Jekyll had access to many of the most influential figures in Victorian art and design. Meetings with William de Morgan, William Holman Hunt, Frederick Leighton and G.F. Watts were listed in her diary during a formative period in her own work. One of her paintings was accepted for the Royal Academy Summer Exhibition in 1865 and, as with Morris and Webb, her craftsmanship and design work extended across any media that attracted her interest. When she was in her thirties she was commissioned to design interiors for the Duke of Westminster at Eaton Hall. There was a commission at Kensington Palace and she designed and made silverwork for Burne-Jones, Queen Victoria's daughter, Princess Louise, and Lord Leighton. Lord Leighton described her embroideries on linen, exhibited at the International Galleries, as remarkable in their use of colour and arrangement: 'one of them, a design with scrolls of fishes, is so good as decorative invention that I hesitate to attribute it to an amateur'.[6] Jekyll's amateur status proved to be a ticklish problem for patrons hoping to commission paid work from her, as Lord Leighton's letters confirm. The range of her abilities, nevertheless, together with the combination of original artistic design with fine craftsmanship, made her a paragon of the Arts and Crafts movement: she was described by her friend George Leslie in his book *Our River* as a master of

> 'carving, modelling, house-painting, carpentry, smith's work, repoussé work, gilding, wood-inlaying, embroidery, gardening, and all manner of herb and flower knowledge and culture, everything being carried on with perfect method and completeness'.[7]

Jekyll's increasingly severe myopia – a debility that forced her to abandon her artistic career just as she was achieving recognition – affected both her personality and her design style as a gardener, as Jane Brown has perceptively documented. The arts that demanded most of her time – embroidery, painting and silverwork – had to be given up because they strained and exacerbated her already serious myopic condition. When her father died in 1876 she and her mother decided to return to Surrey after an absence of eight years and a period of frustration and disappointment drew to a close. Jekyll had disliked living in Berkshire, describing it as a time 'of what felt like exile – a perpetual homesickness and inability to be acclimatised'. Nevertheless, she had made a garden at the family home in Wargrave. George Leslie described it as 'a perfect wilderness of sweets, and old-fashioned flowers bloomed there in the greatest profusion; there were lavender hedges of marvellous growth'. He recalled how Jekyll had reaped him an armful of lavender, with a sickle of her own construction.

A new house was designed and built on Munstead Heath for Jekyll, a few miles from their former home at Bramley. By the time she and her mother moved – 'To Munstead for good' – on 26 September 1878 Jekyll had already formed an important friendship with William Robinson and begun writing for *The Garden*.

Robinson and *The Wild Garden* were important influences on Jekyll's gardening philosophy. Many of the herbaceous plants that were championed in *The Wild Garden* – hellebores, eryngiums, echinops and daylilies – became staples in Jekyll's garden designs and his commitment to natural planting was absorbed into her philosophy. The success of Robinson's books and his magazines, particularly *The Garden* and later *Gardening Illustrated*, expanded and sustained a massive new market for gardening publications catering for professional and amateur gardeners. Within nine months of the launch of *Gardening Illustrated* in 1879 Robinson could claim a larger market for it than for the rest of the British horticultural press put together; by 1881 the magazine had a circulation of 30,000 copies per week.

When Jekyll began to write about gardening her style and her status as an amateur were uniquely suited to this voracious readership. She exploited the impact of Robinson's sometimes fierce gardening radicalism. Her social and cultural background, her painterly conception of colour and composition and her connections in the world of arts and crafts as well as country-house society made her uniquely qualified to unite the artistic philosophies that Ruskin had instigated with Robinson's popular and progressive doctrines. Where Robinson and Blomfield had drawn a sharp division between the architect and the gardener, Jekyll, through her own practical and aesthetic appreciation of both building and gardening, and through her partnership with Lutyens, reunited them. Under Jekyll's jurisdiction gardening was elevated to an art, and it became an integral part of the Arts and Crafts movement.

Like William Morris, Jekyll had an acute sense of place and her knowledge of the hollow lanes around Munstead – their tangible history, visible in the exposed roots of ancient trees – was a vital factor in her work and her restored sense of well-being. She designed a substantial garden for herself and her mother at Munstead House. The creative energy and practical expertise that were thwarted by her myopia were applied with vision and dexterity to garden making. The sense of regeneration on her return to Surrey and the liberation of designing a composition on a grand scale, which could be dramatically changed in an afternoon's work with a border fork at the right time of year, contrasted with the concentration of nervous energy required in painting and silverwork, where a single mistake could ruin an entire piece. For Jekyll the garden at Munstead became the practical and experimental element in a complex equation of writing, designing and gardening, as well as encouraging an understanding of design in others.

Edwin Lutyens (1869–1944) was introduced to Jekyll at afternoon tea in the garden of Harry Mangles, an azaleodendron dealer, in the spring of 1889. He was twenty and barely qualified, having studied architecture for two years at the South Kensington School of Art before training for a further two years in the London office of Sir Ernest George. Although it was more usual to be pupilled for a period of five years, Lutyens had joked his way through pupillage, quickly absorbing 'all that was best worth learning'. It seems probable that the meeting between Jekyll and Lutyens was deliberately manufactured. She had bought some land across the road from her mother's house and was looking for an architect to design a house for her. He had recently set up in independent practice and was urgently in need of commissions. One of his first designs was for a cottage for Harry Mangles at Littleworth Cross, with tall brick chimneys and half-timbering, in the style of an old Surrey cottage. Jekyll must have been shown the drawings and been told all about the young architect before making an exacting study of him over tea. Lutyens later recorded his impression of their first meeting and his sense of privilege at meeting so celebrated a figure:

> 'She was dressed in, what I learnt later to be, her Go-to-Meeting Frock – a bunch of cloaked propriety topped by a black felt hat, turned down in front and up behind, from which sprang alert black cock's-tail feathers, curving and ever prancing forwards.
>
> Quiet and demure, of few words and those deliberately chosen and deliberately uttered in a quiet, mellow voice – with keen, bright eyes that missed little in their persistent observation. She spoke no word to me, but on leaving, with one foot on the step of her pony-cart and reins in hand, she invited me to Munstead on the very next Saturday.'[8]

Like Jekyll, Lutyens had grown up in Surrey. Delicate health had caused him to be educated at home with his sisters, rather than follow his brothers to boarding school. Later he told Osbert Sitwell:

> 'Any talent I may have was due to a long illness as a boy, which afforded me time to think, and subsequent ill health, because I was not allowed to play games, and so had to teach myself, for my enjoyment, to use my eyes instead of my feet.'[9]

He explored the lanes around his home in the village of Thursley. Fascinated by buildings, he made sketches on a small plate of glass with a piece of soap sharpened to a point. He was interested in the old buildings with uneven red-tiled roofs sweeping down almost to the ground, with half-timbered or tile-hung gables; but he was interested in the way that new buildings were made, too. He watched them during construction and haunted the builder's yard and the carpenter's shop. Jekyll would have been drawn to his practical curiosity – a quality she shared – and to his sensitivity to the stylistic trends and building traditions of Surrey. It seems probable that she took Lutyens on, sensing that she would be able to work with him. She could be confident, as a woman twenty-five years his senior with a wealth of ideas and experience of her own, that he would respect and interpret her exacting artistic and philosophical demands.

Her own garden at Munstead Wood was in place long before the house was designed. The land was bought in the early 1880s, on the opposite side of Munstead Heath Road to Munstead House, so that her many visitors – 'gardeners, artists, architects, and all such as worked with hand or brain', who according to Lutyens came to Jekyll 'for help, discussion and advice' – need not continue to disrupt her mother's quiet life. In her reminiscences Jekyll described the fifteen-acre plot with characteristic precision and tenderness:

> 'It is roughly triangular in shape, widest to the south, and slopes down to the north-west. There had been a close wood of Scotch Pine lately felled in the upper nine acres, then a wide strip of Chestnut coppice, and at the narrow end a small field of poor sandy soil.'[10]

There are no plans for the garden, suggesting that – like William Robinson's – Jekyll's relationship with the landscape of her home was profoundly intimate; the

RIGHT: *Munstead Wood, 'designed and built in the thorough and honest spirit of the good work of old days'.*

garden would have been laid out on site, in response to the innate qualities of the land and its history. She was very clear that design should evolve out of natural conditions. In a letter to Robinson, written in the early 1880s when he employed an architect to design a house for him without first having a site (before Gravetye was found), she wrote: 'I can never satisfactorily imagine a house without knowing the particular site. A house must grow up between the ground on one side & its master on the other & must marry both.'[11] Although the letter was written before Jekyll had met Lutyens, she would already have been working on the garden at Munstead Wood, and she must have been preoccupied with the future design of her own house as she wrote: 'My ideal house, after an enclosed porch would have a good size habitable hall or room. If space or means could not allow it as an extra sitting room it would be the place to dine in & the stairs would rise from it.' The ideal of the 'living hall', making reference to the great hall of the medieval house, was to become the focus of the Arts and Crafts house.

There was a three-year period of professional courtship between Jekyll and Lutyens before the house for Munstead Wood was designed. His description of their second meeting gives a clear and affectionate insight into their friendship, just as that of the first portrays her formality:

'I was there on the tick of four, and was received by a somewhat different person – very much at home, genial and communicative, dressed in a short blue skirt that in no way hid her ankles, and the boots made famous through their portraiture by W. Nicholson; a blue linen apron with its ample marsupial pocket full of horticultural impedimenta; a blue-striped linen blouse box-pleated like a Norfolk jacket, the sleeves fastened close to her round wrists, giving her small and characteristic hands full freedom. She wore a straw hat turned up and down at back and front, trimmed with a blue silk bow and ribbon.'[12]

This first visit to Munstead was a prelude to many more, and 'the week-end at Munstead became a habit'. They took the pony and cart, with Jekyll in the driving seat, 'for many a voyage of discovery' into Surrey and Sussex, seeking out the old houses, farmhouses and cottages, discussing their methods of construction, and talking with their inmates about their lives and the cottage industries that supported them. We cannot know the extent to which Jekyll was consciously preparing her young architect for the design of Munstead Wood, although the Scottish architect Robert Lorimer suggested that she had 'pretty well run him' until he was twenty-seven. Their friendship was tested in 1893 by the design of Woodside at Chenies, Buckinghamshire, the first house and garden to be officially designed by Lutyens and Jekyll together, and the result was a success. Jekyll had a clearly formulated architectural philosophy of her own, founded on the ancient building traditions and practical considerations that she had studied from her childhood in the lanes of Surrey. Her own description of Munstead Wood, published in *Home and Garden* in 1900 and written a year and a half after moving in, reveals her to have been exceptionally closely involved not only in the planning of the house but in every aspect, technical and aesthetic, of its design and construction.

Home and Garden, her second book, began with an account of 'How the house was built'. It is a deeply personal and unusual description, as though the house had already existed in her imagination and in the materials of local woods, long before Lutyens called it up in drawings and stone. She wrote:

'In some ways it is not exactly a new house, although no building ever before stood upon its site. But I had been thinking about it for so many years, and the main block of it and the whole sentiment of it were so familiar to my mind's eye, that when it came to be a reality I felt as if I had already been living in it a good long time.'

She was adamant that the house should be

'designed and built in the thorough and honest spirit of the good work of old days ... The house is not in any way a copy of any old building, though it embodies the general characteristics of the older structures of its own district.'

Everything about it was 'strong and serviceable, and looks and feels as if it would wear and endure for ever'.

It was made clear that she was not the architect of Munstead Wood:

'Many of my friends, knowing that I dabble in construction and various handicrafts, have asked whether I did not design my house myself. To which question, though I know it is meant to be kind and flattering, I have to give an emphatically negative answer.'

She wrote that amateurs might derive supreme satisfaction from designing their own houses, but that there would always be 'bungles and awkward places' unless the 'higher knowledge' of an architect was consulted. Although Edwin Lutyens was not named in the book, Jekyll wrote of him: 'The architect has a thorough knowledge of the local ways of using the sandstone that grows in our hills, and that for many centuries has been the building material of the district, and of all the lesser incidental methods of adapting means to ends that mark the well-defined way of building of the country, so that what he builds seems to grow naturally out of the ground.' She admitted to having had a say in the position of the house and 'more or less how the rooms should lie together', specifying that she wanted 'a small house with plenty of room in it – there are seven bedrooms in all – and that I disliked small narrow passages, and would have nothing poky or screwy or ill-lighted.' When the plans were drawn up every detail was discussed: 'Naturally in the course of our discussions we had many an amicable fight, but I can only remember one when one might say that any "fur flew."' It was over an aesthetic point that would have added to the cost of the building but not to its utility, and Jekyll, not in the habit of using long words, famously ended a torrent of objections with: 'My house is to be built for me to live in and to love; it is not to be built as an exposition of architectonic inutility!'

Unusually, the house was built without a written contract. Jekyll wrote with pride of 'a perfect understanding existing between the architect, the builder, and the proprietor', which, she claimed, saved the expense of posting a clerk of works on the job 'to see that the builder does not cheat the proprietor'. In fact, she posted herself on the job, undoubtedly striking anxiety and respect in equal measure into the hearts of builder and architect alike. She was living in The Hut, a small cottage only eighty yards from the building site, designed for her by Lutyens in 1894 as temporary accommodation.

Every aspect of the work was studied with relish. In *Home and Garden* she described the craftsmanship of building in terms that matched the quality of observation of her architect contemporaries. It is in her description of the sounds of building, however, that Jekyll's extraordinary combination of poet and practitioner can be heard. Her keen hearing compensated for her short-sightedness and she claimed to be able to identify trees by the sound of the wind in their leaves. This is her account of the sound of bricklaying:

'The chop and rush of the trowel taking up its load of mortar from the board, the dull slither as the moist mass was laid as a bed for the next brick in the course; the ringing music of the soft-tempered blade cutting a well-burnt brick, the muter tap of its shoulder settling it into its place, aided by the down-bearing pressure of the finger-tips of the left hand; the sliding scrape of the tool taking up the overmuch mortar that squeezed out of the joint, and the neat slapping of it into the cross-joint. The sharp double tap on the mortar board, a signal that more stuff was wanted. Then at the mortar-mixing place the fat popping of the slaking lime throwing off its clouds of steam; the working of the mixing tool in the white sea enclosed by banks of sand – a pleasant sound, strangely like the flopping of a small boat on short harbour wavelets ...'

It goes on to describe the carpenter's work and the 'melodious scream' of his plane.

Jekyll's building philosophy was quintessentially Arts and Crafts. Had she been a man, she would have been heralded as a pioneer figure in architecture as well as in gardening. Her involvement in every aspect of the craft of building was comparable to that of Webb, and her integrity in the use of natural materials was a perceptive and imaginative application of Ruskin's most passionate principles. The inner structural frame of Munstead Wood was of timber – not the casually selected wood of a timber yard that a London builder would be obliged to use, but oak, chosen for its natural forms, which Jekyll could remember from her early childhood growing above a carpet of bluebells less than two miles from the new house. For Jekyll building materials were part of a personal as well as a local history. She understood the time and conditions that it took to create them, as well as the tools and traditions that shaped them into a building:

'I used to see these great grey trees, in twilight looking almost ghostly against the darkly-mysterious background of the sombre firs. And I remember always thinking how straight and tall they looked, for these sandy hills do not readily grow such great oaks ... I am glad to know that my beams are these same old friends, and that the pleasure that I had in watching them green and growing is not destroyed but only changed as I see them stretching above me as grand beams of solid English oak.'

She described the way in which the country builder would go into the woods to select his timber, season it slowly in his yard, and then take the architect's drawing and choose each piece exactly for its purpose.

The garden at Munstead Wood was already mature when the house was being built. It was designed with broad confident lines and the same clear, rational thinking, refusing to be swayed by conventions, which distinguishes Jekyll's writing. The layout of the main beds and the relationship between the plan of the house and that of the garden were relatively haphazard compared with later gardens by Jekyll and Lutyens. In later collaborations the main borders were aligned with the axes of the house. At Munstead the geometry of the garden is more arbitrary and it skews away from the angle of the house, partly because Lutyens contradicted Jekyll's initial ideas for the orientation of the building, specifying a north-south axis so that the principal rooms would face south.

Munstead Wood is particularly interesting because it reveals the gardening styles of the two designers quite separately. Large areas of the garden were laid out before Jekyll and Lutyens met, and even when they were planning the house together it must have been

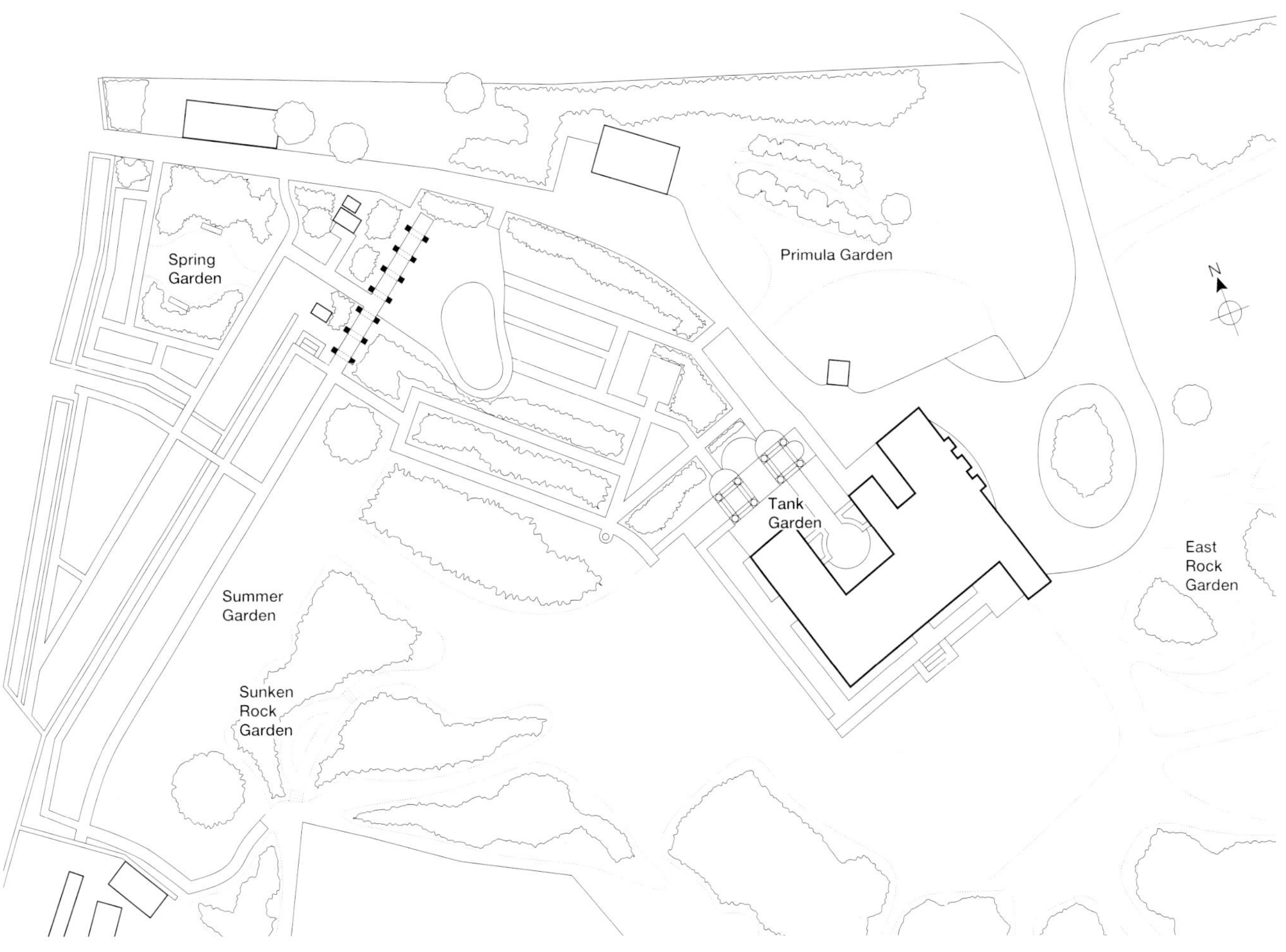

Above: *Garden plan, Munstead Wood, Surrey, Gertrude Jekyll and Edwin Lutyens. Garden designed from 1883.*

some time before Lutyens plucked up enough courage to suggest alterations to the garden. Once the main borders were cut, planted and maturing, Jekyll would have been disinclined to dig them up and start again to conform to an idea of architectural unity. The areas closest to the house – the north court, tank pool, and the south and west terraces – represent one of the first garden collaborations between Jekyll and Lutyens. There is a tangible sense of mathematical precision and crisply defined detail about the Tank Garden that is absent in the main structure of the garden farther from the house, where Lutyens's intervention is less evident.

One of the most extraordinary things about the garden at Munstead Wood is its planning. It was usual for the main flower borders to be laid on the south side of the house, becoming less formal towards the boundaries, and the orientation of Lutyens's building might have anticipated this kind of treatment. At Munstead, however, the rules were decisively broken. The main borders are on the north-west side of the house, some partially concealed behind high walls or sunk out of view into hollows. No concessions were made to the general practice of designing a floral display like a doily around the footings to the house, which could be viewed in its entirety without stepping outside. Instead the borders are organized into 'walks' that lead the visitor away from the building, to explore all the different parts of the garden. This was unconventional enough, but it paled in significance compared with the treatment of the south side of the house. Instead of looking out across a parterre of carpet bedding, or at the very least a clearly structured arrangement of flower beds, the principal rooms opened on to a natural clearing within a copse of mature birches. There was a deliberate impression, lost once the relatively short-lived trees had fallen, of a centuries-old house, cocooned within the woodland like a house in a fairy-tale. The birches were underplanted with young azaleas and rhododendrons, which Jekyll selected for their colour (many of them are unnamed varieties) from the seedlings at Waterer's Nursery near by. Three grass paths, following lines suggested by the trees rather than by an architect's drawing, led into her beloved woodland; one of these, the Green Wood Walk, she described as her 'most precious possession'.

The house had to be approached on foot; there was no driveway for ponies and traps: 'I like the approach to a house to be as quiet and modest as possible, and in this way I wanted it to tell its own story as the way in to a small dwelling standing in wooded ground.'[13] The footpath entered the enclosure of the house by degrees, first through an arched opening in the east wall, accentuated by Lutyens with radiating straight lines of tiles laid end-on in the stonework, and by Jekyll with a generous covering of *Hydrangea petiolaris*. The opening gave entrance to a long, covered porch: 'This serves as a dry approach to the main door, and also as a comfortable full-stop to the southern face of the house, returning forward square with that face.'[14] Even before the porch was entered, however, Jekyll and Lutyens had shattered the carefully laid down rules of country-house design: the visitor was immediately faced with a view across the porch to the secluded areas of the garden beyond. Inside the porch there was a timber window frame, unglazed, looking along the south terrace, and next to it a door into the garden framed by two large tubs of mop-head hydrangeas: 'Anyone entering looks through to the garden picture of lawn and trees and low broad steps, and dwarf dry wall crowned with the hedge of Scotch Briers.'[15]

Jekyll was partly reconciled to the attractions of her garden for an inquisitive public. She described Munstead Wood in words and photographs in her books at a time when garden visiting, with or without advance warning was becoming increasingly popular. This public exposure was frequently read as an open invitation. In the preface to *Home and Garden* Jekyll's readers were gently reprimanded:

'while it is always pleasant to hear from or to see old friends, and indeed all who work hard in their own gardens, yet, as a would-be quiet worker, who is by no means over-strong, I venture to plead with my kind and numerous, though frequently unknown friends, that I may be allowed to retain a somewhat larger measure of peace and privacy.'

The public and professional nature of her work as a gardener might well have caused her to set the privacy of her house, rather than her garden, at a premium. Although it was unorthodox to present the visitor with a framed picture of the garden before the front door was in sight, for many of Jekyll's visitors the garden was the main objective. She designed secret places into which she could escape. The tradition of a house with a front to be viewed by passers-by and a back secluded away for family use did not apply to Munstead Wood. Lutyens designed a long sandstone terrace along the south face of the house, with wide steps linking the clearing with the oak door to the drawing room, and another running alongside the west front. Both were flanked by narrow borders so that Jekyll could plant right up to the walls of the house: roses and *Clematis armandii* on the west wall, underplanted with *Geranium renardii*.

The quiet side of the house, and the most formal part of the garden, was on the north side, where Lutyens set a deep shady courtyard between two wings. At the far end the first-floor corridor, half-timbered with a continuous line of leaded-light windows, was jettied out, providing shelter in all weathers for the sitting area below. Under the lip of the projection Jekyll trained a *Clematis montana* into a garland, which the current gardener at Munstead has struggled to reinstate. It has to grow from the west to the east side, and this has proved difficult because the clematis wants to grow upwards towards the light. Jekyll furnished the courtyard with troughs of hostas and white lilies, forced in the greenhouse so that they would flower simultaneously with the clematis. At the centre of the courtyard a symbolic pool is suggested by a circle of rippled, water-marked sandstone, framed by low box-edged borders. At a lower level, to the north of the courtyard, the suggestion of water is realized in a deep, square tank, finely proportioned in relation to the stone platforms and steps leading down to either side: the calming effects of water are complemented by the harmonious order of geometry. Below the tank a yew hedge, clipped to shape and forming a semi-circle, echoed the circle of stone in the courtyard. Beyond these geometric patterns, however, the hard landscaping and architectural refinement that were Lutyens's contribution had to be reconciled with the more fluid planting considerations of Jekyll's established garden.

The junction between the new garden designed around the house and the older borders laid out by Jekyll is marked by a triangular pattern of paths dominated by a solid seat with a tall birch behind it, where Jekyll's cats liked to sleep in the afternoon sun. When she remarked to a friend, Charles Liddell, that it would be convenient if the different parts of the garden had names, he instantly christened the seat 'the Cenotaph of Sigismunda'.

'The name was so undoubtedly suitable to the monumental mass of Elm, and to its somewhat funereal environment of weeping Birch and spire-like Mullein, that it took hold at once, and the Cenotaph of Sigismunda it will always be as long as I am alive to sit on it.'[16]

Later, when Lutyens was asked to design a monument to mark the anniversary of the Armistice, he recalled the 'Cenotaph for Bumps' (Aunt Bumps was his name for Jekyll), and the word was brought back into use to describe a non-denominational memorial.[17] Although the original birch has long since fallen and when Jekyll's borders were grassed over in the 1960s the seat itself was buried in pieces under turf, it has now been reinstated and a new birch planted in place as part of the reconstruction of the garden.

Jekyll's garden crystallizes around a long sandstone wall, which defines the main axis and separates the Spring and Kitchen Gardens from those nearer the house. The main borders are laid out at right angles to the wall and alongside it: from the Cenotaph of Sigismunda, the Nut Walk and the main aster beds run perpendicular to the wall towards a pergola, which in turn was set parallel to the wall. Jekyll divided the garden into parts with long straight paths, and planted each area to celebrate a different season. In the corner

LEFT: *The triangular pattern of paths with the Cenotaph of Sigismunda to the left that marks the juncture between the garden around the house, laid out by Jekyll and Lutyens together, and the more established garden planned by Jekyll alone.*

RIGHT: Narcissi *and white tulips underplanted with* arabis *in the Spring Garden..*

farthest away from the house there was the Spring Garden, sheltered from cold winter winds by the tall sandstone wall and planted with delicate early bulbs and spring flowers, backed by more architectural plants like yuccas and acanthus to take effect later in the year. This part of the garden was in flower from March to early May. It was planned with meticulous forethought and attention to detail so that the disasters that beset so many spring borders (flowers flattened by wind and rain, or a display too delicate to create a good effect) would be averted. In the middle of the Spring Garden a roughly circular lawn was furnished with simple bench seats shielded by hazels and a covering of tall oaks that sheltered the garden, admitting light during the winter but creating shady growing conditions later in the year. The borders on three sides were planted with spring flowers: primulas, drifts of pale narcissus, doronicum, tulips, wallflowers and forget-me-nots. *Clematis montana* was trained through the hazels and twined over ropes to hang in

garlands between them. As the bulbs and wallflowers faded, yellow tree peonies underplanted with lamb's ears came into flower and the climbing rose 'Mme Alfred Carrière', trained over arches, drew attention towards the main areas of the garden.

On the other side of the sandstone wall the June Garden was planted in cottage style around The Hut, with old shrub roses and the scented China rose 'The Garland', which Jekyll planted in many of her gardens. She used simple, old-fashioned plants: white foxgloves, lupins, snapdragons, irises and lilies. She was conscious, in her planting, of the symbolism of flowers and their associations through history, adding attributes of her own to the conventional reading of flowers. The lily was synonymous not only with purity, but also (surely as an interpretation of its growing habit) with 'uprightness' and 'singleness of purpose'. The 'beauty and sweetness' of the rose, according to Jekyll, merited 'a type of strength, of righteous purpose, and of bountiful beneficence' in addition to its historic importance as a national emblem and a heraldic device. As she went on to write:

'Is it not a badge proper to the good knight, whose nature is strong and brave and tender, cheerful and courteous; who goes forth to battle for the weak, to establish good rule in place of oppression; whose work is to "cleanse the land," to "clear the dark places and let in the law"?'

Jekyll's rigorous professionalism identified her more closely with the role of the 'good knight' than with the

LEFT: *Jekyll's understanding of texture and form in the foliage of the west terrace is complimented by the use of local building materials – Bargate stone, oak, and clay tiles laid end-on.*

innocent damsel generally conjured up as his partner in the medieval symbolism of the Arts and Crafts movement; the absence of the latter in her consideration of the lily is notable.

Roses and lilies were planted in abundance around The Hut. A short tunnel of yew framed the entrance to the cottage, giving way to a lower hedge for the three yards leading to the door, 'for daylight's sake'. To combat 'one of the perennial griefs of the garden' – that it could not grow the lime- and loam-loving Madonna lily – Jekyll gave one end of the border between The Hut and the path 'a good deep dressing of lime rubbish' and the white lilies were planted next to *Pyrus japonica*. *Rosa chinensis* and *Rosa moschata* were trained over hoops, underplanted with white aquilegias and *Myrrhis odorata* in the front border to one side of the cottage. On the opposite side, before The Hut was even built, a *Clematis montana* and a rambling rose were planted to climb through:

'a Holly of rather upright shape some twenty feet high ... The Clematis went up quickest, and for two or three years made a fairly good show, but has not done very much since; but the Rose now fills the top of the Holly ... the flowery ends come tumbling out ... tender, pink-tinged masses of the little Rose-clusters are seen upon their ground of the prickly shining Holly leaves and of the softer sombre Yew.'

Close to the June Garden the Hidden Garden was concealed behind unclipped yew and holly, sunk out of view in a natural depression, with no obvious entrance so that it could be mistaken for a clump of bushes. This was Jekyll's refuge. Stone steps and sandy paths led down into a hollow, set with rocks and planted with drifts of columbines, cerastium, catmint and irises, backed by larger shrubs: tree peonies, the daisy bush, *Olearia*, and rhododendrons.[18]

Although The Hut and the Hidden Garden occurred as incidentals within the garden plan, the main border running alongside the sandstone wall held the overall design together. In July and August it was the main focus of the garden. It was fourteen feet wide, two hundred feet long, and the wall behind it was eleven feet high. Rambling roses, magnolia and a succession of flowering shrubs were planted against the wall to establish a backdrop to the border, and a path between the back of the border and the wall allowed access to both. The plants were massed together in elongated drifts that in plan look like sausages, overlapping so that combinations of colour and form would read as a continuous sequence. Stately yuccas (*Yucca filamentosa* and *Y. recurvifolia*) were used to terminate the composition at both ends and to flank the path that bisected the border and led into the Spring Garden. Next to them, swathes of white flowers – snapdragons and lilies on one side, backed by white everlasting peas, tall white dahlias on the other side, behind *Campanula lactiflora* – gave way to the blue and mauve tints of delphiniums and asters. Jekyll was fond of the tall spires and woolly silver leaves of 'the two grand Mulleins, *Verbascum olympicum* and *V. phlomoides*'. In the main border she graded her colours from the cool tones of the mulleins to the stronger yellows of achillea, rudbeckia and yellow dahlias. At the heart of the border the yellows turned to oranges and reds: red-hot pokers were massed in front of deep red hollyhocks; dahlias ranging from 'Orange Fire King' to 'Cochineal' faded to the orange tones of daylilies.

Jekyll is famous for having composed her borders with a painter's eye for composition, with drifts of colour gradually ranging through the spectrum. Her friendship with the Impressionist painter Hercules Brabazon Brabazon and a familiarity with the complex rules of colour theory that influenced such of her contemporaries as Monet, Pissarro and Cézanne influenced her planting plans. However, in gardening (as opposed to painting) account had to be taken of the manner in which a flower's colour would alter as it developed from bud to faded bloom and as the seasons affected the scale and the tones of its foliage. Jekyll was confident and adept in her use of strong colours, but they were never employed as bright, isolated splashes. They intensified gradually in a crescendo and then diminished. In the Spring Garden scarlet tulips were massed at the entrance from the main garden, toning with orange crown imperials and the softer effect of brown wallflowers. Colour theorists like Michel Chevreul advised the artist to draw on nature for inspiration, to study the combinations of strong autumn tones in order to produce a harmonious effect. Here Jekyll had the advantage. Chevreul dictated a hierarchy of specific colour combinations, a set of rules that were considered essential to the attainment of beauty. It was decreed that white was the colour of light, making all things more beautiful, and that the combination of pale blue and white was most sublime.

These theories were composed for painters, however, who were concerned with two-dimensional compositions. In garden design white has a foreshortening effect, and in softer lights it has a dominant luminosity. Writing to an American colleague in 1913, Jekyll described the limitations of Chevreul's theories:

'That French chart is helpful to a certain degree, but when I looked through it a few years ago I could not but feel that in some ways it was misleading because in many cases it seems to attempt to define the undefinable.'[19]

Her triumph was the adaptation of complex artistic theories to a large scale and to a three-dimensional context, susceptible to changing conditions of light and natural growth. In her borders white was used at the extremities, to contain and compress a composition. It was scattered over walls or looped into garlands in the form of climbing roses and clematis or massed to give a scattered effect of dappled light in delicate clouds of gypsophila. She taught that gardeners, looking at the effects of distance on colour, must learn to differentiate between what they knew a colour to be close to, and the way it truly appears to be. She confessed to using a large leaf with a hole in it for this purpose,

'first looking at the distance without the leaf-frame in order to see how nearly I can guess the truth of the far colour. Even in the width of one ploughed field, especially in autumn when the air is full of vapour, in the farther part of the field the newly-turned earth is bluish-purple, whereas it is rich brown at one's feet.'

Her study of the effects of distance on colour must have been discussed with Ruskin. Many years later one of her gardening colleagues recalled being asked by Jekyll the colour of some distant grass and answering that it was green: 'And Miss Jekyll said to me that she had given the selfsame answer when asked the selfsame question by John Ruskin. "No it is not, Mr. Ruskin told me," said Miss Jekyll. "Were you to paint that grass, green is not the colour you would take from your watercolour box. It would be primrose yellow."'[20]

Jekyll's gardens were more akin to symphonies than to paintings in their complexity and layering of effects. Her expertise as a plantswoman, her ability to plan immense herbaceous borders that would grow, as if by magic, into harmonious configurations of colour and form, and her master planning of the garden into a succession of spectacular displays make her an awe-inspiring figure in garden history, particularly given the fact that so much of her work was pure invention. There were no comparable designers for Jekyll to study and emulate. Her success was founded on an intimate understanding of the individual needs of plants, amounting to a kind of empathy, and on close observation. The strengths and susceptibilities of every plant were understood and each was provided with an ideal growing environment. She was determined that

'There is no spot of ground, however arid, bare, or ugly, that cannot be tamed into such a state as may give an impression of beauty and delight. It cannot always be done easily; many things worth doing are not done easily; but there is no place under natural conditions that cannot be graced with an adornment of suitable vegetation.'

She was indefatigable in her determination that every part of the garden should be made beautiful, from the coke enclosure to the tool shed:

'sheds that would be otherwise unbeautiful can be adorned with rampant Vine and Jasmine and the free-growing Clematises and Virginia Creeper. For my own part, I wish I had more of such places in order to have a wider scope for such plantings; while in other gardens I groan in spirit to see the many opportunities wasted, and unsightliness reigning supreme where there might be pictures of delightful beauty.'[21]

A stone seat framed with yew was positioned at the end of the main flower border so that Jekyll could sit and look along its length. From one side of the seat a pergola continued the axis of the main border, leading to the Nut and Aster Walks to the house. An avenue of hazel trees, underplanted with shade-loving anemones, hellebores and primroses, flanked a wide straight path to the west side of the house. Parallel to this, the aster beds were planted to take effect in the late summer:

'Where space can be given, it is well to set apart a separate border for these fine plants alone. Here the starworts occupy a double border ... planted and regulated with the two-fold aim of both form and colour beauty.'

The larger white daisy, *Chrysanthemum uliginosum*, was planted with cultivars of *Aster novi-belgii*. Jekyll wrote that only a lack of suitable space prevented her from planting more special regions for good plants that were interesting only for a limited season. At Munstead there were gardens for primroses and for peonies as well as asters. She would have added gardens solely for tulips, carnations, columbines, ferns and wallflowers to these, as well as the more conventional rose garden, if space and resources had permitted. Of her pleasure in the aster garden, she wrote:

'There is more than usual pleasure in such a daisy garden, kept apart and by itself; because the time of its best beauty is just the time when the rest of the garden is looking tired and overworn ... the fresh, clear, lively colouring of the lilac, purple and white daisies is like a sudden change from decrepit age to the brightness of youth, from the gloom of late autumn to the joy of full springtide.'

Jekyll made her own strict rules of gardening. There were no short cuts to her success. Early each spring every plant in the aster borders was lifted and divided and she included in her published list of 'Things worth doing' the practice of growing together as many forms of a single species as possible, so that in their blooming season the gardener could judge 'which was really the best and most beautiful; for in equal or even greater proportion with the growth of critical appreciation, there comes an intolerance of rubbish.'[22] She warned that the 'shelves-full' of helpful gardening books 'that had no existence in my younger days' were no substitute for practical experiment in the garden, chiding her readers:

'Now that there is so much to choose from, we should not let any mental slothfulness stand in the way of thinking and watching and comparing, so as to arrive at a just appreciation of the merits and uses of all our garden plants.'

Nor did she approve of impulse buys, even of favourite plants:

'In my own case I should wish to grow many more than just those I have, but if I do not find a place where my critical garden conscience approves of having any one plant I would rather be without it. It is better to me to deny myself the pleasure of having it, than to endure the mild sense of guilt of having placed it where it neither does itself justice nor accords with its neighbours, and where it reproaches me every time I pass it.'[23]

She wrote of the folly of many of her clients who, having already purchased their favourite plants, asked her where to put them. Her response was typically

RIGHT: *The north face of Munstead Wood showing the shady courtyard behind the Tank Garden, and the new birch replacement for the Cenotaph of Sigismunda to the right of the Aster Walk.*

uncompromising: 'That is not the way in which I can help you; show me your spaces and I will tell you what plants to get for them.'

In an age when horticulturists all knew and visited one another Munstead Wood, like Gravetye Manor, became one of the most influential gardens of its day. It was painted by George Samuel Elgood and by Helen Allingham, the artist friend of both Jekyll and Kate Greenaway. H. Avray Tipping, Miss Ellen Willmott and Edward Hudson, the founder of *Country Life* magazine who was to become a committed client of both Jekyll and Lutyens, were among the many distinguished visitors. As her eyesight deteriorated and Jekyll became increasingly unwilling to travel more than a few miles from home, prospective and actual clients for her garden designs came to Munstead in order to secure her services, so that the garden was a constant source of reference and inspiration. An intricate network of society connections ensured that potential clients for garden designs and country houses were informed of Jekyll's work. Some clients, however, like the aptly named Lady Chance, came across her work and that of Lutyens by accident. Having bought a neighbouring piece of land in 1897 and then commissioned designs for a country house, the Chances found that they disliked their architect's plans so much that they were on the point of abandoning altogether the idea of building when

'a miracle happened ... Passing through a sandy lane we saw a house nearing completion, and on the top of a ladder a portly figure giving directions to some workmen. The house was a revelation of unimagined beauty and charm, the like of which we had never seen before,'

and the figure descending the ladder was Gertrude Jekyll.[24] 'Later, as a result of this meeting, we became the owners of a Lutyens house [Orchards] with a Gertrude Jekyll garden.'

Demand from the public to see the famous garden became so overwhelming that a decade after the house was built Jekyll wrote to a friend:

'The question of visitors has for many years been a great difficulty. I have tried what you propose (omitting the fee) but find it quite useless to attempt to keep to one day. If any offer of a day is made, it seems to give people a kind of right of entrance, or they take it to be so, and they will come at their own convenience.'

Many of the visitors, Jekyll complained, were prompted by curiosity rather than by any sympathy with what she was trying to achieve. They wrote and visited from all over the world, reducing Jekyll to a plaintive state: 'You can have no idea what I have suffered (actually in health) from the pertinacity of Americans and Germans and of journalists.' She concluded: 'For health's sake my only course of late has been to refuse all but old friends.'[25] Not all her American visitors were pertinacious or unwelcome, however. Jekyll found an enthusiastic and sympathetic readership for her gardening books in North America, and as Europe became embroiled in the First World War it was in America that her philosophy and practical guidelines were most successfully interpreted and put to effect.

Although her actual designs for American gardens were limited to a very few, and all of those by correspondence, the opportunities in terms of scale and resources in America, and the progressive attitudes of gardeners there, ensured that her ideology was interpreted and developed without interruption even after the war in Europe had shattered the affluence and illusions of the English country garden. Jekyll actively encouraged her American followers. She never visited America, but the importance of her books, her patient benevolence towards at least some of the American visitors to Munstead, and her correspondence with American gardeners were recognized in the award of the George Robert White Medal of Honour from the Massachusetts Horticultural Society. She wrote to Francis King in Michigan:

'it is a great happiness and a rich reward of effort and long years of work, to find such sympathy and appreciation, and I am truly glad to know that you are writing and giving addresses on ways of gardening that I know would be after my own heart.'

The following year she agreed to write a foreword to King's book *The Well-Considered Garden,* and later, when King sent her a book on American gardens, she praised the Italianate gardens of 'Drumthwacket' in Princeton, advising that Italian models were particularly appropriate to the Californian climate.

Jekyll's correspondence with King demonstrates a lively and enquiring interest in the climates, conditions and vernacular architecture of a country that, at the age of seventy, and with failing eyesight, she could never hope to see. As a perfectionist she must have recognized the opportunities that America could offer during a period of increasing hardship in English gardening: 'It is good to see how seriously good gardening is being practised on your side and how neither pains nor cost are spared.' She gravitated towards 'houses of the old Colonial type', believing them to be compatible with the quiet of an English garden,

'for the time when these houses were built was one of singular refinement in all matters of building and decoration – there was that delightful combination of dignity, modesty and restfulness that made itself felt through everything'.[26]

As early as 1895, while Jekyll was living in The Hut and the main house at Munstead Wood was still in the planning stages, she had been visited by the American garden designer Beatrix Farrand. For the remainder of her career Farrand was committed to developing in America the colour harmonies and planting propositions that Jekyll had initiated, and it was Farrand, in 1948, who purchased the bulk of Jekyll's garden plans and preserved them for posterity, finally donating them to the University of California at Berkeley in 1955.

Jekyll's reverence for nature; her determination to shape a design around the indigenous conditions of a garden site; the deliberate selection of plants whose growing requirements were perfectly suited to the site and soil; and her vision of a garden as an annual sequence of carefully orchestrated visual events – sometimes spectacular, sometimes intimate, always exquisitely natural – placed her at the heart of the Arts and Crafts movement. Her practical knowledge of traditional country crafts and her determination to record and perpetuate these through photographs, descriptions and her own practical efforts were akin to the concerns of Morris and Webb in the Society for the Protection of Ancient Buildings, although Jekyll did not limit herself to the protection of building crafts. Like Morris, she opposed industrialization. Where Morris wrote manifestos and marched the streets wielding banners, however, Jekyll's reaction was typically private and personal. She wrote an unpublished novel entitled *The Death of Iron* in which an England suddenly deprived of iron had to rediscover elemental ways of living.[27] In her work as an artist and craftswoman Jekyll personified the Arts and Crafts ideal of unity in the arts. As a woman of independent means she chipped steadily away at prejudices against professional status for women, and she lifted the art of gardening into the realm of socially acceptable activity where previously it had been largely the domain of the professional gardener. Through her partnership with Lutyens she set a standard of excellence in the integration of house and garden that still remains unsurpassed. The collaborative designs of Lutyens and Jekyll span the complete development of the Arts and Crafts garden, progressing, from 1906 onwards, towards increasingly formal and mannered effects that marked the transition from an Arts and Crafts philosophy into a style, and from 'Arts and Crafts style' to that of the classical revival.

Above: *William Nicholson's portrait of Jekyll, commissioned by Lutyens in 1920.*

As an architectural patron Jekyll gives us an informative insight into the romantic ideals, shared by her contemporaries, that motivated so many commissions for the 'deliciously simple' Arts and Crafts country cottage. Describing the 'Dear little Hut' designed for her by Lutyens, she wrote:

> 'How I loved the small and simple ways of living, the happy absence of all complications, the possibility of living close down to nature – I know no better way of saying it – that seemed to leave one more freedom to think and to do!'

There was a clear correlation in Jekyll's mind between the simple life and good health. Describing her bed, set beneath the pitch of the roof so that she could listen to the 'musical, tinkling sound' of rain at night, and standing on the carpetless brick floor, she concluded: 'there was no feeling of hardship, and the whole way of life was evidently wholesome, for during the two years that I occupied the cottage I was never a day ill and only had one slight cold.'

Many of Jekyll's contemporaries, Morris and Webb included, found that their regard for craftsmanship and honest labour, and their abhorrence at the social and aesthetic consequences of industrialization, led inevitably to socialism. Jekyll offered a genteel alternative. She would have read the condemnations of the idleness of the rich by designers like Walter Crane. In her own writings she confessed:

'I only know that to my own mind and conscience pure idleness seems to me to be akin to folly, or even worse, and that in some form or other I must obey the Divine command: "Work while ye have the light."'

Her practical determination to live close to nature in harmony with the old country ways, adopting the traditional role of employer and protector of the village people around her, set a laudable and achievable example for women of her own and subsequent generations who found themselves disorientated and discomfited by sweeping social changes beyond their control. The country retreat had a missionary appeal, even if was only for weekends. For a significant minority Jekyll's example was even more profound. In an age when spiritualism and alternative religions were blossoming, her abstemiousness, her pleasure in difficult tasks, the profundity of her communion with nature, and not least her celibacy, represented a possibility that serious gardening might signal a pathway on the road to redemption.

Footnotes

1 Jane Brown, *Gardens of a Golden Afternoon*, Allen Lane, London, 1982, p.23
2 Quoted in Francis Jekyll, *Gertrude Jekyll: A Memoir*, Jonathan Cape, London, 1934, p.26.
3 Ibid., p.27.
4 Ibid., pp.28–9.
5 Ibid., p.30.
6 Quoted in Francis Jekyll, op. cit., footnote, p.87.
7 George Leslie, *Our River*, p.37.
8 Francis Jekyll, *Gertrude Jekyll: A Memoir*, Jonathan Cape, London, 1934, foreword by Sir Edwin Lutyens, p.7.
9 Originally quoted in Osbert Sitwell, *The Scarlet Tree*, 1946, p.266.
10 Gertrude Jekyll, 'About Myself', *Gardening Illustrated*, 27 August 1927.
11 Quoted in Mea Allan, *William Robinson 1838–1935*, Faber and Faber, London, 1982, pp.142–3.
12 Francis Jekyll, op. cit., pp.7–8.
13 Gertrude Jekyll, *Home and Garden*, Longmans, Green & Co., London, 1900; reprinted by Antique Collectors' Club, 1982, p.22.
14 Ibid., p.220.
15 Ibid., p.220.
16 Ibid., p.106.
17 Lutyens's reintroduction of the word is described by his son, Robert Lutyens, in *Sir Edwin Lutyens: An appreciation in perspective, by his son*, Country Life Ltd, London, 1942, p.30.
18 Jane Brown's excellent book *Gardens of a Golden Afternoon* gives planting plans for most of the beds at Munstead Wood.
19 Letter to Francis King, 19 August 1913, quoted in Francis Jekyll, op. cit., p.169.
20 This anecdote from Herbert Cowley is given by Laurence Fricker in his account of Dartington Hall in *Beatrix Jones Farrand (1872–1959), Fifty years of American landscape architecture*, Dumbarton Oaks, Trustees of Harvard University, Washington DC, 1982, p.79.
21 Gertrude Jekyll, *Home and Garden*, Longmans, Green & Co., London, 1900; reprinted by Antique Collectors' Club, 1982, p.354.
22 Ibid., p.344.
23 Ibid., pp.344–5.
24 Lady Chance's recollections of Jekyll are quoted in Francis Jekyll, op. cit., pp.160–3.
25 Letter to a friend dated 10 July, 1908, quoted in Francis Jekyll, op. cit., p.136.
26 This undated letter from Jekyll to Francis King (presumably post 1913) is quoted in Francis Jekyll, op. cit., p.170.
27 See Francis Jekyll, op. cit., p.135 for a brief description of this book.

Chapter Seven

Nature and Tradition

The ideal of a partnership between architecture and nature, exemplified in the work of Jekyll and Lutyens, and the combination of a formal framework containing an abundance of natural planting, became inherent in the Arts and Crafts garden. A reverence for nature and for the traditions of building and craftsmanship – as indicators of ancient social structures as well as anchors of aesthetic integrity – was equally fundamental to Arts and Crafts designers. The visual consequences of this reverence link together gardens that belonged to very different social contexts and political motivations. The gardens of Earlshall, Hidcote and Rodmarton Manor can be compared on stylistic grounds. A detailed study of the ambitions of

Right: *The Long Garden at Rodmarton Manor with summer house designed by Ernest Barnsley.*

their clients and designers, however, reveals that the traditional cottage, castle or manor house could be claimed for the cause of the romantic nationalist, the fashion-conscious socialite or the pioneering socialist, and that all of them might claim some allegiance to the Arts and Crafts movement.

In Scotland, Georgian and Victorian fashions in garden design had made less of an imprint than in Engand and the bones of old-fashioned gardens, so sought after by Morris and his contemporaries, were littered around baronial castles, shrouded by decades of neglect. One of these, Kellie Castle, became the home of Robert Lorimer (later Sir Robert Lorimer) during his adolescence; it was to have a profound effect upon his development as a craftsman, a garden designer and an architect. Lorimer (1864–1929) became preoccupied with regenerating a form of garden design that was indigenous to Scotland. In the 1880s and 1890s his interest in the gardens of old castles was not limited to the romantic appeal of their old-fashioned quaintness, as Rossetti's had been two decades earlier, or to their archaeological importance as evidence of the whims and traditions of previous generations. He was concerned with the evolution of a specifically Scottish ideology within domestic design, founded on the traditions of centuries of building and adapted to the modern requirements and ideals of contemporary life. His gardens received high acclaim and were very influential; a part of their attraction, however, was their deliberate remoteness.

The origins of Kellie Castle, near Pittenweem in Fife, can be traced back to the mid-fourteenth century. It was the home of the Earls of Kellie until their line died out in 1829, after which the castle fell into a state of neglect. The Gothic appeal of a ruined castle was almost irresistible to the Victorian sensibility, to such an extent that even two decades after the building was restored *Country Life* still lavished more attention on the condition of the castle when Robert Lorimer's father, Professor James Lorimer, 'came, saw, and fell in love with the old place as it stood, gaunt and desolate, in the middle of a turnip-field' than on the details of its restoration.[1] The article continued:

> 'for the most part it was left to the rooks and the owls who built their nests in its crumbling chimneys and dropped down piles of sticks which reached far out into the rooms. Great holes let the rain and snow through the roofs, many of the floors became unsafe, every pane of glass was broken, and swallows built in the coronets on the ceilings, while the ceilings themselves dipped, and in some places fell in. Dandelions, grass, and nettles grew in the rooms, and trees rooted themselves in the walls'.

Robert Lorimer was fourteen when Kellie Castle was leased to the family and restoration work began. Like Lutyens, who was five years his junior, periods of his childhood were circumscribed by illness. He spent part of the rebuilding period at Kellie convalescing after an attack of scarlet fever and his attention focused, perhaps with a degree of frustrated intensity, on the fabric of the building and its historic craftsmanship. Lorimer had a workshop in the oldest tower, originally a keep. He studied the fine plaster-work of the ceilings and made measured drawings of the entire house, outside and in. He practised carpentry and woodcarving, studying the ancient vocabulary of Scottish craftsmanship until it was an inherent part of his individual style. His brother John (later to become a painter) made a drawing of him 'with sleeves rolled up at work, carving with hammer and chisel'. Robert made his first garden design for Kellie in 1880, when he was sixteen. It was drawn out

Above: *Mixed borders line a grass walk to the thistle gate at Earlshall.*

in a pencil plan, indicating an early tendency towards the discipline and remote control of the architect. The qualities of clarity and objectivity, however, which were to define the planning of his gardens, were equally matched by a practical and romantic passion for gardening.

The garden at Kellie was inspired by the walled gardens of seventeenth-century Scottish castles. In part it was reclaimed from the derelict remains of a garden

'still encircled by a tumble-down wall ... a wilderness of neglected gooseberry bushes, gnarled apple trees, and old-world red and white roses, which struggled through the weeds summer after summer with a sweet persistence'.[2]

The custom of creating a walled enclosure, often running from the turnpike stair to wrap around one or two sides of a castle, and letting the landscape continue right up to the building on the other sides, was a Scottish tradition. It was founded on good sense: in the harsh Scottish climate prevailing winds could literally blow the shrubs out of the ground. By locating the garden on the sheltered side of the castle and building tall walls around its remaining boundaries, more favourable growing conditions could be ensured. In such a climate, however, and with the dramatic backdrop of towering castle walls, romantic associations of the garden as a magical or spiritual sanctuary were encouraged, as Lorimer wrote in 1899: 'A garden is a sort of sanctuary, a chamber roofed by heaven; the garden is a little pleasance of the soul by whose wicket the world can be shut out from us.'[3] The stone garden walls at Kellie were rebuilt, and fruits and vegetables were planted among the flowers within their enclosure, again in accordance with practical Scottish traditions:

'Such surprises – the little gardens within the garden, the months garden, the yew alley, the kitchen garden too, and nothing to be ashamed of, to be smothered away from the house but made delightful by its laying out.'[4]

Lorimer's garden at Kellie was not ordered by elaborate architectural features. There were no terraces, no cascading stone steps. The main structural elements were emphatically natural, as though, even in adolescence, he had formulated for himself the basic rules of gardening. He was to express these much later in a paper 'On Scottish Gardens' given to the Architectural Association in 1899, in which he explained that the axes of the garden were defined by 'intersecting walks of shaven grass, on either side borders of brightest flowers backed up by low espaliers hanging with shining apples'. Lorimer's brother John recalled how Robert 'designed the long grass walk with circular centre for which I found an astrolabe with a ship on top'. At the east end of the garden there was 'a charming little yew garden with yew hedges shaped like birds, where there was a pillar with Cupid above with bow and arrow'. High box edging divided the grass walks from borders massed with 'quantities of simple flowers'. When in 1904 Gertrude Jekyll described the garden in its maturity, in *Some English Gardens*, she was impressed by the single hollyhocks in 'big free groups' and by the fertility of the garden:

'How the flowers grow in these northern gardens! Here they must needs grow tall to be in scale with the high box edging. But Shirley Poppies, when they are autumn sown, will rise to four feet, and the grand new strains of tall Snapdragons will go five and even over six feet high.'

Jekyll's description was surely based on paintings by George Samuel Elgood, who illustrated her book, and on conversations with Lorimer, rather than a visit. She confined her account to general recommendations for tall plants that would do well in box-edged borders: Canterbury bells, lilies, astilbes, the bluish leaves and feathery flower heads of *Bocconia* (now *Macleaya*) *cordata*, with columbines to take effect earlier in the year.

Kellie was famous for its roses. *Country Life* described them breaking 'like a wave over the summer garden' and Jekyll wrote of the 'various pretty simple ways' in which they were trained around frames and over walls.

'Some of them, like the Scotch Briers, grow in Rose bushy masses; some have an upright habit; some like to rush up trees and over hedges; others again will trail along the ground and even run downhill. Some are tender and must have a warm wall; some will endure severe cold; some will flower all the summer; others at one season only.'

At Kellie, she wrote, roses were 'balloon-trained' to give height to the garden: 'the framework being a central post from which hoops are hung one above the other. The Rose grows up inside the framework and hangs out all over'. They were trained over arches, endorsing the understated structure of the grass walks, grown through fruit trees, and planted in mixed borders among the vegetable beds.

In *Some English Gardens* Jekyll complimented Robert and his brother John on being 'artists of the finest faculty ... they have done for this grand old place what boundless wealth, in less able hands, could not have accomplished', and by the time her book was published she had drawn up three planting schemes for Lorimer houses.[5] In private, however, she said that: 'the difference between working with Ned [Lutyens] and Lorimer was as between quicksilver and suet'.[6] Lorimer's gardens became more pedantic as his career progressed. In his early work, however, they were inspired by a poetic understanding of Scottish baronial traditions and a sensitivity to the remains of ancient gardens, liberally mixed with modern planting ideals.

Lorimer's involvement in the restoration of Kellie and the remaking of its garden brought him to the attention of a family friend, Robert Mackenzie, who in 1890 had purchased the neighbouring castle of Earlshall, eleven miles from Kellie, and in urgent need of repair. At this time Lorimer was completing his architectural training in London. He had gathered a firm grounding in Arts and Crafts principles in the London practice of George Bodley, and although he would have been a year too late to hear J.D. Sedding's paper on 'The Architectural Treatment of Gardens' at the Art Workers' Guild (he remained sceptical about the 'artificial crudeness' of much of the Guild's work) he would have seen Sedding's newly published *Garden-Craft Old and New* and been introduced to the ideology as well as to some of the pioneering members of the Guild. When Robert Mackenzie gave

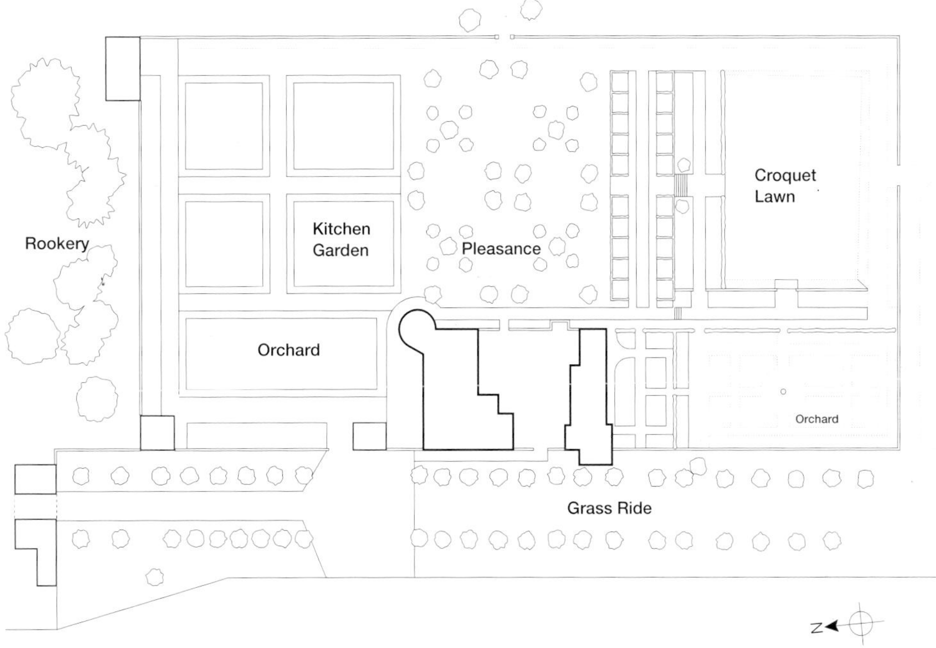

RIGHT: *Garden plan, Earlshall, Fife. Designed by Robert Lorimer from 1892.*

him his first independent commission, to restore Earlshall and design a new garden within the walled enclosure on the site, Lorimer was able to complete his training in the office of the late James Maclaren, and set up in independent practice in Edinburgh.

The garden at Earlshall is one of the most vivid and comprehensive statements of the Arts and Crafts movement. Lorimer manipulated traditional elements appropriate to the sixteenth-century stone tower-house into a sequence of interconnecting outdoor rooms. Areas of grandeur and authority gave access to intimate and mysterious spaces. The working parts of the garden, producing fruit, vegetables and herbs, were mixed in with flower borders, and long vistas connected the kitchen garden with the social platform of the croquet lawn and the rose terrace beyond. Lorimer was given a free hand and an ample budget to create this exquisite garden out of a potato field. The

ABOVE: *Lorimer designed interior details, including stained glass for Earlshall, in addition to designing the garden and its buildings and repairing the castle.*

Right: *The gatehouse, designed by Lorimer in 1901 as an imposing entry point to the castle and its garden.*

Right: *Earlshall viewed from the topiary lawn. Entry into the garden is through a pass-door in the dark sheltered courtyard between the cottage 'Dummy Daws' on the left and the castle building.*

old walled garden, probably dating from the early seventeenth century, had been ploughed up by tenant farmers and used for growing root crops and grazing livestock before Mackenzie purchased the castle. Lorimer's instinct was to reinstate the original framework: 'The natural park up to the walls of the house on the one side, on the other you stroll right out into the garden inclosed; but what paradise can such a place be made.'[7]

The castle was set like a centrepiece in the west wall of the garden and the sixteenth-and seventeenth-century grey stone garden walls were repaired and rebuilt on the remaining three sides to form a perfect rectangle. The three and a half acres enclosed within it were organized, like rooms in a house, into five main areas connected by long straight terraces paved with grey stone, and by wide corridors enclosed by clipped yew and holly hedges. Initially Lorimer had intended the castle to look out over a formal parterre. His plans were changed when an obsolete garden was discovered in Edinburgh, full of mature topiary pieces. The head gardener at Earlshall was offered an incentive of five pounds for every tree that took, representing a fortune in terms of gardeners' salaries; every one of the thirty-six mature yews was successfully transplanted between 1894 and 1896. The standard yews were planted at regular intervals, forming four saltires (diagonal

crosses) in front of the castle. Although the traditional manner of growing topiary is within borders, often underplanted with annuals and perennials, at Earlshall they were planted directly into the lawn, so that they sit like chessmen on a board. There is a story that Nathaniel Lloyd, visiting Earlshall before his own fifteenth-century house, Great Dixter in Sussex, was remodelled in 1910, was so impressed by the topiary lawn that he asked Lutyens to copy the idea.[8]

The approach to Earlshall and the dramatic possibilities of its garden were devised with a discerning appreciation of the effects of shadowy, mysterious enclosures set against open spaces fully revealed in light. In 1901 Lorimer designed a tall stone gatehouse, defining the entrance to the castle grounds and focusing the experience of entry from the dappled shade of a cobbled yard, through a massive arched opening, on to the sudden revelation of a long straight avenue of limes. Because the gatehouse is on the north side of the castle the visitor invariably passes from shadow into light – from the medieval associations of cobble stones and austerity to a wide paved path and orderly refinement. Once within the castle grounds the visitor is faced with another equally intriguing contrast. The west side of the lime walk is bounded by open meadows stocked with cattle. The east side is closed by the high walls of the castle and its garden. Instead of terminating at the castle walls, the avenue runs parallel to them, towards an opening into woodland. At a turning circle set into the paving, halfway along its length, the visitor is offered a short pathway to the left and a second distinctive point of entry, reminiscent of ancient fortifications: a narrow pass-door with a gridded inspection window through which admittance might be granted or denied.

From the sunshine and the possibilities of open fields or woodlands, the pass-door plunges the visitor into a densely shaded well court, enclosed on three sides by the walls of the castle and its cottage, called 'Dummy Daws' because in the eighteenth century it was supposedly the home of a coachman named Daws who was dumb. Lorimer designed a low balustrade across the fourth side of the court, defining the boundary between the old and the new areas of the garden and offering glimpses to the clipped yew of the

Top: *The straight path and turning circle from the gatehouse at Earlshall running parallel with the garden wall.*

Above: *Robert Lorimer's stylish arbour focuses the axis of a yew walk.*

Right: *The rose terrace overlooking the croquet lawn to the right, with the orchard enclosed by tall hedges to the left.*

topiary lawn beyond. Through an opening in the balustrade the visitor steps from shade into sunlight again, and from the confines of the cobbled court on to a wide path with vistas opening to the south and the east, defining the open expanses of the garden. The garden is revealed sequentially, always inviting further exploration. There are changes in both scale and pace. Adjoining the topiary lawn to the south, a long straight yew walk encourages the visitor, on first impulse, to hurry along its length towards a curved wooden seat in the shelter of a fine stone arbour. Once the walk is entered the apparently solid blocks of yew can be seen to enclose a series of miniature bays separated by yew buttresses and originally planted with old-fashioned flowers: delphiniums, phlox, irises and lilies, each bay exacting individual inspection.

From the yew walk the garden opens out again, with steps down into a vast sunken croquet lawn bordered by spectacular herbaceous beds. Lorimer designed a rose terrace along one side, continuing the wide path from the well court, raised up above the level of the lawn. The terrace is defined by a long low wall so that effectively the lawn is bounded by walls on three sides and by the tall clipped yew hedge on the fourth. Rambling roses are grown over the walls and a summerhouse is tucked into one corner of the tall garden walls. On the west side of the terrace an orchard is laid out with lines of fruit trees underplanted with naturalized drifts of spring bulbs. The structure of the orchard was originally underpinned with straight grass paths running parallel to the main axis of the garden. At its centre a sundial was raised on a circular mound, and this in turn could be seen through arched openings in holly and yew hedges, as a distant focal point from the croquet lawn and from a small garden close to Dummy Daws.

At the heart of the garden the majestic topiary forms echo the massive sculptural shapes of the castle walls. They respond, in gardening language, to the castle's inscrutable accoutrements of age and invincibility. Viewed from above, from the castle windows, they look as though they might exchange places with one another, very sedately, in the night. Lorimer designed a fine gateway on the far side of the topiary lawn, leading to the woodland beyond. Beneath the pediment on the garden side is carved an inscription from Shakespeare: 'Here shall ye see no enemy but winter and rough weather'; on the reverse side the inscription reads: 'He who loves his garden still keeps his Eden.' Earlshall is close to the sea and a shell motif is carved above the letters. Surmounting the pediment, however, there is a curious stone phallus, the significance of which defies interpretation.

The kitchen gardens are laid out to the north of the topiary lawn, not sequestered away from view but continuing the main axes of the garden. Four square beds, framed by espaliered fruit trees, form a larger square quartered by wide grass paths. Within the beds vegetables and flowers are grown together. In the north-west corner of the vegetable garden Lorimer designed a two-storey Dowry House. Two rooms on the ground floor housed the apple store with floor-to-ceiling racks of wooden trays and the dairy house where butter was prepared on marble slabs. The whole building has an air of playfulness: hearts are pierced into the doors of the apple store and a basket of apples is carved into the stonework over the door on the floor above. Lorimer had a curious affection for monkeys and they were carved clinging to the gable above the window. The interior of the first-floor room, panelled from floor to ceiling and with a marble chequered floor, dispels any illusion that this was simply a

ABOVE: *Shakespeare is summoned to define the sanctuary of Earlshall's enclosed garden in the Legend Gate.*

ABOVE: *Monkeys play on the tool-house roof.*

Above: *Viewed from the castle windows, the topiary lawn with a sheltering band of woodland beyond the garden walls.*

functional garden store. It was an idealized and gentrified model of the traditional farm or estate garden store, where produce was dealt with on the ground floor and cramped living accommodation provided for peasant labourers above. The Dowry House, tucked into the corner of the garden away from the responsibilities of castle life, promised a romantic retreat into the wholesome simplicity of rural labour. The cramped living quarters were translated into a simple sewing room for the mistress of the estate, and the stores below were perfectly ordered to preserve or to prepare, in the old country way, the natural bounty of the grounds. Perhaps Lorimer's monkeys played a mimicking game.

There were monkeys, too, on the roof of the tool house in the second corner of the kitchen garden, where Robert Mackenzie's favourite Shetland pony (useful for pulling the lawn mower) was tethered. A fine herringbone path links the two buildings, flanked to one side by a south-facing mixed border backed by the stone garden wall. Although the tool shed is relatively functional in character, Lorimer was careful to secure it within his grand design. An arched opening at one end is the focus for the eastern axis of the garden, linked to the legend gate by an avenue of pleached limes, and the monkeys, set against the backdrop of the woodland trees outside the garden walls, can be glimpsed from all over the garden. Lorimer introduced carved monkeys again in his later gardens. Since the Middle Ages the monkey or ape had signified the imitative role of the artist, copying nature, and this would have been appropriate to the follies of a garden designer. There was an older, less flattering reading of the monkey, however, as a symbol of lust, or of the wild man of nature. An ape with an apple in its mouth signified the Fall of Man and although

Above: *Robert Mackenzie astride his favourite Shetland pony with his castle in the background.*

Lorimer's monkeys might have had a special significance for him, he and his clients would have been aware of the academic interpretation of his symbols. Perhaps the garden as Eden had more than a literary interest for those above the apple store.

Earlshall evolved gradually as Lorimer matured as a designer. Although the structure of the garden was probably laid out by 1894, the content and detailing of its individual 'rooms' were altered and refined until the close of the century; the garden buildings date from about 1899, the gatehouse from 1901. The clarity of its planning and its intrigue and subtlety made it an exceptional garden in its own time. However, like many ambitious gardens designed around the turn of the century, when labour was cheap and resources were plentiful, Earlshall was allowed to deteriorate as the twentieth century progressed; in the 1980s it was reported with a degree of resignation: 'sadly these once beautiful gardens will soon disappear'. The fact that Earlshall did not disappear, that it was reclaimed and restored as a garden of outstanding value, can be attributed partly to the enduring qualities of Lorimer's plan, but above all to the energy and tenacity of the present Baroness of Earlshall.

In the early 1980s, when she took responsibility for the garden, the croquet lawn was a mess of molehills, moss and weeds, the herbaceous beds surrounding it were blackened and dead, deliberately poisoned by a disaffected predecessor: 'If I hadn't been so ignorant I'd have been frightened of the responsibility.' Instead she and her gardener, Henry Colliar, cleared and replanted the lawn. The herbaceous beds were reinstated more gradually, almost entirely from cuttings and divisions from plants in the rest of the garden. Waist-high weeds and nettles had to be removed from the orchard, but most of the original fruit trees had survived. Inevitably there have been some changes. The topiary forms grow larger each year because when trimming topiary it is necessary to limit the cutting to the current year's growth. If old wood is cut into, instead of regrowing, that branch can sprout again from the trunk, undermining the shape of the piece. Even if the accuracy of the trim is within a millimetre of the old wood, over the decades each piece becomes larger, and where there have been periods of neglect the whole shape of the piece can change.[9] All the yew at Earlshall is trimmed annually by Henry Colliar. The garden is maintained with a sensitive appreciation of its historic importance, coloured by a passion for its living, chang-ing character. In her guide to the garden the Baroness writes: 'Gardens are ephemeral and owe their existence to the care lavished on them by the current owner.' Earlshall has been particularly fortunate in this respect.

The study of nature and tradition, of sixteenth- and seventeenth-century buildings and their ancient gardens and surrounding landscapes, became one of the central concerns of the Arts and Crafts movement. Lorimer's gardens in Scotland must be seen as part of a national preoccupation with preserving and regenerating ancient structures and their settings, and with a determination to retain the regional characteristics, all the architectural dialects, of communities that had been almost totally isolated before the influx of the railways. Traditional structures and their landscapes had a political as well as a nostalgic charge. In the hands of William Morris an Elizabethan manor house could become a standard for centuries of unchanged rural tradition synonymous with British history, and simultaneously a haven for the future – the righteous destination of pilgrims of a socialist age. After the sale of Red House, Morris had adopted the 'beautiful and strangely naif' Elizabethan manor house Kelmscott, in Oxfordshire, as his country retreat and it was later claimed that in doing so he had 'discovered' the Cotswolds. He certainly attracted attention to the area. In *News from Nowhere*, published in 1892, Kelmscott was represented as the archetypal old stone house that had 'grown up out of the soil and the lives of them that lived on it'. Its formal garden was immortalized on the frontispiece, with standard roses flanking a straight stone path to the front door. Artists and designers followed Morris's trail to the Cotswolds 'for environment and for inspiration'. They were joined by some of his most fashionable clients.

Throughout the Arts and Crafts period there was a dialogue between artists earnestly questing, through design, to reinstate meaning and purity into contemporary life, and a fashion-conscious clientele eager to patronize their work as the very latest thing in a long catalogue of styles. Designers like William Morris, Gertrude Jekyll and C.F.A. Voysey had a celebrity status in the drawing-rooms of the commissioning classes. A Morris interior, a Jekyll garden or a Voysey cottage had a currency in terms of fashionable desirability that was quite distinct from the aesthetic and philosophical intentions of its author. However, very few designers could afford to reject even the most superficial offers of patronage. Equally, the labour-intensive, hand-crafted individuality that was essential to Arts and Crafts interiors, furniture, embroidery, metalwork and so on made their products so expensive that they were accessible only to wealthy clients. The mass market that many designers were committed to serving could only afford mass-produced goods; this conundrum continued to undermine the validity of the Arts and Crafts movement and tormented its more serious practitioners.

Country Life and *The Studio* magazines adopted certain designers and actively promoted their work, presenting their houses and gardens, explaining them and setting them in a context that would have a particular appeal for their readers. Some designers, like Lorimer and Lutyens, were comfortable with their fashionable status. Their continuing success was founded on an ability to manipulate and exploit specific trends (as well as social opportunities), while retaining close working relationships with specialist artists and craftsmen who could be employed in their projects. They translated the ideology of Morris and Ruskin into a sophisticated visual language and in doing so turned a philosophy into a style. Lutyens in particular refined the components of Arts and Crafts with a vivacity that created some of its most brilliant buildings and gardens. The difficulties of retaining artistic integrity and at the same time keeping pace with a fashion-conscious market drove those more obstinately committed designers to drink (Mackintosh), to the piety of martyrdom (Voysey), to teach (Lethaby), and to life in the obscurity of remote rural communities (Ashbee, Gimson, Ernest and Sidney Barnsley).

The dual effects of voguish interest and progressive artistic endeavour can be seen polarized in the development of artistic communities in the Cotswolds. Morris's admiration for the village of Broadway and its unspoilt cottages, described as 'a work of art and a piece of nature – no less', was instrumental in encouraging a small community of fashionable artistic figures to settle in the area. From 1885 a group of American artists including illustrators for *Harper's Magazine* Frank Millet and Edwin Abbey and the expatriate painter John Singer Sargent, adopted the village as a perfect retreat. They were visited by Henry James, whose description of 'Our Artists in Europe' published in *Harper's Magazine* in 1889 put Broadway firmly on the tourist route for visiting Americans. In 1895 the acclaimed American actress Mary Anderson bought The Court Farm in the village. In addition to friendships with Morris and Burne-Jones, her 'at homes' were frequented by Elgar and the garden painter Alfred Parsons, who designed a garden for her and later settled in Broadway. This community of intellectual and artistic refugees was self-consciously set apart from the local population; serious attempts at integration would probably have been thought undesirable if they had been thought about at all. Broadway became a fashionable resort for an artistic elite and its rural charms were eulogized, but the economic stability of the village and the guardianship of its traditions were not at issue.

One of the main attractions for Mary Anderson's guests came to be the garden at Hidcote, within a few miles of Broadway:

'My Italian friends regard Hidcote as the most beautiful garden they have seen in England. Its wonderful blending of colours and its somewhat formal architectural character please them particularly.'[10]

Hidcote was a high-society garden, visited in its heyday by the Duke of York, Princess Mary, the Duke of Gloucester and the Duke of Kent, as well as by some of the greatest gardeners of the twentieth century. It was designed by its American owner, Lawrence Waterbury Johnston (1871–1958), who was born in Paris and educated at Cambridge before he applied for British nationality and served in the army as a major. Johnston's redoubtable mother, Gertrude Winthrop, twice widowed but never to be parted from her son (she lived with him for nearly twenty years at Hidcote), bought the tiny village of Hidcote Bartrim as part of a 280-acre lot of working farm land at auction in 1907, with the intention that 'Laurie' should settle to the life of a gentleman farmer. He was only marginally interested in farming, however, choosing to take the horses and spend a morning ploughing on occasion, but leaving the bulk of the responsibility for the farm and its running to a farm bailiff, George Wheeler. Instead he developed a passion for gardening that was practical, adventurous and supremely individual. Although he had no formal training as a designer, no particular commitment to preserving vernacular or historical traditions, and no expert training in horticulture, he built up a national reputation as a plant collector and created one of the most celebrated and influential gardens of his day, described more recently as the epitome of Arts and Crafts garden design.

The design of Hidcote was informed by a sophisticated stylishness. Johnston was able to manipulate the quintessential elements of an English cottage garden with a foreigner's objectivity. Cottage gardens on his estate probably served as models for

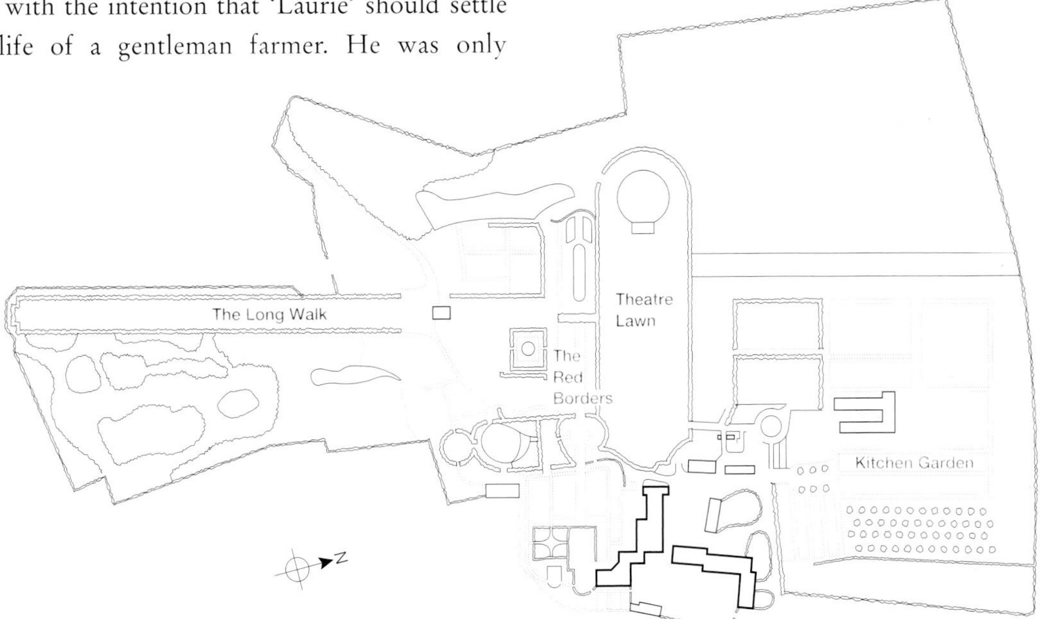

ABOVE: *Garden plan, Hidcote, Gloucestershire. Designed by Lawrence Johnston from 1907.*

Left: *'Smug broody hens' in the Bathing Pool Garden at Hidcote, described by Vita Sackville-West as bringing 'the cottage-garden' idea to Lawrence Johnston's design.*

some of the dense compositions close to the house, but Johnston was not restricted to any single source for inspiration. Hidcote draws on French as well as English gardening traditions and the structure of the garden is boldly defined by wide, generous avenues, which *Country Life* likened to a central gallery with apartments opening from it for the display of 'duly selected and ordered objects of art and *vertu*'.[11] At Hidcote the objects of art were rare and exotic plants. Johnston exploited the fashion for dividing the garden into a series of outdoor rooms in order to combine open (and consequently exposed) views to the distant landscape with sheltered microclimates in which his extraordinary collection could be grown to best advantage. The need to protect the elevated site from prevailing cold winds – and to accommodate a pronounced sloping away of the ground to the south and a rising incline to the west – were dealt with intuitively, although *Country Life* concluded: 'I suspect that the scheme took a lot of worrying out and was of lengthy incubation.'

There are no planting plans for Hidcote and early photographs suggest that the garden was not designed as a single entity. Instead it was altered and extended over a twenty-year period, with three distinct phases of concentrated activity followed by more subtle settling-in times. Johnston used to confide in his gardener that his mother would allow him only £600 per month, and that this was far too little to run both his estates (Hidcote and his winter villa in France). The gardener's wife was in turn visited by Gertrude Winthrop, who used to call and chat about her son. She said that he was hopeless with money and she had to limit his spending drastically.[12] Even after her death the budget was controlled – for Johnston was never allowed access to his mother's capital; she bequeathed him only the interest.

He was not restricted by any Arts and Crafts regard for native plants and conditions. Where the soil would not suit, he changed it:[13] one gardener remembers digging out a border in the 1930s to a depth of three feet then filling it with barrowloads of old, nearly black, sawdust from a nearby sawmill, mixed with clinkers to make a lime-free soil so that azaleas and rhododendrons could be grown in the Old Garden and the Lower Stream Garden. The hard landscaping and garden structures were designed for maximum visual effect. Structures were makeshift where time or money was limited. The Lower Stream Garden and the area known as Westonbirt (so called because so many of its trees and shrubs, selected for autumn colour, were supplied by the Westonbirt nursery at Tetbury) provide relatively wildareas at the perimeter of the garden, opening on to pasture land, but the ideal of a progressive relaxation towards wild nature is contradicted by the straight formality of the Long Walk, which signals Johnston's authority from the pavilions almost to the horizon.

RIGHT: *The Long Walk, viewed from one of the pavilions.*

In its heyday it was the autocratic eccentricity of Hidcote that distinguished it from other gardens, a combination of absolute determination and whim. Ostriches, flamingos and golden pheasants strutted and displayed themselves.[14] The bathing pool, which has a rather forlorn obsolescence today, was designed for swimming: it was regularly drained, cleaned and filled with a special Mediterranean-blue dye. On most mornings in the summer the four daughters of Major and Mrs Muir of the neighbouring Kiftsgate, accompanied by their governess, would visit for a dip. The head gardener's daughter recalls the summers at Hidcote in the 1920s and 1930s as

'glorious times – the Manor was always full of visitors – all gardening enthusiasts, of course. I'm afraid my family hardly saw anything of my father when the Major was in residence – evenings and weekends Dad was always with him, in his study or wandering round the garden, planning the next addition to the gardens.'

It was the head gardener who showed Johnston's visitors the garden while he was away, and during the winter months, while Johnston was in France, he and his family would move into the manor to look after the spaniels. Royal visitors to the house brought their own servants, and at least part of Johnston's reputation as an elusive figure must be attributed to a necessary insistence on privacy for his guests. He is known to have been fond of tennis (Hidcote boasted two courts and its own private coach) and fast cars, of which he owned three. Twice a year he took the Masaratti to his club, Boodles in London.

One of the most ecstatic descriptions of Hidcote was written by Vita Sackville-West (1892–1962). She was a regular visitor to the garden, recalling Johnston's gifts and guidance as well as the 'dripping luxuriance' of his planting.[15] The references to nature and tradition were clearly identified:

'Would it be misleading to call Hidcote a cottage garden on the most glorified scale? ... It resembles a cottage garden, or, rather, a series of cottage gardens, in so far as the plants grow in a jumble, flowering shrubs mingled with Roses, herbaceous plants with bulbous subjects, climbers scrambling over hedges, seedlings coming up wherever they have chosen to sow themselves.'

She was quite clear, however, that the cottage element was illusion rather than reality; that it was a device by which Johnston had transformed the exposed ten-acre site into a rich variety of parts, each separate from the others and yet working together as a unified design. The use of hedges rather than walls, 'tall living barriers', deepened the impression of 'luxuriance and secrecy' and Sackville-West noted the use of texture and colour in mixed hedges of yew, box, holly, hornbeam and beech, the shine of the holly leaf against the flatness of yew and the overall effect of 'a green-and-black tartan'.

Right: *The Stilt Garden looking eastwards towards the pavilions with the Red Borders beyond.*

She was particularly attracted to Johnston's botanical flamboyance and the element of stage management in his garden rooms:

'In one such enclosure, I recollect, no larger than a fair-sized room, where moisture dripped and the paths were mossy and the walls were made of the darkest Yew, scarlet ropes of *Tropaeolum speciosum* trailed all over the hedges, more amazingly brilliant in that place full of shadows, than ever it had appeared on a whitewashed cottage in Scotland.'

She described the magnolias, carpenteria, hydrangeas and the 'Hidcote' hypericum, 'lavishly planted all round the walls' in the forecourt. The original manor house and the collection of various outbuildings haphazardly grouped around a forecourt were given the barest mention as supports for the *Solanum crispum* and the creamy white flowers of *Schizophragma hydrangeoides,* which Johnston had trained over the buildings.

The picturesque informality of the front of the house is sharply contradicted to the rear, where the space is organized into the wide grass walk representing the principal vista of the garden. The formal prerequisites of stone steps, a pair of brick pavilions symmetrically disposed, and a fine wrought-iron gate framing a view of the distant landscape are classically arranged in a composition that owes nothing to cottage (or even English) traditions. Johnston's disregard for the niceties of convention may have been responsible for a daredevil inclination to juxtapose gardens that are alarmingly different in scale as well as character. To one side of the grass walk 'a *very* large grass lawn' known as the Theatre Lawn has a spare monumentality, which Sackville-West described as 'spacious, simple, and peaceful'. On the other side Johnston arranged a warren of small separate gardens that might easily have been adapted to 'such diverse habitations as are to be found in our small country towns and even in the garden city'.

Vita Sackville-West disliked the 'tortured shapes' of topiary at Levens Hall and the elaborate chessmen of Hever Castle. She would have had little time for the topiary lawn at Earlshall, but at Hidcote the 'smug broody hens, bumpy doves and coy peacocks twisting a fat neck towards a fatter tail' were in the 'country tradition'. She complimented Johnston's taste and restraint in using 'just enough topiary to carry out the cottage-garden idea' with the same critical, incisive intelligence that recognized the 'old-fashionable' qualities of his roses. Her analysis of Hidcote, and her evident affection and respect for a gardener twenty-one years her senior, is a homage from one extraordinary garden designer to another; it accentuates the parallels between Hidcote and her own garden at Sissinghurst (planted from 1930 onwards), and offers an insight into the elements of Hidcote that were considered most exciting in its own time. The pleached hornbeams that frame the main vista beyond the pavilions were noted for their French flawlessness. They are planted in two double rows, clipped above bare straight trunks, giving rise to the name 'the stilt garden'. The Wilderness – 'a bosky place made secret by the overhanging trees, with a trickle of water somewhere invisibly near at hand, and the smell of damp peaty soil' – was described as the perfect space for growing *Hydrangea aspera maculata* in the summer and as an astonishing bonfire of colour in the autumn. Around the centre path of the kitchen garden old roses were planted in wide rows, three and four bushes deep; Sackville-West described them on a June day, 'the bushes weeping to the ground with the weight

Right: *Country Life likened the formal vistas at Hidcote to a central gallery with apartments opening from it within which treasures were protected.*

of their own bloom, a rumpus of colour, a drunkenness of scents'.

It was the dense, unorthodox quality of planting that most impressed Sackville-West. By the time she reached the kitchen garden, she wrote,

'I had become so wildly intoxicated by the spilling abundance of Hidcote that I was no longer in any mood to worry about exact nomenclature, but only in the mood to enjoy the next pleasure to be presented.'

Vita Sackville-West, like Lawrence Johnston and Gertrude Jekyll, was liberated by her position as client, designer and expert practical gardener, answerable to no one. She would have brushed aside the modern historian's concerns over disparities in scale and stylistic references, and she would have been right to do so. Hidcote defined its own terms. It was immensely successful and influential as an idiosyncratic design, superbly planted with a unique collection of rare and familiar plants, all grown under optimum conditions.

The article was published to mark a significant transition from private to public access to Hidcote. In 1948, ten years before Johnston's death, it became the first garden to be accepted by the National Trust, to be preserved as a garden of outstanding merit. Anna Pavord's excellent guidebook describes the difficulties of the transition: Johnston's reluctance to let go, and the challenge of making the garden work throughout the visiting season. 'People see gardening as flowers on stems. They don't see green as a colour.'[16] Some of Johnston's dramatic but short-lived effects, like the phlox garden (now the White Garden), had to be replanted to provide a longer flowering season and the elitist, hedonistic qualities of the garden evaporated with its original audience.

Some of Johnston's extravagances defeated the National Trust in its early years of stewardship, when Hidcote had to be maintained at a loss. His winter plant house, ingeniously designed with heating pipes on one side and a glass front that could be entirely removed in the summer, was unique. It housed some of the tender exotics that he had himself collected on plant-hunting expeditions, including *Haemanthus katherinae* (now renamed *Scadoxus multiflorus katherinae*) from Kilimanjaro and *Gordonia axillaris*. *Country Life*, visiting the garden in January 1930, had described the Gordonia's healthy growth and profusion of large white blooms, and marvelled at its rarity. When the cost of essential repairs and fuel costs for the greenhouses (£100 in the first year) forced the Trust to dismantle the winter plant house, a part of the garden's exotic speciality was lost with it. Hidcote had been an important centre for the propagation and distribution of rare plants during Johnston's time. On wet days the seed collected from the garden's exotic collection was cleaned and stored for the head gardener to sow at the appropriate time, or distributed to Wisley, the Botanic Garden in Edinburgh and to Kew.[17] Tender plants like *Dendromecon rigida* and *Arbutus canariensis* were used in the main borders and covered with cloches in winter. Although Johnston himself generally spent the winters in France, descriptions of a camellia house 'with space left in it to accommodate a luncheon table' suggest that he returned early in the spring. The National Trust has had to contend with its public's expectations and prejudices in addition to making necessary changes to the conditions of entry (access is now from around the side of the house, whereas Johnston's visitors went directly through it). The main structure of the garden, however, and its principal effects are well preserved.

Hidcote looks Arts and Crafts: what Sackville-West summarized as 'the nice distinction between formality and informality' is refined to perfection; but the connections between practice and philosophy, craftsmanship and tradition, which are inescapable in the work of William Morris and Gertrude Jekyll, are superseded by his botanical and individual preoccupations. Johnston, with a magpie's eye for glittering detail, might have been attracted to a semblance of Arts and Crafts reverence for tradition.

A few miles away to the south, however, William Morris's influence was very differently interpreted by a group of designers inspired by his political as well as his aesthetic teaching, who committed their working lives to regenerating the social impetus and the craftsmanship of rural life. In their work and in the communities they generated these designers deliberately rejected 'the sham grandeurs and vain ambitions' of fashionable society. Although they had met and trained together in London, they abandoned the comfortable comradeship of the Art Workers' Guild and the earnest technical and philosophical discussions of SPAB. They were haunted, according to Lethaby, by 'that old feeling that "one must live near to Nature"'.[18] There was a strong element of denial in their exodus, as well as a positive determination to establish an alternative set of values through the example of their own work and in their lifestyles. These designers and craftsmen were enacting, in the vigour of their youth, the same steadfast assertion of ancient values and crafts that Gertrude Jekyll represented in her isolated old age at Munstead. The integrity of their work, like that of Jekyll, was unassailable. For the patrons who supported them and visited their showroom, and for their fellow designers, the appeal of their position was manifest: it represented a logical conclusion, politically and artistically, to the teaching of Morris and Ruskin. At the same time it confirmed the viability of the ultimate retreat, an escape into purism, away from the social disparities and urban degradation of industrialization.

The gardens of Ernest Gimson (1864–1920) and the brothers Sidney and Ernest Barnsley (1865–1926 and 1863–1926), who set up workshops, first at Ewen and then at Pinbury Park, near Cirencester, in 1893, had a pared-down simplicity that made the cottage gardens of their contemporaries appear brash or trivial. They were deliberately remote from mainstream developments in garden design, declining to court the attentions of *Country Life* magazine (although *Country Life* caught up with them in 1909). Gimson and the Barnsley brothers were the self-appointed disciples of Philip Webb, their rejection of publicity probably stemming from Webb's refusal to allow his work to be published during his lifetime; their work was widely known and respected, nevertheless, through a network of sympathetic artists and clients. During their training years in London the Barnsley brothers had formed a vital link between the architectural practices of J.D. Sedding and R.N. Shaw, both important training grounds for young Arts and Crafts designers. Sidney Barnsley was articled to Shaw, where he met W.R. Lethaby, while Ernest was articled to Sedding, together with Ernest Gimson. Sedding's office was next door to the Morris & Co. headquarters at 447 Oxford Street, so that in addition to a thorough grounding in practical craftsmanship (Sedding is reputed to have been an obsessive carver), garden craft and architecture, Barnsley and Gimson were encouraged to attend the weekly meetings of SPAB, where they came directly under the pervasive influence of Morris and Webb.

Webb's influence on the younger generation of architects, focusing on the study of ancient buildings, was fundamental. W.R. Lethaby, who was introduced to the Society by Gimson, wrote in a contribution to Gimson's biography in 1924:

> 'the Society was itself a remarkable teaching body ... it became under the technical guidance of Philip Webb, the architect, a real school of practical building – architecture with all the whims which we usually call "design" left out.'

He described the deepening of Gimson's love of old buildings into 'a passionate reverence' and the conviction that 'ancient architecture was an essence & reality'. In his diaries he recorded pilgrimages to the 'great-roofed barn at Harmondsworth' and to Fountains Abbey near Ripon, where they drew pinks growing in the crannied grey stone walls. He remembered Gimson saying: 'I am thinking of architecture all the time I am awake' and that together they agreed on a definition of architecture as 'building touched with emotion'. The emotional charge of those training years, and the comradeship of the Barnsleys with Gimson and Lethaby, all living within a short walk of Webb's office and lodgings, shaped an attitude to architecture that was loaded with political and social direction.

Gimson and the Barnsley brothers established a workshop at Pinbury Park that was to train and employ local craftsmen in the production of furniture and metalwork, made to their designs but founded on traditional patterns. In doing so they shored up the failing economics of traditional cottage crafts, grappling at the same time with the cost implications of hand-made designer products. There were several wheelwrights in the area, so a local tradition of craftsmanship existed and could be redirected into the manufacture of furniture. Gimson and the Barnsleys never permitted their designs to be manufactured by machine. By combining the production of affordable pieces with exclusive one-off designs they were able to sustain a viable workshop.

Gimson and the Barnsley brothers were extremely fortunate in their patronage. From 1902 their first landlord at Pinbury, the major landowner in the area Lord Bathurst, allowed them to use Daneway House, a fourteenth-century manor house, as a showroom and workshop. The atmosphere around Daneway was described by *Country Life* as savouring 'strongly, overwhelmingly of solitude'. Unlike the village of Broadway, which was 'almost too well known, perhaps', around Daneway the air was 'quite uncorrupted', according to *Country Life*. They were given two tracts of land, beneath Sapperton Church and close to Daneway, on which they could design and build houses for themselves.

Ernest Gimson's house was considered so spartan when it was visited by H. Avray Tipping for *Country Life* that although he missed meeting Gimson he concluded it must be the home of a socialist. He was careful to qualify his assumption, never confirming or refuting it, but leaving it hanging as a possibility, translating it into a form that his readers might more easily countenance:

> 'I judge from the house that its designer is something of a Socialist. His Socialism, however, is not that of the back street of the modern town; material, violent, narrow; but of old rural England, idealised by a somewhat eclectic study of the past, and a placid outlook on to the beautiful in Art and Nature. His ideal must surely be that of the old free village community, altered to suit an age of larger organised masses and of wider humanitarian and intellectual intercourse.'[19]

RIGHT: *Upper Dorvel House, Sapperton. An old cottage extended by Ernest Barnsley with a garden of box standards and box-edged borders.*

Gimson's socialism, according to Avray Tipping, was a thinly veiled reiteration of William Morris's socialism, but whereas Morris had been arrested for his militancy (and by 1909 when this was published he had been dead for over a decade), Tipping presented Gimson's politics as humanitarian, hardly more threatening than 'a pervading sympathy and neighbourliness of feeling'.

Upper Dorvel House, designed by Ernest Barnsley for himself, was no more ornate than Gimson's house, but it was strongly recommended in a second article by Tipping as a perfect example 'of what should be done by those who want to build anew and simply in the Cotswold district'. Both Ernest and Sidney Barnsley treated vernacular architecture with such reverence that their own buildings are barely distinguishable from the seventeenth-century and later cottages of the village. At Upper Dorvel House Ernest Barnsley had to contend with a site that was 'awkward in shape, access, aspect and gradient, and having a plain and featureless cottage standing in its midst'. The 'plain and featureless cottage' was incorporated into the new house, with wings added to either side; a long curved drive with a yew hedge crowned with simple topiary forms turned the difficult access to advantage; and the site was terraced, exploiting the gradient to provide the house with a fine view across the valley. Mr Barnsley, it was said, had met his difficulties not with hostility or destruction, but 'in a friendly way', entering into partnership with them. The new wings of the house were built of local stone, quarried nearby to match the original cottage, and although the adaptation of the older building gave the house a sprawling ground plan (Sidney Barnsley used to joke about his brother's 'mansion' up the lane) the interiors retained an unassuming simplicity. Ornament was fastidiously avoided except in the main beam of the hall (part of the structure of the original cottage), where Gimson enriched the plasterwork with running scrolls of vine, oak and rose leaves, and 'detached sprigs of such flowers as flourish in the garden borders'.

The garden itself has a crisp, sculptural decisiveness. Barnsley's astute sensitivity to period detail made him adapt the seventeenth-century knot garden to the intimate scale and setting of a cottage. The influence of Sedding's ideas on garden craft, instilled in him during his training a decade earlier, is also apparent. *Country Life* described the garden in 1909 as

> 'a plat whose horizontal lines are in sympathy with the vertical ones of the house, for its straight paths surround square and oblong flower-beds and borders, to which clipped box shrubs and hedges give point and variety.'

Special note was made of the cheapness of laying out and maintaining such a garden: 'It is a question of taste, of a true sense of the fitness of things, rather than of money'.[20] The box standards and neatly clipped hedges set close up against the front of the house were described as 'the requisite semi-formal link between the straight lines of the building and the tumbled Cotswold landscape' and the article was illustrated by a plan in which the layout of the garden was drawn as an integral part of the house.

Ernest Barnsley's commitment to integrating the design of house and garden, his social experiments in collaboration with Sidney Barnsley and Gimson, and his regard for building in accordance with centuries of tradition, attracted an extraordinary commission in 1909. The building of Rodmarton Manor evolved over a twenty-year period, beginning with the design of a house and garden, and concluding in the creation of an idealized rural community of craftsmen and women.

RIGHT: *Rodmarton Manor, near Cirencester, built between 1909 and 1929 in defiance of industrialisation.*

Country Life, which was still reporting the philosophy, as well as the facts, of country-house building with remarkable consistency in 1931, described the project as the realization of the ideal that 'William Morris so strenuously preached, but which even he never carried out with such completeness'. Rodmarton Manor was commissioned and designed as a defiant gesture against industrialization. To those who argued that the old way of building was obsolete it presented tangible evidence that a large house could still be built

'using only local materials and without any kind of mechanical assistance ... Every stone and slate of Rodmarton has been quarried near by, brought to the site in farm carts, and then cut, shaped and laid by local masons. In addition, all the oak for the floors and roof timbers has been felled and seasoned on the estate, and local craftsmen have carried out all the carpentry and joinery. Even the furniture has been made and designed in the neighbourhood, and much of it in the Rodmarton workshops.'[21]

Below: *Garden plan, Rodmarton Manor, Gloucestershire, Ernest Barnsley and William Scrubey, 1909–29.*

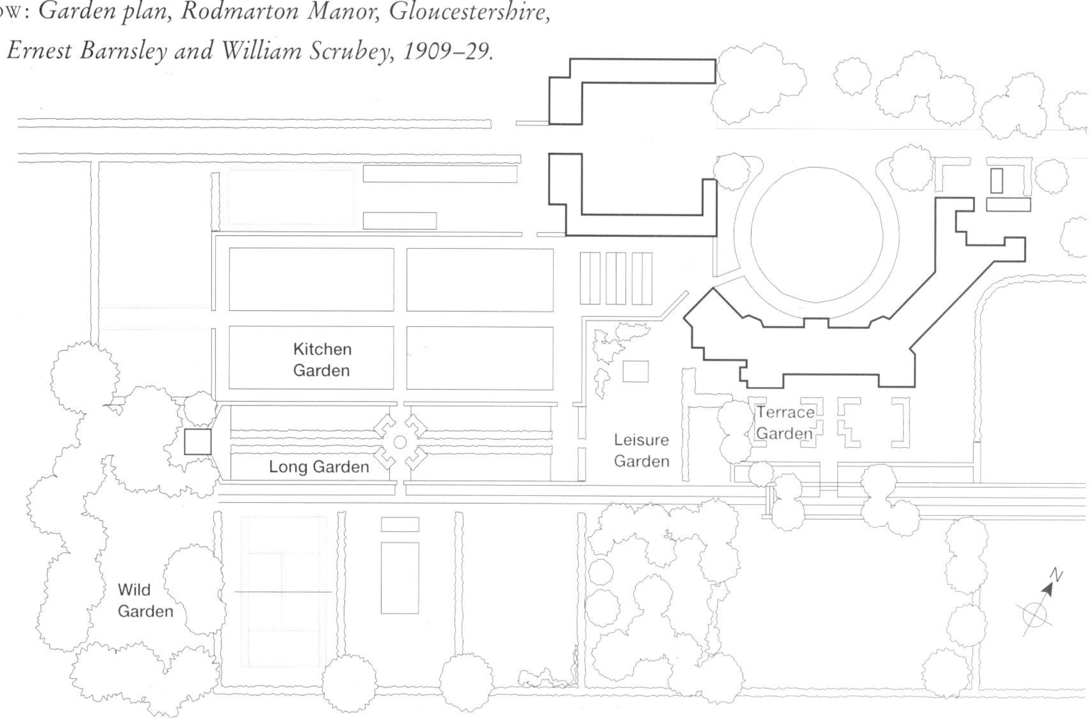

The garden at Rodmarton was designed by Barnsley in collaboration with William Scrubey, head gardener at the Manor for almost fifty years. The clients, the Hon. Claud Biddulph and his wife Margaret, were agreed that it should be laid out while the house was under construction and Margaret Biddulph's expertise as a trained horticulturist (she had grown flowers commercially before her marriage) played an influential part in the evolution of the design.[22] The structure of the garden is crisp and formal, reflecting Barnsley's style. Two long straight driveways, the 'Holly Drive' and the 'Beech Drive', arrive at a circular lawn in front of the house. The far side of this green forecourt is enclosed by the stone manor house and its high garden wall, arranged as four sides to an octagon; the near side is sheltered by an arc of lime trees, planted in 1919 and pleached until the 1950s. To one side of the house a gateway into the garden is incised with the names not of the architect and his client but of William Scrubey and the foreman-carpenter for Rodmarton, Alfred Wright. Beyond the gate the clarity and openness of the forecourt give way to a garden full of secret compartments and densely planted enclosures. Although, like Earlshall, the plan was devised as a series of outdoor rooms, clearly defined by long straight walls and hedges, the intimacy of Rodmarton is beguiling; it contradicts the grandeur of its scale.

Rodmarton is not preserved as a relic of the days of William Scrubey and Ernest Barnsley. It has remained in the Biddulph family through three generations, and although the main plan and features of the garden have been preserved, in parts it has been altered in response to changing family needs and a reduction in the

RIGHT: *A screen of pleached limes frames the view from the Winter Garden.*

number of paid gardeners from ten to one. A swimming pool has taken the place of one of three original tennis courts, and in the 1950s a rough grass area was made into a Leisure Garden, paved and planted with roses with the intention of creating a low-maintenance area. It is this Leisure Garden that is first encountered within the garden gate. A sequence of garden rooms runs in succession along the south face of the house. From the Leisure Garden a dense screen of pleached limes shelters and secludes a shady Winter Garden, planted against the south-west corner of the house with hellebores, snowdrops, hepaticas, fritillaries, hostas and Japanese anemones. To the south the pleached limes frame a vista across a small topiary lawn, beyond the confines of the garden to the distant Stonehill Wood. After the soft informality of the Winter Garden the topiary lawn is sharply defined, with boundaries of low dry-stone walls and a straight central path of circular stepping stones, flanked by parallel rows of topiary, which reinforce the directional emphasis of this garden, away from the house. The house itself is planted with roses, clematis, wisteria and other climbers, and large stone and wooden tubs are arranged on the terrace, planted with marguerites and agapanthus. Today Rodmarton is unusual because, as at Upper Dorvel House, the garden presses right up to the building. The qualities of space and openness usually secured by the provision of a generous terrace have been transformed into a more intense relationship between house and garden by the planting of yew hedges on what was originally an expanse of lawn. The relationship between the garden and the landscape beyond, in contrast, is open and expansive.

ABOVE: *Ernest Barnsley's design for a summer house at the end of the Long Garden, with its steeply pitched roof and finial, is like a house in a child's drawing.*

ABOVE: *The size of a small room, this vine-covered arbour is half concealed in the south-east corner of the garden.*

Barnsley cut a ha-ha along the southern boundary to keep the Biddulphs' cattle out of the garden (although occasionally they found a way in) without obscuring selected vistas from the garden across open pastureland. The individual garden rooms are screened from prevailing winds by high walls and hedges, which also serve to divide the garden; banks of trees are used selectively around the perimeters to provide essential shelter and a backdrop to garden features, but the absence of a single boundary wall defining the space within the garden contributes to an element of intrigue and adventure. In the south-east corner a sunken garden is hidden away out of sight. There is a pattern of intimate, contemplative spaces that are given axial views across areas of garden that are very different in character. Barnsley's treatment of architectural features within the garden is in sharp contrast to that of Lorimer or Lutyens, however: it is essentially unarchitectural. Instead of creating a vista with an arbour at its focus, at Rodmarton the arbour is half-hidden. Its architectural importance is secondary to its value as a retreat, solidly sheltered with stone walls and roofed with timber stretchers covered with vines. This principle of sublimating the architectural elements is reversed with a liberal dash of complexity and contradiction at the very heart of the garden. In a garden where spectacle is deliberately undermined by a more resonant, introverted character, the single most extravagant gesture is completely concealed within high stone walls and tall yew hedges. The Long Garden is not central to the plan. It is sandwiched between the tennis courts and the vegetable garden, west of the house. There are no telltale vistas, flagging it from other parts of the garden: it is always encountered as a surprise. Barnsley designed a summerhouse with a steep stone roof, like a house in a child's drawing, to focus the axis of the Long Garden. Four long rectangular herbaceous beds flank a straight stone path (originally edged with wide grass borders) that bisects the garden. At the centrepoint a small circular pond is surrounded by tall quadrants of yew that embrace simple stone bench seats (hiding places even in so open a plan). Eight mounds of clipped box (much larger and more angular now than in early photographs) are set like sentries, marking the extremities of the path and its juncture with the circular centrepiece; and the summerhouse surveys the entire garden from its western tip.

Sheltered by the high south-facing stone wall, tender plants can be grown alongside other hardier specimens. Areas of wall are covered by *Clematis x eriostemon* 'Hendersonii' and *C.* 'Huldine'. Shrub and climbing roses form the backbone of the borders. The herbaceous borders were completely overhauled in the 1990s. They had become so overgrown, and perennial weeds such as bindweed were so problematic, that the present owners decided to clear each of the borders sequentially. The first bed was dug up in the autumn of 1992, healthy plants were divided and stored in the kitchen garden, and the border was manured and left fallow (so that weeds could be treated with herbicide as they appeared) for eighteen months before being replanted in the spring of 1994. Each year, work began on the next border so that the garden was never completely disrupted (it is open to the public between May and August) and the work could be spread over a period of years. As the borders were replanted the best of the old perennials were used with new plants that would extend the flowering season; structural plants like euphorbias and *Cynara cardunculus* are planted in bold swathes among roses, phlox, asters, sedum and daylilies.

ABOVE: *Fruit tress trained across the inner brick face of the kitchen garden wall.*

Adjacent to the Long Garden an enormous rectangular kitchen garden is walled on all four sides. The walls have a double skin; stone on the outer face and long shallow bricks facing inwards. Originally every wall of the kitchen garden was lined with espaliered and cordoned fruit trees. Vine eyes were fixed into the mortar of the brick wall and the bricks, which absorb and retain the heat of the sun, helped to ripen the fruit. The training and pruning of these trees probably fell to William Scrubey and his gardeners,

RIGHT: *The outer skin of the kitchen wall, faced with stone, encloses the Long Garden.*

but Margaret Biddulph's influence was apparent in the tradition of growing flowers as well as food for the house in the kitchen garden, a tradition that is still retained today.

Both Claud and Margaret Biddulph were exceptionally committed to re-creating ancient building traditions and the craft-based structure of a rural community. Rodmarton was a country retreat of sorts, a withdrawal from modern life. By reviving the traditions of a pre-industrial age its masons and joiners were condemned to a lifetime of manual labour that might have been liberated by the use of modern machinery, but the lengthy building schedule, spanning two decades when comparable buildings of its time could be built in as many years, created a long-term structure for the development of skills that was to ensure a lasting effect. Despite the interruption of the First World War the steady progress of the building of Rodmarton survived the general demise of the Arts and Crafts movement. In 1931, shortly after it was completed, *Country Life* described the it as almost

'a village in itself ... In fact, the whole place bears an astonishing testimony to the life and vigour which Mr. and Mrs. Biddulph have given to a tiny village by their enthusiastic encouragement of the arts and crafts.'

The slow progress in building the house caused the Biddulphs to settle so comfortably into one wing of the building that when the principal rooms were completed they were reluctant to move. Instead the immense hall was adopted as a theatre room for village concerts and amateur theatricals, and the palatial drawing-room became the villagers' workroom, furnished with long trestle tables and benches. Canework, embroidery and furniture-making were all conducted at Rodmarton. This invasion of the drawing-room, the most refined and feminine area of the house, by wood-workers and basket-makers represented a complete subversion of Edwardian hierarchies. If Avray Tipping had paid a visit he would have suspected not socialist but communist sympathies. At Rodmarton it was part of a natural progression of events, returning (although unconsciously) to the tradition of a medieval hall, where workers ate in close proximity to the family. The practice of arts and crafts outlived its architect. Ernest Barnsley died in 1926, as did his brother Sidney a few months after him. Gimson had died in 1920. The traditions of furniture-making that they had initiated and revived were carried on by successive generations.

The garden at Rodmarton, like the plan of the house, has all the characteristic hallmarks of Arts and Crafts. It is conditioned by a clear formal plan divided into a series of 'outdoor rooms', there are axial walks with vistas to the landscape beyond, twin herbaceous borders are sheltered by tall walls and yew hedges, and there are even tennis courts. There is an 'Attitude' at Rodmarton, however, which distinguishes it from its contemporaries, and from Hidcote in particular. Despite being a large garden of about eight acres, the usual elements of grandeur and display are absent beyond the entrance court. Perhaps the insularity of each component part is an honest interpretation of a tradition in garden design that other architects had failed to recognize. The less sophisticated gardens of the seventeenth-century and Tudor periods, gardens of rural manor houses, were not all sharply aligned with arches and vistas so that the entire garden could be surveyed, or at least anticipated, from the terrace. Rodmarton was designed as a manor house made up of many parts, and the same philosophy inspired the design of its garden. Perhaps, too, it was as radical in its attitude to nature as it was to tradition: we know that most of the building materials for the house were literally quarried and felled from the site. Is it possible that the character of the garden was determined by the natural topography of the land? Again the evidence is provided by *Country Life,* describing the landscape in 1909: 'this tumbled region of hill and dale, full of folds and laps, produces a series of pictures, each one of considerable extent and great variety, but exclusive of the others. The ridges form boundaries, dividing the country-side into a set of provinces retaining their own independence and individuality.'[23] For the most part, the garden at Rodmarton is arranged on a level site. There was no question of retaining the humps and bumps, or all of the extant trees, on the virgin site. Barnsley was never brazen in his designs.

Footnotes

1 Anon., 'Country Houses, Gardens Old and New. Kellie Castle, Fife, the residence of Mrs Lorimer.', *Country Life*, 28 July 1906, pp.126–31.
2 Ibid.
3 Sir Robert Lorimer, 'On Scottish Gardens', paper delivered to the Architectural Association in 1899.
4 Ibid.
5 For 'Whinfold' and 'High Barn' at Hascombe in Surrey; and 'Brackenburgh' at Calthwaite in Cumberland.
6 Letter from Emily Lutyens to her sister Betty Balfour in 1901, Lutyens Family Papers, RIBA.
7 Sir Robert Lorimer, op. cit.
8 Peter Savage, *Lorimer and the Edinburgh Craft Designers*, Paul Harris Publishing, Edinburgh, 1980, p.12.
9 I am grateful to Chris Crowder, head gardener at Levens Hall in Cumbria, for describing the history and care of topiary to me.
10 Madame de Navarro (née Mary Anderson), *A Few More Memories*, London, 1936.
11 H. Avray Tipping, 'Country Houses, Gardens Old and New. Hidcote Manor, Gloucestershire. The seat of Mr. Lawrence Johnstone' (sic), *Country Life*, 22 February 1930, pp.286–94
12 This information is outlined in a letter of 29 November 1978 from the head gardener's daughter Mrs M.R. Lees to the RHS. It was in the 1920s that Johnston's allowance was £600 per month.
13 Jekyll, too, changed the soil in gardens to accommodate specific plants on occasion.
14 Jack Percival, gardener at Hidcote between 1932 and 1936, assures me that these exotic birds were looked after in special heated quarters during the winter months.
15 The following quotations are from Vita Sackville-West, 'Hidcote Manor', *Journal of the Royal Horticultural Society*, Vol.74, November 1949, pp.476–8
16 I am especially grateful to Paul Nicholls at Hidcote for sharing his knowledge of Johnston and the garden with me, and for introducing me to the people who remember its history.
17 I am grateful to Jack Percival for describing his work as a gardener at Hidcote to me.
18 W.R. Lethaby, Alfred H. Powell, and F.L. Griggs, *Ernest Gimson, His Life & Work*, Shakespear Head Press, Stratford-upon-Avon, 1924, p.8.
19 H. Avray Tipping, 'Lesser Country Houses of To-Day. A house at Sapperton designed by Mr. Ernest Gimson.', *Country Life*, 6 March 1909, pp.348–54.
20 H. Avray Tipping, 'The Lesser Country Houses of To-Day. A house at Sapperton by Mr. A. Ernest Barnsley.', *Country Life*, 10 April 1909, pp.522–7.
21 Arthur Oswald, 'Rodmarton, Gloucestershire. The Seat of The Hon. Claud Biddulph.', *Country Life*, 4 April 1931, pp.422–7.
22 See Rosemary Verey, 'The garden at Rodmarton Manor', *The Garden*, Vol.107, 1982, pp.263–8.
23 ' Country Houses, Gardens Old and New. Daneway House, Gloucestershire, the property of the Earl Bathurst.', *Country Life*, 6 March 1909, p.344.

CHAPTER EIGHT

THE GARDEN WITHIN THE HOUSE

The balance between nature and tradition that shaped the Arts and Crafts movement in Britain was very differently weighted in North America. Frank Lloyd Wright (1867–1959) recalled his wonder, as a boy, at primitive American architecture – 'Toltec, Aztec, Mayan, Inca' – whole civilizations that architects, looking to Paris for their education, had neglected to observe. While British designers had assumed a conservationist role, albeit a dynamic one, Americans were more liberated in their attitudes to history, craftsmanship and the opportunities as well as the iniquities of a Machine Age. Frank Lloyd Wright, describing 'the sovereignty of the individual', claimed that unlike the English and Europeans, who faced

RIGHT: *48 Storey's Way, Cambridge, encapsulating Baillie Scott's ideal of the modern cottage and its garden designed as an integral whole.*

backwards towards traditional forms that they felt compelled to preserve, 'an American is in duty bound to establish new traditions in harmony with his new ideals of Freedom and Individuality'.

If tradition represented a plethora of opportunities rather than restrictions, nature proved equally invigorating as a source of inspiration: the grandeur and scale of the American landscape and its extremes of climatic conditions presented a very different spur from the soft pockets of rural England that William Morris and his followers had pledged to protect. Californian designers considering the inherent conditions of the landscape were faced with a native desert. The traditions of a migrant population included those of Hispanic, Japanese and native American as well as European gardening and building cultures. Indigenous plants like cacti could be grown to a size and luxuriance that brazenly defied the harmonious possibilities of the English herbaceous border. Conversely, the lush perennials of the traditional border rapidly shrivelled in the heat. Where a return to first principles was sought and nature and tradition were consulted, designers were presented with a dazzling variety of stimuli, impelling them to forge an approach to garden design that would honour the philosophy of Arts and Crafts and at the same time interpret cross-cultural and environmental conditions that were uniquely American.

The ideal of uniting art and nature, of designing a house and garden as a single entity, had grown up in America independently of the Arts and Crafts movement in Britain, but been motivated by comparable social and artistic conditions. Although the writings of Ruskin and Morris, followed by those of Robinson and Jekyll, were all extremely influential, the interpretation of their work by American designers was quite different from that of their British counterparts. It formed only a part of a complex determination to evolve a design philosophy that would respond specifically to the American landscape and the vigour and diversity of its people, and which would utilize, rather than deny, the potential of the machine. The concept that states like California had a vitality 'as both a physical place and a state of mind' and the resurgence of that state of mind in garden design has already been considered in David Streatfield's excellent book California Gardens: Creating a New Eden. On one level, English planting plans continued to be incorporated into highly eclectic estate gardens. At the same time extraordinarily creative designers like Frank Lloyd Wright and Charles and Henry Greene were formulating intense new relationships between landscape and architecture.

The integration of the American house with its garden could be adapted to the various American climates. In temperate regions the proposition of a garden as an outdoor extension to the plan of the house – a series of spaces designed to accommodate intimate or social encounters, into which the activities of the house could comfortably overflow – was practical as well as progressive. In the Mediterranean-type climate of California the dappled shade of a pergola, a colonnade or the still sanctuary of an inner patio created an interface, neither inside nor out, which could be enjoyed for most of the year. In the Midwest, where temperatures reach opposite extremes in winter and summer, gardens were absorbed into the architecture of the house where they could be sheltered from scorching heat in summer and protected from severe frosts in winter. The ideal of a garden within the house, or of a series of rooms open to the sky, was particularly suited to the growing conviction that a single vision (that of the architect) should inform every detail of the domestic sphere. The shape and plan of the house, the materials and method of construction and the inspiration for its decorative patterning were all founded on a profound regard for nature, so that the interlocking forms of house and garden became emblematic of a fundamental unity.

Frank Lloyd Wright did not design gardens as separate entities; he wrapped the wings of his houses around them, creating green courtyards, sunken gardens and covered terraces so that interior and exterior spaces were barely divisible. The principle of shelter, fundamental to architecture, was essential to garden making in the Midwest. Wright wrote of the climate around Chicago as 'a matter of violent extremes of heat and cold, damp and dry, dark and bright'. His Prairie Style houses, so called because they adopted the spirit and horizontal lines of the prairies, were protected by shallow-pitch roofs with deep overhanging eaves. By setting the house walls well back beneath the eaves they were sheltered from driving rain, and the interiors were shaded in summer. The walls could be 'light screens' giving access to balconies from the bedrooms or opening on to verandas and terraces on the floor below. These intermediate spaces belonged to both house and garden. Sometimes, as in the case of the Robie House in Chicago, designed in 1906, the roof projected so far that entire terraces were covered. Wright was interested in the overall relationship between the house and its landscape, and, at a detailed level, in making the garden a working part of the house. At the Robie House the sunken garden court is very compact, but the billiard room and the children's playroom open directly on to it. The playroom benefits from the covered terrace that can be used in almost all weathers and is bounded by walls to prevent the children from straying on to the nearby road. The corners of the terraces are punctuated with brick and concrete planters, incorporated into the walls and made to Wright's designs; on his plans and perspective drawings he showed them festooned with trailing plants.

Wright eliminated the distinct separation between indoor and garden spaces. Although progressive Victorian houses often presented a vista across the garden from the drawing-room, it was unusual to find glazed doors opening directly from the principal rooms directly on to outdoor terraces. At both the Robie House and the Avery Coonley House in Riverside, of 1906–9, Wright dissolved entire walls into glazed screens. Bedrooms as well as living-rooms open on to verandas and terraces, and at Avery Coonley roof lights illuminate the interiors with a pervasive natural light. The garden and the landscape beyond are constantly glimpsed from the interior, and a painted frieze of a birch forest, flanking the fireplace along the vast north wall of the living-room, makes an explicit reference to nature within the house. Wright was fond of emphasizing the low lines of his houses by drawing them in perspective, set within a frame of slender tree trunks. The vertical lines of organic growth contrast with the horizontal planes of the houses, and the roofs are sheltered beneath a natural canopy of branches and leaves. There is an implication in these drawings that the house and its natural environment form an organic partnership. At Avery Coonley this concept was extended to the interior structure as well as its decoration: the living-room frieze shows only the pale birch trunks, underplanted with ferns; on the ceiling above, the shelter of a birch copse is suggested by a tent-like structure of wooden rafters, with passages of natural light filtering through the patterned roof lights.

Above: *Perspective, Avery Coonley House, Riverside. Frank Lloyd Wright.*

Left: *The emphatic horizontal planes and balanced proportions in house and garden form a single unified composition.*

In the garden the clear horizontal lines that Wright drew across his elevations to reflect the predominant horizontals of the prairie plains are in turn mirrored in a sheltered pool, which is generously scaled and proportioned to complement the house. The garden site was densely wooded in parts, running down to the banks of the Desplaines River, and Wright located the house close to a copse of mature trees. The rooms are arranged in long narrow wings that spread into the grounds so that rooms can be glazed along two or three sides, giving the effect of being surrounded by the garden. These wings penetrate and define the garden spaces. A sunken garden is framed by the extended wings of the house with a pergola closing one side. There is a dynamic relationship between the natural landscape of riverside and woodland, and the garden contained within an architectural structure. Straight paths and terraces are dappled with the shade of nearby trees; the wings of the house overhang and in some areas span across the garden spaces.

Wright's simple troughs and flattened urns, cement rendered in keeping with the main building, determine the position and to some extent the type of planting within the overall architectural strategy. They are incorporated into the balcony walls and the piers around the house, climbers trail down from the upper storey, and Wright introduced the same fixed planters into the interior architecture of the living-room. At Avery Coonley every element of the domestic environment was determined by Wright – the lighting, furniture, textiles and carpets – as well as the hard landscaping of the garden. Within the house and around its perimeter, elements of the garden are disciplined to conform to a master plan. The house itself, however, exercised Wright's advocation of an 'organic' architecture, voiced in a public address given in 1894:

'Let your home appear to grow easily from its site and shape it to sympathise with the surroundings if Nature is manifest there, and if not, try and be as quiet, substantial, and organic as she would have been if she had the chance.'

The need to establish a bond between architecture and landscape, which underpinned the entire Arts and Crafts movement, achieved its most dramatic exposition in Frank Lloyd Wright's Fallingwater at Bear Run, Pennsylvania. The house has no artificial garden. It is poised within the landscape, projecting out over a natural waterfall. A hatch in the living-room floor leads down to the river beneath the house and the top of the bedrock boulder, on which the client's family used to picnic before the house was built, breaks through the floor in front of the living-room hearth. Wright told his client: 'I want you to live with the waterfall, not just to look at it, but for it to become an integral part of your lives'. The waterfall cannot be seen from the house, although on the terraces, cantilevered out over the fall, the sound of water is ubiquitous:

Above: *Poised above a waterfall at Bear Run, and with terraces pierced by mature trees, Fallingwater carries Wright's convictions about the natural house to a sublime conclusion.*

'The waterfall never becomes merely an image for the house's inhabitants, as it does in the famous perspectival view from below, but remains something that underlies our entire experience, permeating all our senses'.[1]

The walls of Fallingwater are constructed of local stone, quarried close to the site and taking their thickness from the natural depth of the strata. Wright let the glazing into grooves cut into the stonework, eliminating the need for frames, and the stone floors, waxed to resemble the water below, are deliberately continuous between interior and terrace spaces. This use of natural materials indigenous to the site, and the pleasure in contrasting surface textures, is energized by Wright's determination to explore the most modern building technology and materials available to him. The house depends on a reinforced concrete structure that was considered so daring when it was built in 1935 that at one point the interference of engineers and a pusillanimous builder caused Wright to withdraw his staff and drawings, writing to the client in fury: 'I have put so much more into this house than you or any other client has a right to expect that if I haven't your confidence – to hell with the whole thing.' Wright extended the concrete roof slabs into massive trellises, holes are cut into the cantilevered terraces where mature trees grow through the building, the river and the rock structure of the falls permeate every element of the house. Unlike the Robie and Avery Coonley Houses, Fallingwater does not fit into the period of Arts and Crafts; the individuality of Wright's genius cannot be channelled into any single movement. Fallingwater offered a sublime conclusion, nevertheless, to part of the Arts and Crafts quest. There is no garden because the relationship between the house, the rocks, the river and the woods is so direct that any intermediary space would be superfluous.

Japanese gardens and the spiritual import of simplicity and craftsmanship were studied and interpreted in America with a keenness that was lacking in Europe. The reconstruction of the Ho-o-den pavilion at the Chicago World's Columbian Exhibition in 1893 gave young designers like Frank Lloyd Wright and the brothers Charles and Henry Greene (1868–1957 and 1870–1954) direct contact with Japanese construction methods, and introduced the concept of the garden as a symbol of landscape – a centre for contemplation. The plurality of American traditions promoted a diverse and liberal attitude to imported cultures. In the gardens of Greene and Greene, stepping stones and quiet pools made open references to Japanese gardens. However, in the primary relationship between the garden and the house and in the bold detailing of structural beams and rafters, Greene and Greene adapted Shinto traditions to a progressive Californian ideal; there was no superficial style-mongering.

The Gamble House in Pasadena, California, designed in 1907–8 for David and Mary Gamble of the Proctor & Gamble family, is Greene and Greene's masterpiece. The spiritual importance of nature is expressed in an organic silhouette of a 'Tree of Life', richly coloured in Tiffany glass, across the massive front door. Throughout the house the natural strength and beauty of wood is accentuated in an exposed timber structure and panelled interiors. The structural detailing of ceilings, staircase, windows and doors is painstakingly expressed in teak and mahogany. Wright's propositions for machine production are rejected in favour of the finest standards of hand craftsmanship, taken to such extremes that the edges of the bricks in the study fireplace are hand-rounded, to complement the rolled edges of the joinery. Although no written testimony defines the meditative intentions of the design, it is apparent that there was more going on in the design of the Gamble House than a fastidious attention to the smallest detail and a straightforward

Right: *Dining room in the Gamble House by Greene and Greene. The stylized vine in the stained glass window echoes a real vine growing outside.*

preference for natural materials. Greene and Greene made literal references to Japan throughout the building and its garden; whether there was an underlying translation of Eastern philosophy and religion cannot be seen, although it might be surmised.

The presence of nature within the house is both explicit and profound. At a decorative level, the dining-room windows are leaded and stained with designs of delicate stems and flowers of a blossoming vine, conjuring with the image of real vines, which cast shadows across the window from their growing place outside. Through the stained glass, here and in the front door, the Greenes bathed the interiors with coloured light, defining time and the seasons by focusing the movement of the sun around the house, and its relative strength and height. Randell Makinson described the transforming effect of light through the Tree of Life glass into the hall:

> '... on certain favoured mornings, the early prowler will find the sun striking almost horizontally ... already dappled by its passage through the trees across the road opposite, blazing through that fantastic Tiffany glass in the entrance doors and filling the house from front to back with a luminance not to be found anywhere else ... that rather formal central space of the house is transformed, for maybe an hour, into something so perfectly "cliche" – Aladdin's cave or sacred grove'.[2]

Spatially, the first floor literally extends and opens into the landscape and it is tempting to make an analogy with the branches of a tree. Greene and Greene designed open-air sleeping porches, covered decks that project out from each of the principal bedrooms, so that the family and their guests could sleep out under the stars. By this means the scents and sounds of the garden, and the orange groves that the Gambles owned nearby, had a nightly presence within the house. There was a practical dimension to these outdoor sleeping rooms, however: the Greenes' father was a physician specializing in respiratory illnesses and they had grown up with the doctrine, gathering currency at the beginning of the twentieth century, that sunshine and fresh air were essential to health.

The sleeping porches and the terraces on the ground below transform the elevations of the Gamble House into a series of open and closed spaces, of shingled walls, brightly lit beneath the California sun, and intriguing passages of deep shade. The timber structure of the porches, and the exposed beams and rafter tails of the shallow-pitch roofs, refer to Japanese domestic and temple buildings. The inspiration for the garden is equally clear. Two large terraces, tiled and furnished with Greene and Greene tubs and illuminated at night by delicate lanterns, are partially covered by the sleeping porches. Originally the rear terrace was dominated by two mature eucalyptus trees. Stepping stones of random sizes form a curved path across the lawn and a small pool, surrounded by walls of clinker bricks and uncut stones, continues the Oriental symbolism of the path in a sequence of stepping stones, placed with their tops rising just above the surface of the water.

RIGHT: *The fragile remains of a Japanese tea-house, installed at New Place for the publisher Sir Algernon Methuen, nicely contradicting the design philosophies of Jekyll and Voysey.*

In Europe re-creations of the spirit of Japanese gardens were rare. An interest in more general Eastern philosophies and a fascination for Spiritualism and for alternative religions like Theosophy were often expressed in highly personal and specific symbolic forms that were designed into the garden and the house. In England the Japanese garden was more often adopted as a fashionable interlude. It found its way into the Arts and Crafts garden through the insistence of clients rather than the choice of serious designers like Jekyll. Familiar with the rash of pagodas and lantern features, Jekyll dismissed them as a pretentious craze and counselled restraint:

'The sober, thoughtful gardener smiles within himself and lets the freaks of fashion pass by ... If he has travelled in Japan, and lived there for some time and acquired the language, and has deeply studied the mental attitude of the people with regard to their gardens, and imbibed the traditional lore so closely bound up with their horticultural practice, and is also a practical gardener in England – then let him make a Japanese garden, if he will and can; but he will be the wise man if he lets it alone.'[3]

At New Place in Haslemere, Surrey, Jekyll's counsel would have been supported by that of the architect for the garden, C.F.A. Voysey (1857–1941), who also believed that a symbol should only be used where its meaning was properly understood (although he evolved his own personal language of symbolism). Voysey designed the garden and its house in 1897. Jekyll refined the planting five years later. A determined client deftly found a way around both of their arguments. He invited a team of Japanese gardeners and craftsmen to design and install the Oriental part of the garden, after Voysey and Jekyll had made their contributions and departed.[4]

Above: *Lead statue by Reginald Fairfax-Wells in the formal walled garden at New Place.*

Right: *New Place and its garden were designed by C.F.A. Voysey in 1897 to fit around the contours of a steeply sloping site. The bench is a rare example of Voysey's garden furniture.*

New Place is an affirmation of the influence of the client, in addition to that of the architect and gardener, in the making and maintenance of a garden. The publisher Sir Algernon Methuen commissioned the house and its garden to be designed as a single entity. C.F.A Voysey was already a leading protagonist among those with the conviction that every detail of a house, from the curtains at the windows to the size and shape

of the borders, should be designed by the architect. At New Place he measured the natural contour of the site, a steep slope rising from west to east, and plotted the floor levels for the house and the outdoor rooms of the garden together in a single drawing. The site was organized into a series of level terraces divided by sloping banks or stone retaining walls and the house absorbed the change in level, gaining a lower ground floor in one wing. Although the structure of the garden was defined at a single stroke, however, Voysey returned to New Place after the completion of the house in 1899 to design a gardener's cottage and a summerhouse, and again two years later to revise the formal garden.

Above: *Voysey's garden gate pays homage to the fine eighteenth-century gates in the brick arcade.*

Right: *The roughcast render and buttresses of Voysey's arbour and the green painted bench within echo the architecture of the main house.*

Voysey arranged the garden as a series of six rooms. On the highest terrace, to the east of the house, a formal walled garden was divided into four squares with a circular water tank at its centre, now surmounted by a statue. He intended to house a second 'cast lead statue', almost certainly the Peasant Woman and Child by Reginald Fairfax-Wells, in a niche in the centre of the east wall. In the executed design, however, its axial position was changed and it was given its own plinth. A tennis lawn was provided on the south side of the formal garden. A splendid brick arcade, designed to house a pair of Italian gates delicately entwined with iron vine leaves and thought to be the eighteenth-century, divides it from a long narrow bowling green below. Voysey thoughtfully built stone bench seats into his arcade and at the north end of the bowling green an arbour, originally thatched, was provided for players to shelter or gossip in while they waited their turn. By the early 1920s the brick arcade was clothed with Azara microphylla, an evergreen shrub with glossy foliage and vanilla-scented flowers.

Voysey had little horticultural knowledge. He provided a framework for the garden, intimately associated with the plan of the house, and the details of planting were worked out either with the client or with a specialist landscape architect. The overall planting effect that he wanted was indicated: on his plan one of the borders for New Place is simply marked 'flowers big and tall' while the specification for 'more or less wild' areas farther from the house, and for a bank planted with indigenous 'Briars, Blackthorn, other wild shrubs' suggests that his sympathies lay with Robinson and Jekyll rather than with Blomfield. His gardens are exceptional for the clarity of their planning and for the continuity between interior and exterior rooms. The separate garden areas are open or closed,

finely proportioned to connect with different parts of the house. Although there are deliberate alignments and vistas within the garden, less formal diagonal views are explored using the architecture of the garden to frame a view of the house, or across the semi-wild woodland areas to the landscape beyond. Methuen was a keen gardener and the view from his study, along a straight path to a sheltered arbour, must have been a constant temptation.

At the centre of the house a south-facing hall was designed in Arts and Crafts tradition as a principal living space as well as a circulation area. Almost the entire south wall was lit by generous windows. Voysey designed an inglenook, not around the fireplace, but overlooking the garden, defining an intimate, sunlit space that was echoed outside in the garden court by a covered settle, sheltered from easterly winds and facing west to enjoy the afternoon sun. The transition from the hall, through a half-glazed door, to the garden was skilfully organized into a series of stages by the provision of a sheltered court, enclosed by the wings of the house on three sides. Voysey was particularly sensitive to the sensations of feet: he believed that a rapid succession of different surfaces had a distressing effect on the walker, and although New Place was too grand a house to be treated, as his smaller cottages were, with the same slate floors inside as in the garden paths, the semi-circular stone steps into the garden court and the provision of wide paths paved with stones salvaged from Old Christ's Hospital were designed as a temptation to wander from the house to the garden.

The promise of shelter, and a lyrical perception of the psychological effects of enclosure – around a seat, within the grandeur of a brick and stone arcade or beneath a thatched arbour – recur as subtle preoccupations throughout the design of New Place. The wide drawing-room bay window, and the billiard room on the floor below, are fitted with window seats. Any bay window literally projects the interior into the garden space; at New Place, however, the proportions of this vertical three-storey wing are picked up in the high retaining wall of the sunken garden that it overlooks. Voysey repeatedly used a heart motif as a symbolic reference not just to love, but to noble thought and feeling. Heart-shaped letterboxes decorate his front doors; hearts are pierced into his chair backs and wrought into the tips of hinges. At New Place the sunken garden, viewed from the drawing-room, was to have featured a centrepiece of four heart-shaped beds, filled with rue. Lady Methuen, however, wrote to Gertrude Jekyll that she thought this 'hardly practical ... and I do not care for the scent.' If the rue beds were ever cut, they were grassed over again when Jekyll was invited to redesign Voysey's rose garden, and the planting of borders to either side of the sunken garden suggests her authority.

The pale mauve flowers of Abutilon vitifolium complemented the grey stone of Voysey's retaining wall, facing west and so establishing a sheltered microclimate. This was grouped with double white peonies against the tall, pale blue flowers of delphiniums and Anchusa azurea 'Opal'. In the opposite border, away from the shelter of the wall, anchusa and catmint were planted together. Voysey habitually specified that several hundred galvanized iron eyes be fixed to the roughcast render of his houses, to be wired for creepers in the final stage of the building. At New Place, in addition to the metal eyes, trellis was used extensively, painted green and planted with Robinia hispida, hydrangeas, escallonias, Sophora tetraptera and Fremontodendron californicum. Some of this planting was probably advised by Jekyll, whose plans for a rose garden, made after a visit to New Place in March 1902, are in the Reef Point Gardens Collection. Beyond the sunken garden her rose garden, filled with standard and dwarf roses, either replaced or refined an earlier design by Voysey. Jekyll and Voysey knew and respected each other's work. Voysey is represented in a battlemented yew hedge along one side of the rose garden, and Jekyll in the planting of Phlomis fruticosa cascading over a retaining wall, growing in harmonious proximity. However, their joint presence is no evidence of a working relationship. Jekyll's contribution to the planting of New Place was made in a second phase of the garden's development, after Voysey's departure. A third phase was instigated after the grounds were laid out and the initial planting was complete, when the client stepped in.

Beyond the formal structure of the garden the land banked away to a water garden bounded by rockeries, which were Sir Algernon Methuen's particular passion. His authorship of an Alpine ABC, an encyclopaedic volume including the extensive range of alpines grown 'more or less with success' at New Place, and the private publication of New Place Haslemere and its Gardens by Methuen in 1921, testify to a contribution that is often underestimated: the long evolution of a garden by the client. Today the moss-covered stones and channels of Methuen's Japanese water garden and the failing timber structure of the tea-house are more poignant than any other part of the garden. After its peak of maturity in the early 1920s, when Methuen opened the garden to the public on summer Sunday afternoons, New Place was gradually allowed to return to nature. No radical interventions disturbed the masonry structure of Voysey's plan, no bright new vision usurped the fleeting brilliance of Jekyll's planting, a thick blanket of coarse grass shrouded Methuen's rockery, and the vineries fell derelict. More recently the areas close to the house have been cleared of undergrowth and the clarity of Voysey's structure predominates again. Elsewhere, the condition of the garden has been stabilized. The proposition that it might be restored to a former condition has been cautiously resisted. There is an uncomfortable element of dishonesty in the replication of something that has been irrevocably lost. Where Jekyll's shrubs and Methuen's trees survive they have grown to a size that says far more about their history than their original position as part of a planting scheme. The preservation of the garden is not presented as a solution to the dilemma of restoring a period garden; it is poised in a fragile state of change, as it has always been.

Voysey's collaborative approach to garden design was not indicative of a half-hearted commitment to nature. He believed that by studying nature the human spirit was developed: 'The more we look into nature, the more we feel the spiritual forces behind us.' His buildings, like those of Wright, were designed to 'play into the hands of nature. As a sympathetic accompanist, both in colour and form, we can show a desire to be subdued and quiet and restful, modestly hiding behind trees.' In his houses, where plain wall coverings were used, Voysey derived his rich colour combinations from nature. Green was recognized as the most soothing colour:

> 'nature never allows her colours to quarrel. Her purple trees, with their gossamer of delicate spring green, dwell lovingly with the blue carpet of hyacinths. Harmony is everywhere.'[5]

Decoration was sparingly used. The effect of a Voysey interior was invariably dependent on the colours and surface textures of oak, slate and stone offset by smooth expanses of white plaster, and of meticulously refined proportions. Where a clock case was painted, or a wall patterned with Voysey paper, the decoration was invariably drawn from nature. The birds and fruiting trees that recur throughout his work are symbols in a complex spiritual strategy, which Voysey believed would ennoble the thoughts and feelings of his clients.

Voysey's concern with stylized symbols, with harmony and repose, and with spiritual growth through the contemplation of nature, are affiliated with the spiritual basis of Oriental design that fascinated Frank Lloyd Wright and Greene and Greene, although Voysey might have been uncomfortable with the association. His contemporary, M.H. Baillie Scott (1865–1945), was more straightforward in his recommendations for the ideal garden and in his manner of infusing the garden into the house. Where Voysey had a tendency to preach in his published writing, Baillie Scott was sympathetic and down-to-earth. His book Houses and Gardens (1906), exquisitely illustrated with watercolours of his own designs, presented the 'average householder' with a handbook of practical ideas and advice. The function of the garden, according to Baillie Scott, was simply 'to grow fruit and vegetables for the household, and also to provide outdoor apartments for the use of the family in fine weather'. He sought to rectify the separation between use and beauty, kitchen and ornamental gardens, declaring: 'If rose leaves, like cabbage leaves, were found to have culinary uses, it is probable that the rose would soon be deposed from its position as queen of the flowers.' In place of the red geranium Scott proposed the 'scarlet runner', as a plant that would be more admired 'were it not for the uses of its slender pods'. He wrote with reforming enthusiasm and a gift for prose:

'The grey-green foliage and great thistle-like heads of the globe artichoke, the mimic forest of the asparagus bed, and the quaint inflorescence of the onion have each a distinctive beauty of their own which would be more widely recognised if these plants were not used for food.'[6]

In his writing Baillie Scott invoked nostalgia for rural ancestral roots; he conjured with images of picturesque cottages and borders filled with roses and lilies against a background of cabbages and potatoes. He told his readers that under the 'specializing influence of modern civilization' in the suburbs and cities they had lost the instinct for cultivating the soil, and then he presented them with a set of guidelines and model plans, inciting them to reject their dingy yards in favour of the garden suburb. His vision of a garden was not limited to the cottage garden, however. He built up a picture of the country garden set against a dark moorland covered with purple heather 'and that lesser kind of gorse which seems to have been clipped into neat round bushes by Nature's invisible shears'. In the background a deep pine wood and a few silver birches would provide so perfect a setting for a house of grey stone that the only garden required would be a terrace enclosed by rough walls of lichened stone. Where a larger plot could be obtained, Baillie Scott's 'garden of average size' would include

'a lawn for tennis, croquet or bowls, an orchard, a kitchen garden, and a flower garden in two main divisions – one a rose garden, which may be square or nearly square in form, and the other, which may be long and narrow, devoted to perennial flowers. All these out-door apartments will be connected with straight paths, and one of these may form a pergola ... the beauty of the garden will depend to a great extent on its vista effects, and for this purpose its paths must be straight.'[7]

LEFT: *The entrance to Undershaw in Guildford, designed by M.H. Baillie Scott in 1908-9.*

Paths would be few, following the shortest routes: 'If one imagines a garden without paths at all one would soon find certain beaten tracks appear, and these would represent the general lines for the fundamental paths.'[8]

Baillie Scott's garden formula was scarcely original by 1906. It was his commitment to planning even the smallest town garden through a persuasive approach, and the consideration of the house and garden as a single entity that enabled him to popularize the Arts and Crafts garden at the turn of the century, bringing it to a much wider, urban population. Baillie Scott fudged the lines between urban and country garden plans. Actual size, he wrote, had little to do with the need to create effects of mystery, surprise, light and shade in a garden. Certain elements could be adapted in scale to suit the conditions of the suburban garden. They included the provision of a central dipping well for watering the garden, the planning of a pergola to pattern a paved walk with shadows and the planting of hazels or willows to shade a grass walk from which vistas could be glimpsed to 'an open sunlit space bright with flowers'. Stone steps and walls were to be given a 'rough and homely treatment', considered not as 'mere masonry, but building which is to be clothed with plant life'. Baillie Scott accompanied his lyrical prose and practical assurances with seductive watercolours of pergolas laden with roses, and hillside cottages set within the orchards and formal gardens of his descriptions. Simple layout plans were provided.

Of all the designers of his generation, Baillie Scott was one of the most gifted and original decorators. Plants from the garden and indigenous trees from the surrounding landscape were brought into the office in the mornings to be drawn in detailed studies. They were simplified and stylized or modelled with life-like intensity as decorative motifs, which could be wrought into metal fire dogs and light fittings, stencilled into friezes, carved into joinery and embroidered or appliquéd on to the loose covers of Baillie Scott's high-backed winged armchairs. At Blackwell, a substantial country house built in 1898 above the banks of Lake Windermere, trees and flowers from the estate are brought into the interiors with extraordinary delicacy and originality. The swirling foliage and berries of the mountain ash are carved into two inglenooks in the hall; whole trees are shaped around the staircase columns and beams, and birds' nests are partially concealed within the foliage screening a minstrel's gallery on the floor above. Only this vast double-height hall, used for entertaining weekend guests and for family activities, has a door leading directly into the garden. The drawing-room projects physically into the garden, commanding superb views of the grounds and the lake through two bays, but the invitation to view – this being essentially passive – was not developed into an opening for action. Traditionally the drawing-room was the feminine domain, presided over by the Angel in the House (until Virginia Woolf killed her off).[9] At Blackwell it is a decorative tour de force in restrained femininity.

The entire room is white. Standard roses and fruiting trees are stylized into slender, elongated columns with capitals carved into foliage, flowers and berries, grouped together to support the soffit of a bay, or a thin white shelf. Above the shelf a deep frieze is embossed with rowan branches laden with berries, and the ceiling, too, is enriched with intertwining branches. Baillie Scott designed fitted seats, enamelled white with the rest of the room, for the window bays and around the fireplace, to minimize the intrusion of ordinary furniture. Delicate shelves and glazed cupboards appear too insubstantial to support anything weighty. There is a parallel between the elegant finesse of this room and the immaculate perfection of women's fashion of the same period – not the rich colours and flowing lines of Liberty gowns, but the fitted white satin and lace confections seen in the paintings of John Singer Sargent and James Tissot, which restricted society women to the cleanest (and by implication the purest) activities. We know too little of the clients, Sir Edward and Lady Holt, to understand whether family dynamics or the independent creativity of the architect motivated the refined delicacy of the white drawing-room at Blackwell. No plans or early photographs of the garden survive to define a relationship between interior and exterior. As a reflection of nature within the house, however, it is one of the most sophisticated and esoteric interiors of any period.

Right: *Standard rose trees and stained glass tulips ornament the white drawing room of Blackwell by M.H. Baillie Scott.*

Baillie Scott was only thirty-three when he designed Blackwell. As his practice matured he became increasingly involved in the garden-city movement and the relationship between his houses and gardens became more intimate and direct. The garden city focused philanthropic and socialist ideals into the provision of model communities that presented a viable alternative to unregulated metropolitan growth. Baillie Scott designed a cottage for the first garden city, at Letchworth, Hertfordshire in 1907, and the following year a terrace of houses for Hampstead Garden Suburb. Although these houses were small, each had its own individually designed garden with a tree-lined path leading to the front door, and to the rear a paved terrace, a lawn and a grass path to a distant arbour, focusing the view from the living-room. In Houses and Gardens Baillie Scott considered the familiar problem of the long narrow terraced garden. He divided it into three: a formal rose garden closest to the house, with paved paths and a central fountain; a water garden beyond, with two pools, one semi-circular, the other rectangular, linked by a central rill flanked by flowers; and farthest from the house a pergola establishing an element of mystery and seclusion. It is a romantic plan, and makes no concessions to limited budgets. The absence of any connecting door between house and garden is a notable omission.

The proposition that gardening and fresh air enhanced good health was developed further in a second design for Hampstead Garden Suburb: fifty flats for young working ladies were surrounded with communal gardens at Waterlow Court and allotment beds were provided. The accommodation was planned as a quadrangle around a green central court, so that every flat had a garden view and a covered arcade gave the court a cloistered quiet.

One of the finest surviving examples of a modest house and garden, planned and executed together as a single entity, is 48 Storey's Way in Cambridge, designed by Baillie Scott in 1912. The entire site is defined by a central axis that determines the layout. In front of the house this axis is marked by a straight stone path, edged with pebbles, leading with unwavering precision to the wide oak front door. Baillie Scott's instinct for poetic detail is expressed in a vine carved across the middle rail of the door. Perhaps he was aware of Voysey's use of the vine as a symbol of hospitality. The entrance to the house immediately reveals the alignment of a second door, leading to the rear garden, fulfilling one of his conditions: 'on opening the front door, one enters a wide and low passage, and beyond its cool shade, one catches a glimpse of a garden vista.' There is an impression of sunlit rooms, sandwiched between the two gardens, and the path as central axis carries through the living-room to continue in the rear garden. Although the site is suburban in scale, Baillie Scott divided it into a clear sequence of outdoor rooms. The front garden acts as a candid introduction to the house. Its visibility from the street through a white-painted picket fence and the pattern of rectangular lawns and borders, planted in cottage style with lavender, iris and peonies, reflect the scale and character of the house. Four columns of clipped yew add a note of grandeur to the approach to the front door, marking an intersection of paths, and to either side, mounds of clipped box signal the entrances to secondary garden rooms, divided by walls of privet. While the formal, central garden area relates to the main living-room and staircase areas of the house, these long narrow garden rooms originally gave access to a bicycle store on one side and the scullery and coal store on the other.

The length of the rear garden enabled Baillie Scott to give practical expression to his theories. The rear elevation of the house is trellised around bay windows so that climbing roses scent the living- and dining-room bays and in May the garden door is festooned with wisteria racemes. Conservatories were seldom permitted in Arts and Crafts houses because of their association with Victorian artifice. In place of their hothouse environment Baillie Scott substituted a

Above: *The neat formality of the front garden at 48 Storey's Way is scaled and detailed to complement the house.*

Left: *Baillie Scott provided shaded walks and 'open sunlit space bright with flowers' in the long rear garden of 48 Storey's Way.*

'garden room' at each side of the house: a partially enclosed space covered with stretchers that extend into pergolas flanking an open area of lawn. Beyond the formal garden, surrounded by tall yew hedges, Baillie Scott designed a wilder area with spring bulbs and flowering shrubs. Nut walks and a vinery afford the glimpses from shade to sunlight idealized in Houses and Gardens. Fruit and vegetable gardens are decorated with borders for cut flowers, and in the orchard, which marks the farthest limit of the garden, a simple arbour is located from which to look back along the straight central path. Although the interiors at 48 Storey's Way are not adorned with the elaborate flower and foliage decorations that distinguish Blackwell, the prominence of the bay windows within the principal rooms, and the continuity of style, scale and axial planning between house and garden, ensure that the presence of the garden is as integral to the interior of the house as its white cottage-style elevations are to the effect of the garden.

The idea of a garden room within the house was carried to an extraordinary level of sophistication at The Hill House in Helensburgh, Scotland. The architect was Charles Rennie Mackintosh (1868–1928) and The Hill House, designed in 1902 for a generous plot at the top of a hill in a wealthy suburb, was his second domestic commission. Mackintosh was fortunate in having a sympathetic client, the publisher Walter Blackie. At this time Mackintosh was working in close collaboration with his wife, the designer Margaret Macdonald Mackintosh (1865–1933), whom he later credited as the inspiration for half, if not three-quarters, of his architectural work. They were commissioned to design the building, its interiors and all the furnishings for the house. Inevitably they designed the garden as well, although this part of the design was only partially implemented once the building work was complete.

The Hill House is justifiably celebrated for the unity of all its component parts in a single stylish artistic statement that was supremely elegant and at the same time startlingly original. The full significance of its interiors is only just beginning to be understood as evidence of the original paint finishes and decorations is revealed beneath subsequent layers of paint. Blackie was a publisher of fairy-tales and at the turn of the century these children's stories were laden with symbolic meaning. Two years after the completion of The Hill House the German art critic Hermann Muthesius described Mackintosh as a creator of fairy-tales. For almost a century this remark was interpreted by historians as a light-hearted, mildly derisory quip. It is more likely, however, that Muthesius was referring to a visual and metaphorical narrative at The Hill House that was clearly understood by architect, client and critic.

The drawing-room at The Hill House was an early-morning rose garden, caught, as if by magic, within the walls of the house. A wide south-facing bay window lights the room and offers views out over the garden to the Firth of Clyde beyond. Within the bay two standard roses stood in pots and a window seat (heated from beneath on winter days) was originally stencilled with patterns of stylized roses and flanked by tall slender 'columns' that counterbalanced the long horizontals. Trellis was used extensively in the gardens and the vertical floor-to-ceiling windows that light the two sides to the bay are leaded to give a corresponding grid effect. They were hung, like all the windows in the drawing-room, with fine white linen or toile curtains, appliquéd with a stylized pattern of elongated stems connecting in a sparse pattern of buds or petals, and rising from square bases – a stylization, perhaps, of the standard roses that the Mackintoshes used to define the main pathways in the garden as well as to decorate and scent the bay.

The trellis patterned with rose buds became a recurrent motif in the Mackintoshes' work. The delicate curves of an unfurling bud set against the rigid geometry of a grid and the elongated curve of a stem or the straight vertical fretwork of a support provided a fertile source for the concentrated panels of ornament in uncompromisingly plain settings that characterize their work. In The Hill House drawing-room the order and restraint of single buds and flowers arranged between trellises, and the cultivated conformity of the standard rose, is contrasted with the wild untrammelled beauty of the briar rose. Above the fireplace a gesso panel by Margaret Macdonald Mackintosh depicts a fairy-tale princess encapsulated within a protective enclosure of vigorous thorny wild roses. The theme of a sleeping beauty, reclaimed and safeguarded by nature until she could be liberated by a chivalrous prince, was a provocative metaphor for the age. At The Hill House it played a personal as well as a metaphysical part in the decoration: the profits from fairy-tales probably financed the house. Mrs Blackie's spinning wheel, deliberately positioned on the

ABOVE: *Perspective drawing of The Hill House from the south-west by Charles Rennie Mackintosh, 1903.*

RIGHT: *The Hill House from the east showing a petal or leaf motif carved in stone above a bedroom window.*

staircase, alluded to the theme again and it is significant that although rose and trellis motifs recur throughout the house, it was in her domain, her bedroom and drawing-room, that the decoration was predominantly white – silvered as if by morning dew. Mr Blackie's bedroom, the dining-room and the hall are much darker and more contained in character. In late nineteenth-century literature woman is seen as a redeeming force, unsullied by the corruption of industrialization and commerce; there is a clear correspondence between the virgin woman (whether angel, fairy or innocent child) and wild nature.

The drawing-room walls were stencilled with a rose trellis. Strips of silvered paper were stuck on to it to make the verticals, and random petals and leaves were painted on as though they had drifted in with the morning breeze. Recent investigations suggest that the surface of the wall was stippled with silver in places, perhaps applied with a stiff dry brush by one of the Mackintoshes. Early photographs show the furniture draped with beadwork – antimacassars as fine as cobwebs, accentuated by dew.[10] The fireplace was surrounded by luminous silvery-gold mosaic work, and flanked by a vertical shelf whose central spar traced the outline of a sapling tree with horizontal branches terminating in leaves of coloured glass. The room was lit by elaborate lanterns, gilded or chromed and fitted with milky-white opaque glass, or rose buds inset in coloured glass, adding to the fairy-tale effect.

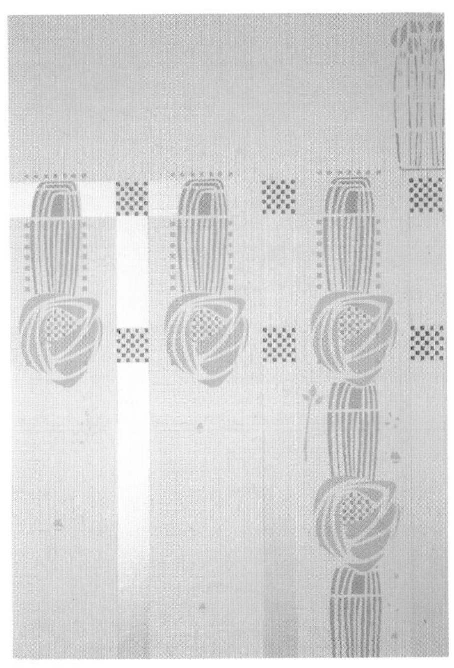

Above: *The drawing room bay, Hill House, where standard roses originally stood in tubs completing the symbolism of rose and trellis motifs that recur through every detail of the interior.*

Right: *Stencilled roses and trellis in the drawing room.*

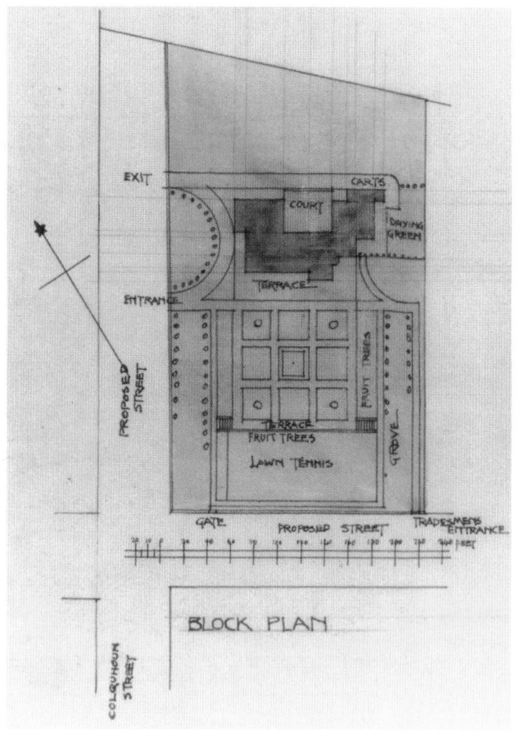

Above: *Mackintosh's block plan for The Hill House showing his original design for the garden.*

The large rug was patterned with a trellis motif and the Mackintoshes designed the freestanding as well as the fitted furniture for the room. A painted cabinet next to the door was patterned with vertical ladders of trellis and in the bay a black-painted table was constructed of three tiers of openwork, each comprising a pattern of squares, so that as the sunlight moved round the bay during the course of the day a changing pattern of light and shadows would be cast across the floor.

The theme of nine squares was inset into the table top. It recurs around the window seat, in the fitted furniture and even in the rugs of Mrs Blackie's bedroom. It had been Mackintosh's intention to extend this pattern of nine squares into the structure of the garden. His plans and elevations include a block plan for the house showing the garden on the south side divided into nine squares, aligned with the main bays of the house. In the centre an inner square is marked, perhaps suggesting a tank pool. A grove was to have run along the east side of the garden and beyond the formal area there was to have been a lawn tennis court. Mackintosh had a tendency to compose his elevations for maximum effect. Gateways and even windows were moved from one drawing to the next to make a better picture. There are details on The Hill House drawings that Blackie probably edited out to keep the costs down. However, his memoirs of Mackintosh record: 'He also gave us the main lines for the lay-out of the grounds; whereafter everything seemed to fall naturally into place.'[11]

Mackintosh's elevations suggest an elaborate garden design: on the south side of the house the garden was terraced with high stone retaining walls espaliered, presumably, with fruit trees. Stone steps led down to the formal garden, flanked on one side by a cylindrical pavilion and on the other by an intriguing arbour. Mackintosh's fluid drawing style makes it difficult to determine whether this arbour had walls of yew, or of masonry covered with creepers. They were to have been crowned with peacocks, but again these might have been topiary or wrought iron. The idea of the house and garden designed as a single coherent whole was reiterated in the boundary wall, which was harled like the house and styled to frame specific views of the elevations. A horseshoe-shaped opening invites a view of the entrance bay. On the south side of the house the wall was lower, curving away from a wooden gate.

Early photographs of the garden show that Mackintosh's plans were only partially implemented. The pavilion and the retaining walls were built, but apparently not the arbour. On the west side the formal garden was entered through an elaborate arched opening in a wall of trellis, not shown on Mackintosh's drawings, and the pattern of sweeping and straight gravel paths that conform to his designs may not originally have been planted with the standard roses that punctuate the lines of his elevations. There was a small courtyard with access from the hall on the north side of the house, formally composed with a circle at its centre. To the north of this, away from the shadow of the house and cleanly divided from the family areas by a long straight path, was a vegetable patch, still conveniently close to the kitchen. The highly individual approach to garden design evident in Mackintosh's drawings was compromised to some extent by the limitations of the Blackies' gardener. Mackintosh's designs dealt skilfully with the difficulties of a steeply sloping and exposed hill-top site. However, the Blackies' gardener (brought with them from their previous small town garden), was less adaptable to the steep incline and driving winds at The Hill House. The task of making an ambitious new garden out of a former potato field still littered with building residue almost defeated him, and there remains a mound in the garden, grassed over now, where he dumped barrow-loads of stones, refusing to take them any farther.

The fairy-tale element in the design of The Hill House and the idea of a garden almost literally drifting into the house with the morning dew – of rose petals caught in the stonework of the elevations and the tiled fire surrounds – made it one of the most enigmatic and influential houses of its time. The importance of symbolism in domestic design was seldom overtly described at the turn of the century and today it is easily overlooked. There are inferences in the writings of the period, and records survive of apparently ordinary clients performing symbolic rites, such as carrying the 'living fire' from an old dwelling to a new one. For certain architects and their clients the design of a dwelling and its integration with nature had a quasi-religious status: the literal retreat to nature was part of a more profound or fanciful philosophy. Although the design of The Hill House was only dimly appreciated in Britain, it became widely known throughout Austria and Germany: Deutsche Kunst und Dekoration published a lengthy article on the house in 1905, illustrated with Mackintosh's drawings and early photographs.[12] Both Mackintosh and Baillie Scott had a formative influence on the Vienna Secessionists and on the promotion of the *Gesamtkunstwerke*, the house and its garden as a total work of art that was developed in European Art Nouveau.

Footnotes

1 Robert McCarter, *Fallingwater*, Phaidon Press,London, 1994, p.22.
2 Randell L. Makinson, *Greene & Greene: Architecture as a Fine Art*, Peregrine Smith, Inc., Salt Lake City and Santa Barbara, 1977, p.21.
3 Gertrude Jekyll and George Samuel Elgood, *Some English Gardens*, Longmans, Green & Co., London, 1904.
4 I am indebted to the present owners for this information.
5 C.F.A. Voysey, 'Ideas in Things', *The Arts Connected with Building*, ed. T. Raffles Davison, Batsford, London, 1909.
6 M.H. Baillie Scott, *Houses and Gardens,* George Newnes Ltd, London, 1906, p.81.
7 Ibid. p.81.
8 Ibid. p.83.
9 Virginia Woolf, lecture to the National Society for Women's Service on 21 January 1931, published in *The Death of the Moth*, 1942.
10 I am grateful to Anne Ellis, Property Manager for The National Trust of Scotland at The Hill House, for sharing her ideas on the drawing-room as an interior garden so generously with me.
11 Walter Blackie, 'Memoirs of C.R. Mackintosh', written in 1943 and first published in the *Scottish Art Review* in 1968.
12 *Deutsche Kunst und Dekoration*, Vol.6, 1905, pp.337–59.

CHAPTER NINE

NEW DIRECTIONS

Attempts to define Arts and Crafts and contain it historically impose limits on the diversity of its ideals and their capacity to inspire successive generations. In its own time, Arts and Crafts coexisted with other fashionable styles. Many of its protagonists, including Jekyll, Lutyens and Lorimer, were as comfortable with classical traditions as with the Gothic that inspired Arts and Crafts and some of their finest work was distinguished by a liberal mixing of sources. While it would be possible to draw the themes of earlier chapters to a reasonably neat conclusion, using the First World War as a historical full stop, there is a more open-ended view of Arts and Crafts that explores the perimeters of the movement and suggests that the

RIGHT: *Moorish and Italian motifs are mixed with English style at Hestercombe.*

war redirected rather than terminated its momentum. The writing of history casts key characters in specific roles, editing away the achievements that do not progress a particular argument. The conventional view of Jekyll as partner to Lutyens glosses over the evidence for her involvement in the women's suffrage movement and her influence in establishing professional training for women gardeners. Gardens that pushed beyond the limits of Arts and Crafts took familiar themes in new directions both before and after the war. Finally, the preoccupation with preservation that characterized the movement can be seen in its continuing form, in the restoration of Arts and Crafts gardens.

The ideas behind Arts and Crafts design and the characteristics with which it is identified were liberally interpreted before the First World War. Lutyens and Jekyll were not dogmatic in their pursuit of the principles that we now associate with the Arts and Crafts movement. Their gardens did not always respect the native conditions of site and soil, and ancient vernacular traditions were sometimes mixed with modern foreign ones. If Lutyens had been more intimidated by stylistic distinctions, the design of Folly Farm, in particular, could not have evolved as it did. If he had been insistent on the integration of the house and its garden, he would not have attempted the garden at Hestercombe at all.

Folly Farm, in Berkshire, began as a small medieval farmhouse. Lutyens was invited to make substantial additions to the house on two separate occasions. A less spirited architect might have taken the original building as a model for a vernacular extension, as Barnsley had done at Upper Dorvel House. Instead Lutyens cut a clean divide between new and old work. In the first extension, begun in 1906, he designed a dapper new house at right-angles to the original building in a contained 'Dutch' style. Inconsistencies between the two buildings and a confusing approach to the front door were deftly resolved in the creation of two new gardens contained within meticulously crafted high brick walls. Lutyens turned the small scale of these gardens to dramatic effect, drawing a series of sharp axial lines to focus the entrance and to establish a setting for the house that is both intriguing and distinguished by its detail. Jekyll's planting plans for the courts survive: box-edged borders planted with old-fashioned flowers – poppies, white campanulas, aquilegias and irises in pale yellows, pinks and blues. Rambling roses, jasmine and clematis were planted to clothe the walls. The main expanse of the garden on the south side of the house, however, was not to be designed for another six years, when an ambitious new owner invited Lutyens back to design a second even larger addition to the house and the main areas of the garden were ordered into an inspired collection of interconnecting spaces.

The genius of Folly Farm, in its final form, lies in its celebration of contrasting styles in close proximity. Just as the 'Dutch' extension complemented the original building by refusing to copy it, the 1912 addition builds on, as if haphazardly, in an informal vernacular style (described by Lutyens as his 'cowsheds') that is neither traditional nor modern. An expressive red-tile roof sweeps down to shelter a massive brick arcade enclosing two sides of a tank cloister in which originally the clear water acted as a mirror for shapely brick piers. Separate 'garden rooms' frame and give context to the contrasting faces of the house, and long axial paths create vistas that work both ways: ordering the views of the garden from the house, while defining the composition of a gable end or a balconied bay from the garden. Lutyens wittily added

ABOVE: *Lutyens's 1906 'Dutch' extension to Folly Farm with its witty 'canal garden' added in 1912.*

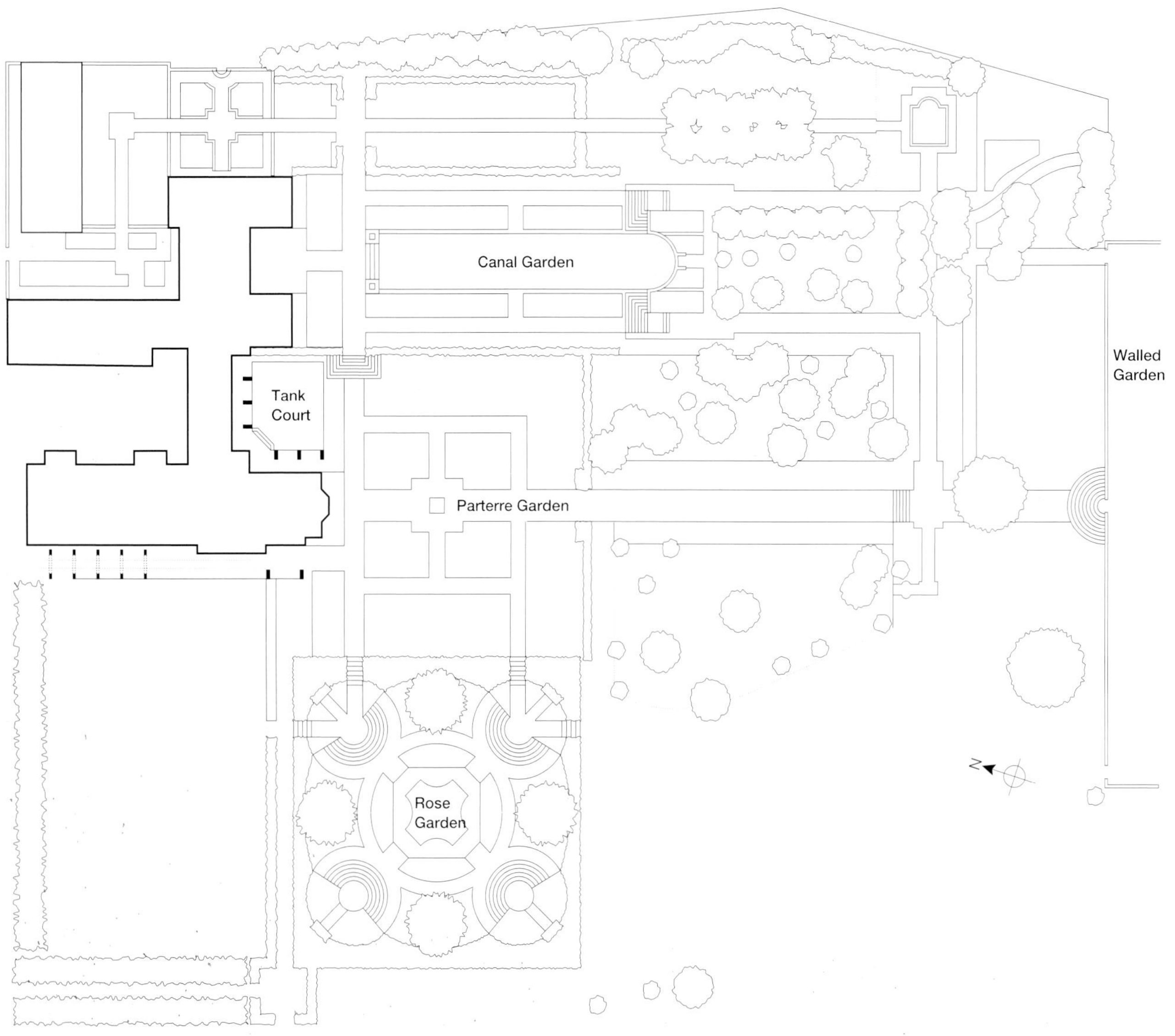

a canal garden to the Dutch face of the house, crisply proportioned and immaculately presented to suit. The rustic gable end of the 1912 addition looks out across a formal parterre, but there are romantic and mysterious elements in the garden at Folly Farm, in addition to the virtuoso displays of architectural accomplishment. West of the formal parterre a sunken rose garden is concealed within high walls of yew. At each of its four corners a circular platform, raised above a cascade of brick and stone steps, invites a secret masque or at the very least stately meditation. From the rose garden the view to the house is dominated by deep sheltering roofs and the long west elevation, which is anchored by its massive chimneys and quixotic in its provision of a balcony for sleeping out on summer nights.

While the garden and the house are interdependent

Left: *Garden plan, Folly Farm, Berkshire. Designed by Jekyll and Lutyens in 1906 and 1912.*

Right: *The sunken rose garden looking across to the 'cowsheds' wing of Folly Farm added in 1912.*

Left: *Lavender spills over onto a herringbone path of hand-made bricks.*

Above: *The great plat at Hestercombe where the architectural frame and its planting are perfectly synthesized.*

at Folly Farm, each drawing attention to the virtues of the other in a masterly sequence of effects, at Hestercombe, in Somerset, Lutyens and Jekyll designed a garden to draw attention away from the house. In this case the house was an existing, perfectly serviceable but ugly, building and the commission was for the garden only. To enjoy the garden at Hestercombe it is first necessary to turn away from the building. Lutyens terraced the sloping site, sinking a 'great plat garden' deep below the original terrace to the house, so that the visitor is drawn to survey the garden from above. Once within the plat, all the axial lines focus on features or openings in the garden, surreptitiously directing attention away from the house above. The garden design looks deceptively simple in plan. The great plat to the south of the original terrace is contained within a square, framed by raised terraces on all four sides. To the north a high stone retaining wall is treated as a vertical border, specially built with planting holes so that the Mediterranean sun-loving plants – lavender, catmint, santolina and rosemary – can send their roots right back into the cool soil behind. Above this wall the 'grey walk' shows Jekyll's love of silver-leaved plants at its most refined.

On the south side of the plat the raised terrace is lower, furnished with a pergola that delineates the edge of the formal garden while filtering the view to the pastoral landscape beyond. The stone pergola piers are alternately circular and square in plan, a favoured device enjoyed by Jekyll and Lutyens to make the subtle distinction between hard and soft shadows. Rambling roses, clematis and honeysuckle are allowed to scramble over the structure, and to pre-empt any critical reaction, asserting that every pergola should have a destination, oval openings were punched into the walls at either end, offering composed views to the landscape. To the east and west of the plat the terraces are formal and symmetrical, ordered by water-filled channels called rills. Jekyll treated these long narrow features as aquatic flower beds, to be planted with irises, arrowheads, water forget-me-nots and water plantain. The structure of the rills, with sunken linings of stone, and edgings tracing a ribbon line that curls into loops in a regular pattern, alludes to the subtle allegiance between the knot-like precision of the rills and the sunken plat between them.

The rills to the east and west are almost identical architecturally, structured by a formal preoccupation with the flow of water. Each rill is fed from above by a spout of water running from a grotesque in the head wall into a circular pool. Circular niches are cut into the wall, and the pool itself is housed within a semi-circular recess in which the form of an ellipsoid is shaped by the base of the pool and the recess walls. The effects of refraction and reflection are deftly calculated, and reflected sunlight patterns the detailed stonework of the curved recess. At the opposite end of the rill water drops down over a short sequence of steps to collect in a much simpler rectangular tank pool. Even here, however, structure and visual effect are inseparable. The steps continue down beneath the surface of the pool, making classical allusions and tempting the feet of children. On both sides of the garden the tank pool interrupts the rhythm of the pergola, so that the long axis of the rill focuses on a framed view of the Blackdown Hills and Taunton Deane. Although both rills cut through a wide area of grass, the planting of the long borders to either side contradicts Lutyens's symmetry. Jekyll specified that the east rill borders should be planted with red-hot pokers, Oriental poppies and irises while those of the

ABOVE: *The spouting arc of water completes a complex play of geometry around the rill pool and its setting.*

west rill are planted with foxgloves, daylilies, shrubs and roses. Closer to the house, at the north end of the rills, this disparity is resolved in two very different architectural treatments of the spaces to east and west of the original terrace.

The garden at Hestercombe is entered from the west side. Steps lead down from the house to an elm arbour, set at the head of a rosary and saved from Dutch elm disease during the restoration of the garden. The curved niche of the arbour, and the half-dome of its organic cover, allude to complex geometric games, the rules of which become more apparent as the garden is explored. From the sheltered intimacy of the arbour, however, the colour and scent of old-fashioned China roses, accompanied by the sound of water trickling along the central rill, seduce the visitor into delaying further investigation. Although the wit and intelligence of the architectural games impress and surprise, they never dominate the experience of the garden. It is only from the balustrade at the far end of the rosary that the layering of terraces can be fully appreciated. The sight of the continuation of the rill on the terrace below, combined with the sound of water spouting from the grotesque head beneath the balustrade, draw the visitor down stone steps to choose between a promenade along the grey walk, or an exploration of the west rill.

In contrast to the old-fashioned Elizabethan character of the rosary, its counterpart on the east side of the original terrace is uncompromisingly classical. From the rill pool rusticated gateways herald a rotunda that is no less impressive for having been designed as an inspired solution to two very awkward problems: the circular plan of the rotunda enabled Lutyens to extend the garden in a new direction, running parallel to the garden's boundary at a tangent to the main axes; in addition, the high rotunda walls obscure an unsightly view of the house. The rotunda orchestrates the classical elements from all over the garden. As a theatrical and unexpected interval it adds coherence to the recurrent classical themes, but, like the rose garden at Folly Farm, it also plays on the idea of a garden as a sequence of fantasies, or elaborately composed settings for drama.

The orangery, inscrutably presented in its own formal gardens to the north-east of the rotunda, stages the final scene. This long narrow building, designed to house a single garden room in aristocratic tradition, steps up the style while reiterating familiar themes. Lutyens used two distinct types of stone, both local, throughout the garden: the grey stone, easily split into uneven pieces, which gives the garden a rough-hewn ancient appearance, was cut out of the hill behind the

ABOVE: *The flow of water along the rills at Hestercombe brings a quiet momentum to the garden's composition and binds its diverse features together.*

house; softer yellow sandstone, which could be dressed or carved to add detail and contrast, was quarried at Ham Hill, near Yeovil. In the orangery, however, Lutyens reversed the balance of proportions, using the yellow stone for the main construction with bands of grey to accentuate the details. By this means he established a startling contrast between the orangery and the rotunda. At a more sophisticated level he squared the circle of the Italianate and the English Elizabethan references that coexist at Hestercombe: instead of the ancient buildings of Rome, the yellow sandstone of the orangery alludes to the Georgian buildings of Bath; architecturally it derives from English Renaissance traditions, famously dubbed 'Wrenaissance' by Lutyens. The audacity of introducing a third architectural vocabulary in order to make an academic comment on the compatibility of two separate languages was beyond the comprehension of most of Lutyens's contemporaries, although not, perhaps, of Jekyll.

Hestercombe was planted with an assurance and sophistication that corresponded exactly to its architectural planning. Details that recur in the hard landscaping of many Jekyll and Lutyens gardens – the setting of terracotta pots to form a pattern of concentric circles within an obsolete millstone and the inclusion of antique Italian statues and urns in the garden – contravene any simplistic assumptions that Lutyens looked after the structure of the garden and all its details while the planting was delegated to Jekyll. The complexity of her planting compositions attest to Jekyll's artistic ingenuity and skill. Her extensive travels and her knowledge of Italian gardens must surely have informed (if not in places dictated) the architectural framework and detailing of the garden. As with the architectural motifs, the repetition of certain plants and predominant colour combinations gives a coherence to the disparate areas within the design. *Yucca gloriosa* recurs in the grey walk, the rotunda border and around the orangery. 'Munstead' lavender, santolina, *Rosmarinus officinalis* 'Miss Jessopps Upright' and lamb's ears – *Stachys byzantina* – are used throughout the garden.

The discovery of Jekyll's original plans for Hestercombe in an old garden shed was one of a number of factors that, in 1973, triggered the restoration of the garden by its owners, Somerset County Council. The existence of a second set of original plans, in the Reef Point Gardens Collection, shows that Jekyll designed variations on the planting scheme, and the publication of photographs of the garden in *Country Life* in 1908 suggests that she might have changed her mind again at planting stage. The restoration of the garden, tackling the problems of crumbling stonework, leaking rills and pools, borders riddled with ground elder and bindweed – especially given that the garden has to work with minimal staff (Hestercombe's eight acres are managed today by two full-time gardeners, with part-time assistance, whereas seventeen gardeners were originally employed) is an extraodinary achievement. Planting schemes were reinstated in the first decade, working through the garden section by section, clearing and replanting. Wherever possible Jekyll's plans were implemented precisely, although shrubs and perennials were substituted in places where annuals had been used extensively (in the great plat, for example) in order to keep the maintenance of the garden within reasonable limits for the gardeners.

Some of the stonework repairs precipitated the rebuilding of whole areas of the garden. In order to repair and reconstruct the broken bases of the east rill,

LEFT: *South facing wall enclosing the sunken plat at Hestercombe, planted as a vertical border with lavender, catmint, erigeron and santolina.*

the stonework had to be lifted completely. When it was reset back at the proper level, the paving and the channel structure were higher by twelve inches. The turves, the edge paths and the borders then had to be raised accordingly, requiring about eighty tons of topsoil, twenty tons of aggregate beneath the paths, new turf and the labour of two gardeners for most of the winter to complete the work. Even lesser stonework repairs invariably involved the gardeners in a lot of extra work. When cappings to the walls were replaced the masons, hefting large pieces of stone, often in wet weather, inevitably damaged plants at the backs of the borders. The head gardener wryly observed: 'Stone masons have the biggest feet out.'

Hestercombe was by no means the last garden collaboration between Jekyll and Lutyens. In its restored condition, however, it is the most brilliant existing expression of their work together, and again it survived the First World War, inviting the attention of *Country Life* well into the 1920s. The interdependence of planting and structure and the composition of contrasting spaces are manipulated with vision and dexterity. Meticulous attention to texture and detail, in both planting and stonework, engages the visitor, concentrating and focusing the experience of the garden. The detailing is never obsessive or pedantic, however; it is challenged or expanded by the dramatic changes in style and scale that invigorate the composition. Hestercombe is drawn into the Arts and Crafts orbit by familiar preoccupations, and by the associations of its designers. The vivacity and daring that distinguish the design take the ground rules of Arts and Crafts and use them as ingredients in an eclectic new direction.

Jekyll is seldom considered in the context of the women's suffrage movement and too often she is cast in Lutyens's shadow. In the first decade of the twentieth century the communities of women meeting or working together in loose affiliations such as garden clubs, or more ardently committed colleges and communes, formed a natural spawning ground for suffrage activity. The ideals of Arts and Crafts – the call for a breaking down of old hierarchies and a new progressive lifestyle founded on simple rural traditions and unflinching reason – could be translated into feminist principles. More prosaically, the energy and ingenuity that distinguished successful women gardeners were equally applicable to political agitation. The evidence for Jekyll's involvement in the suffrage movement is fragmentary. According to her nephew and first biographer, Francis Jekyll, by 1910 she was active enough in the suffrage movement to make banners for the Guildford and Godalming branches, and it is both revealing and frustrating that this is given the scantiest attention, with a slightly derisory tone, in his account:

> 'It was about this period that the agitation for female suffrage reached its height, and Gertrude, though she can hardly have sympathized with its more extreme manifestations, was persuaded to supply banners to the Guildford and Godalming branches, and even to attend a meeting at Compton Picture Gallery under the auspices of Mrs. Watts.'[1]

It is inconceivable that the staunch and autocratic figure of Gertrude Jekyll could have been persuaded to support a movement to which she was less than thoroughly committed. Through her garden making and her writing she set a very public standard of excellence, and she was also actively involved in promoting and providing a means of employment and independence for women through her association with Mrs Watts and Lady Wolseley.

Mary Watts was married to the eminent Victorian painter George Frederick Watts, who had a penchant for much younger women. In 1864, at the age of forty-seven, he had married the sixteen-year-old actress Ellen Terry. They were separated in 1865 and five years later he became involved with Mary, who was thirty-three years his junior. G.F. Watts was at the centre of London's artistic elite: Ruskin, Tennyson and Burne-Jones were among his associates and Mary would have been exposed to the socialist and artistic ideals of Ruskin and his followers. She was influenced by the practical propositions of the Home Arts and Industries Association, which promoted the revival of village handicrafts as a means of sustaining rural economies. Five years after the Wattses left London for Compton, in Surrey, in 1891, Mary founded a pottery that was to

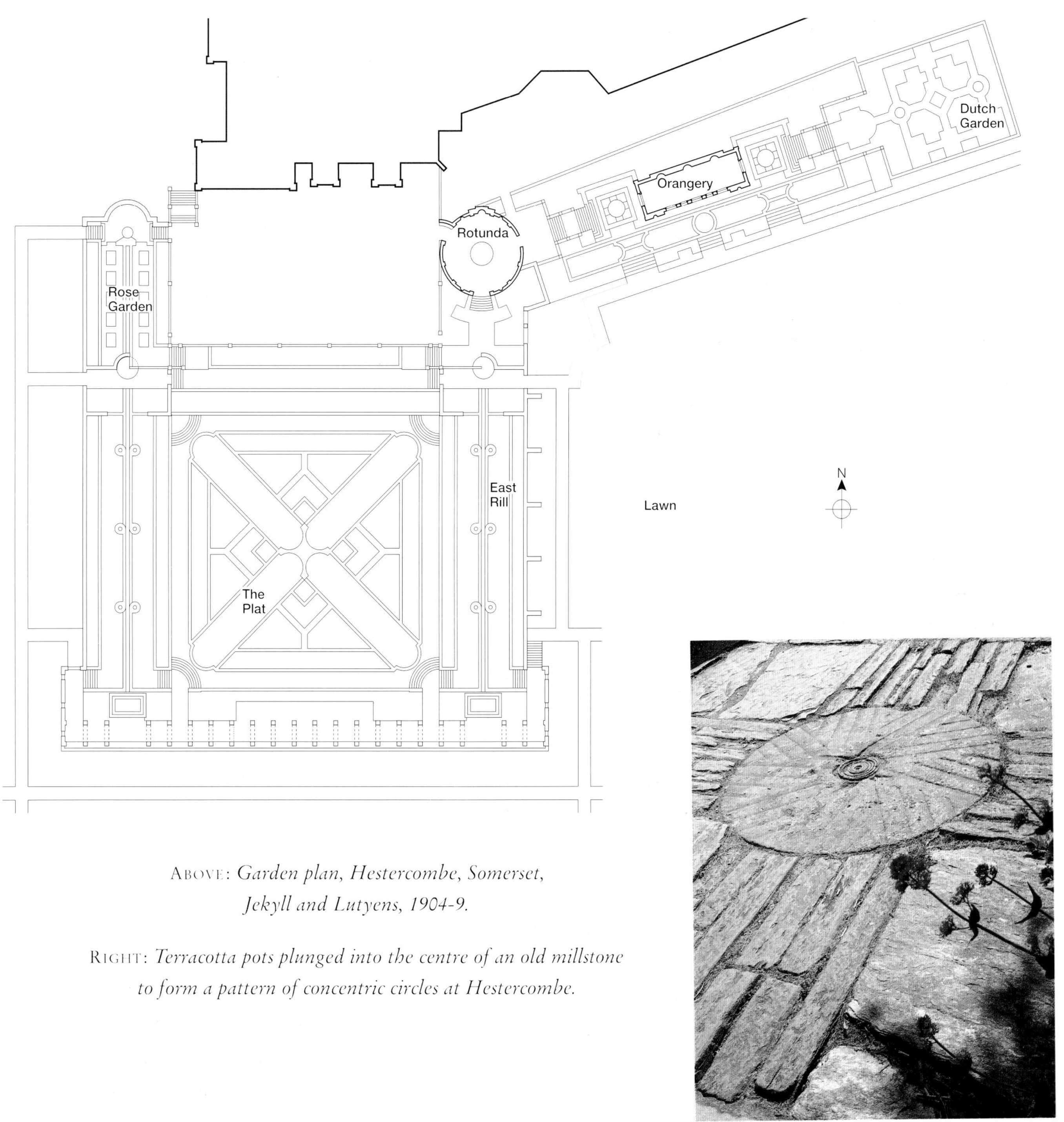

Above: *Garden plan, Hestercombe, Somerset, Jekyll and Lutyens, 1904-9.*

Right: *Terracotta pots plunged into the centre of an old millstone to form a pattern of concentric circles at Hestercombe.*

exercise her own considerable creative talents while also offering a craft training and a degree of financial independence to local women.

The Compton Pottery was to some extent a by-product of a grander philanthropic gesture and of Mary's architectural ambition. Although she had no architectural training, in 1895 she volunteered to design a mortuary chapel as a gift to the village's new burial grounds. The building was to be decorated by local women under her direction, and a kiln was set up at the Wattses' new house, Limnerslease, so that a natural bed of clay in the grounds could be used in the production of ornamental terracotta tiles for the chapel. Evening classes enabled women with other daytime commitments to train as potters. The elaborately patterned tiles, inspired by Celtic motifs, which still cover the exterior walls of this striking building testify to their professionalism and originality. Inside, the chapel walls are richly decorated with symbolic gesso panels, again designed and executed by Mary and her protégées.

The success of the project encouraged Mary to found a commercial pottery for the production of garden ornaments such as urns, sundials, planters, water features and even clay seats. In December 1901 she wrote to a potential manager for the business:

> 'I believe that neither man nor woman can do better than try to make a delightful village industry – beautiful things beautifully made, by people in beautiful country.'[2]

The quality of Watts's 'Artistic Garden Pots', together with her extensive social network, ensured a steady flow of orders from all over England and the Commonwealth, achieving the Arts and Crafts ideal, as *Country Life* reported in 1902, of

> 'a little colony, in the country, of intelligent happy workers, who, trained in eye, mind, and hand, will take pride in making, as the guild of artists did long ago in Italy, their village name known in association with their craft'.

When in 1904 G.F. Watts had a picture gallery built in Compton to exhibit his paintings, Mary added a hostel to the brief, providing workers' accommodation for the flourishing community of potters. G.F. Watts died within months of the completion of the building but the pottery continued, supplying garden ornaments to Gertrude Jekyll and other designers, and it was at this 'Compton Picture Gallery under the auspices of Mrs. Watts' that local women's suffrage meetings were held.

Watts's determination to establish skilled and independent employment for women was part of a more general agitation for professional training and status for women. The society beauty Frances Evelyn Maynard, Countess of Warwick, was more renowned for her romantic affair with Edward, Prince of Wales, than for her activities as a socialist and a feminist, but her ability to match ambitious and progressive ideals with the charitable donations of her well-connected friends was peerless. Lady Warwick was committed to the promotion of professional agricultural opportunities for women. In 1898 she founded a school, the Lady Warwick Agricultural Association for Women, writing to the editor of *Pall Mall*:

> 'I have secured the support of £200 from Lord Wantage, and the Huntleys, Palmers and Suttons, all Reading people, have come forward with sympathy and support, and money, and we hope to start off at the beginning of next term with a dozen students ... Mr Sutton has given the free use of his wonderful seed trial grounds for students, which will be invaluable, and there is a splendidly equipped dairy too.'[3]

Students were given hostel accommodation as well as practical and theoretical training. The Association published its own *Women's Agricultural Times* and a register of vacancies was published in association with the Women's Institute in London.

When the school outgrew its premises at Reading Lady Warwick used her connections to launch an appeal for between £30,000 and £50,000 with Edward VII as patron and a General Committee served by Sir Winston Churchill, Mrs Asquith and Cecil Rhodes among others. In 1903 they purchased Studley Castle, in Warwickshire, and renamed it Studley College; its 340 acres became one of the principal training grounds where women could achieve professional standards in the methods and management of agriculture and horticulture. The College became a centre for nationally recognized examinations and during the First World War it was licensed by the Board of Trade, proving invaluable for its produce in addition to its education of professional women who were capable of running, as well as working, the country's farms. Studley College continued to flourish until the 1960s.

Any account of the contribution of aristocratic women, and women permitted a degree of artistic licence, to the furtherance of professional opportunities for women must include the work of Lady Wolseley, who pledged to devote the remainder of her active life to women gardening students after a night spent with Gertrude Jekyll at Munstead Wood in 1906. Her gardening notes give the impression of an indefatigable garden connoisseur, travelling the country by train, bicycle and occasionally motor car to study the best gardens of the day. Often she arrived without prior warning. Frequently the gardens she visited were the domain of the lady rather than the gentleman of the house, although she made regular visits to William Robinson's garden. Her garden notes for September 1904 record: 'I went with Miss Verrall and some students, to see Mr William Robinson's garden at Gravetye.'[4] She described his use of *Sedum spectabile* to edge a large bed and the 'French system of growing fruit trees' espaliered in the new kitchen garden. Another visit was made the following spring, 'when the owner was most kind to us'. His rose beds, 'carpeted ... with clumps of bulbs, pansies and violas and saxifrages' were praised as 'always effective'. Lady Wolseley was not always generous with her praise, however. Wisley struck her in 1905 'as being useful for botanic purposes, but ill kept', and later in the same year she wrote in her notes: 'I motored with Sybil Burnaby and the Charlie Seymours to Sandringham, as tourists. To me, it was a perfectly hideous style of architecture and gardening.'[5]

Her notes describe the working methods as well as the most successful plant combinations of her contemporaries: a description of the use of scarlet gladioli among the roses and spent blooms at Great Tangley Manor is interesting; the account of Lady Ardilauris's method of planning a pergola in Ireland 'by taking a board and on it dotting little pieces of sealing wax, and then, fixing matches to these to represent the groups of uprights' would make an architect squirm. There is no concession to the idea that garden visiting might have been intrusive. It appears to have been common practice among the aristocracy and their well-heeled contemporaries and, indeed, when Jekyll's *Home and Garden* was reviewed in *The Garden* in 1900, her plea for privacy was reiterated by the anonymous reviewer:

> 'Personally, I know to my cost what this means. In the course of the day perhaps twenty persons call on me. Individually, each visit is a pleasure; collectively, they make work impossible.'

Wherever she travelled Lady Wolseley was always particularly attentive to the prospects for women gardeners. At Lady Sligo's garden, near Guildford, special commendations seem to have been given because the head gardener there was a woman: 'Most perfectly kept and all the things admirably grown, which shows that a woman can be a real success.' In Ireland she noted of one owner: 'This lady was prepared to engage a woman gardener.' The idea of founding a horticultural school for women at her home in Glynde, Sussex, seems to have evolved gradually. From 1901 she had been involved in the informal tuition of women gardening students and she must have been aware of Lady Warwick's agricultural college. Her notes for 23 August 1905 describe a significant expedition by bicycle 'to Compton Mrs Watts Pottery Works, and chose the pots that she is kindly going to give my School. From there, I went on to see Miss Jekyll.' Mary Watts would surely have given advice as well as pots. However, although the school is listed as a definite intention here, it was to take another year and a second visit to Jekyll before the intention became a fact. On 30 July 1906 Lady Wolseley wrote: 'I went to spend a night with Miss Jekyll ... It was the day upon which I finally decided to devote the rest of my active years to garden students, so it was eventful to me.'

The School for Lady Gardeners at Ragged Lands, Glynde, was founded to perpetuate the standards of professionalism for women in gardening that Jekyll (as an amateur) had come to represent. In addition to providing a thorough professional training Lady Wolseley continued to locate and secure head gardeners' positions for which her women students would be considered. As at Compton, the existence of a community of motivated and ambitious women might well have been linked to the suffrage movement, and certainly they were viewed with some suspicion. When Lady Wolseley and her students were visiting Gertrude Jekyll at Munstead Wood in 1912 the meeting was interrupted by a detective who 'demanded an explanation of this female concourse, which had, not very unnaturally, aroused his suspicions!'[6]

In America a network of estate gardens provided the framework for a forum of women to found their own national organization, The Garden Club of America. Special trips were organized, some campaigns for conservation were fought, and members' gardens were recorded in a collection of more than 1,400 hand-painted glass-lantern slides. The first School of Landscape Architecture and Horticulture for Women was founded in 1901, and from 1915 the Cambridge School of Architectural and Landscape Design for Women gradually gave women access to a professional architectural training as well as to landscape studies. In spite of the very real progress towards professional status that horticulture and agriculture represented for women, advances were by no means unilateral. The British architectural profession remained resistant to change so that when asked for his opinion on the place of women in architecture after the First World War, Lutyens, whose sister-in-law had been imprisoned on several occasions for her suffrage activities, immediately quipped: 'As the wives of architects!'[7]

The First World War did not bring to an end the potential for women to become designers and gardeners, although it brought other opportunities that drew them away from the domestic sphere. Women of all social backgrounds were liberated by the war effort, which encouraged them to engage in manual and professional work that had previously been the exclusive domain of men. The Arts and Crafts garden gave women a legitimate outlet for physical energy, organizational prowess and aesthetic expression; through garden societies and regular expeditions to see each other's work it gave them a social focus and to some degree a voice in professional circles; the First World War redirected and amplified those accomplishments. The demise of the Arts and Crafts garden in war time might be seen from a feminist perspective as a casualty of progress. Although in many gardens the emphasis shifted away from aesthetic fulfilment towards the provision of food, the challenges to the gardener, often managing with a reduced staff, were no less acute. For the more ambitious mistress of the house, restructuring the garden coincided with more pressing concerns as she began to turn her attention to the day-to-day running of the country.

The proposition that the First World War blasted a chasm between the 'gardens of a golden afternoon' evoked in Jane Brown's book and the harsher realities of the 1920s and 1930s is valid in general. Many of the Arts and Crafts gardens described in previous chapters, however, survived without serious consequences and continued to change and develop until the outbreak of the Second World War. New Place was at its most spectacular in the 1920s and fresh tracts of garden were still being cut out of the farmland at Hidcote in the 1930s. Although the First World War, like the Great Depression, dominates histories of this period and the loss of life *was* devastating, the continued running of house and garden wherever it was possible, in spite of shortages, was in itself an important psychological contribution to the war effort. Country houses were requisitioned by the armed forces, but for many garden makers the war affected the detail rather than the structure of their lives: gardens were maintained by their owners and by a core staff who were too old or too young to fight.

Labour costs increased, but not as dramatically as is sometimes supposed. The wages for a flower gardener in a private garden near Stamford in 1910 were twenty-one shillings per week – one shilling less than the head gardener's wage, and three shillings more than that of a garden labourer.[8] In 1932, when Hidcote had a staff of six full-time gardeners, the flower gardener responsible for the rock garden was paid twenty-five shillings per week. Accommodation was not provided in either case: the Hidcote gardener lodged with one of the grooms nearby at Kiftsgate, at a weekly charge of five shillings. He remembers that head gardeners from all over the country knew one another. They travelled with their employers, or alone, exchanging seeds and young plants after meetings. Even in 1932 a young gardener's training was taken seriously. The flower gardener at Hidcote was given the names of plants to learn and told by the head gardener that if he couldn't recite them he would suffer the disgrace of being sent home packing to his father (also a gardener). He remembers sitting up late into the night to memorize *Argyroxiphium sandwichense var. macrocephalum* for the following morning. In the event it was three weeks before he was asked to recall the name, but he believes a corner was turned in his career when he managed to do so correctly.[9]

After the First World War the practice of building new country retreats and the customary exodus of the household with all its staff for the summer months were pared down. In Europe progressive designers of the 1920s and 1930s were committed to the opportunities and aesthetics of a Machine Age. The country house was stripped down to the elegant geometry of the International Style or jazzed up in the exotic hedonism of Art Deco. As the defining relationship between 'art and nature' gave way to the more powerful impetus of 'man and the machine', the role of the garden as an intermediary between the house and its landscape was radically altered. Vogues for tennis, bicycling and gardening were supplanted by a passion for speed and sun worship. The bicycle store gave way to the motor house and the Arts and Crafts garden was superseded by the sleek efficiency of the sun terrace, raised to the roof-top or to first-floor level, away from the dirt of nature. Nostalgia for hand craftsmanship and cottage traditions was no longer avant-garde. They continued, nevertheless.

The principles of the Arts and Crafts garden – the confines of a formal structure containing (but not entirely controlling) an abundant, romantic planting style and the extension of the rooms and characteristics of the house into an intimate and intriguing garden structure – did not dissipate at all with changing architectural fashions. It was partly because the style crystallized much older Tudor, seventeenth-century and cottage gardening traditions that it retained a currency garden makers continued to explore and interpret. Vita Sackville-West moulded the idea of the garden compartments of Hidcote into her own intensely individual garden at Sissinghurst Castle in Kent, designed with her husband Harold Nicolson from 1930. Plants as well as inspiration were imported from Hidcote; on one occasion Johnston presented Sackville-West with a huge bundle of lilacs from his nursery beds, saying: 'Take your chance of these. Some of them won't be worth keeping, but you may hit on some that will do.' The resultant double white and pink lilacs were christened 'children of Hidcote'. Sackville-West had visited Gertrude Jekyll at Munstead Wood in 1917. However, the planting at Sissinghurst and the clear organization of the plan that Nicolson formulated responded to the antiquity of the site and its fragments of Elizabethan buildings, to Vita's sense of her own heritage, her upbringing at Knole and, not least, her personal taste. Sissinghurst absorbs the influences of Arts and Crafts. Like Hidcote, its emphatic structural lines are planted rather than built. It has an insularity, however, observing its own maverick rules rather than indulging any imitative admiration for great gardens of the recent and more distant past.

In North America Beatrix Farrand (1872–1959) perpetuated many of the principles that characterize Jekyll's work: the incorporation of thought and meaning into detail, the painterly handling of colour and form through planting, and the concept of the garden as a sequence of intimate, highly personal spaces. Born in New York City, she was educated at home in an atmosphere of privileged artistic and intellectual refinement. Her mother was for a time the closest correspondent of Henry James and hosted one of the liveliest salons in the city. Her aunt was Edith Wharton, famous novelist as well as the author of *Italian Villas and Gardens* (1903). Farrand was encouraged to study landscape gardening by Charles Sprague Sargent, the first director of the Arnold Arboretum. He advised her 'to travel widely in Europe and see all the gardens she could'. In 1895 she visited the great gardens of Italy – the Villa Aldobrandini, the Villa Lante and the Boboli Gardens – before travelling to England. Her journal records visits to the formal Tudor garden at Penshurst and to Hampton Court. The most profoundly influential visit, however, was to Munstead Wood, where Gertrude Jekyll, in residence in The Hut rather than in the house she was to build with Lutyens, was in the process of making the garden.

Farrand did not imitate Jekyll, although she repeatedly acknowledged her importance as a mentor. Soon after her return to New York in September 1895 she established her own practice. She rapidly attained a standard of professionalism and a national reputation at the forefront of landscape architecture, so that in January 1899 she became one of the founder members of the American Society of Landscape Architects. To some degree Farrand was marginalized during her lifetime because she was a woman: until the 1980s she was given the most fleeting attention by historians, who noted her significance as the only woman founder of the American Society of Landscape Architects while neglecting to make any detailed assessment of her work. She was not considered eligible to design the great public parks that made her male colleagues famous. Instead she was restricted to the private sector, specializing in estate gardens.

Farrand's great achievements – Dumbarton Oaks in Washington DC, Dartington Hall in Devon (England), Reef Point in Maine and the university campus designs for Princeton and Yale – extend beyond the confines of Arts and Crafts principles. They are pertinent, nevertheless, to the proposition that the Arts and Crafts movement represented a rich pool of ideals and approaches that could be drawn out and expanded in conjunction with other stylistic references. Farrand's plan for Dartington Hall responded to the ancient site with reverence and with allusions to a much older garden. She planned Dumbarton Oaks as a sequence of unfolding spaces, with hillside orchards, carefully graduated steps and a sharp appreciation of the effects of simple elements, grass and water, to accentuate the innate qualities of pebbles, brick and stone. The rigorous standards and the quiet, intuitive insights that Jekyll exemplified in her work as an amateur achieved a professional conclusion in Farrand's various garden and campus designs. When in 1948 she purchased the majority of Gertrude Jekyll's plans and drawings, preserving them for posterity at her own home in Reef Point Gardens, Maine, she established the basis for a horticultural foundation that continues to facilitate the detailed study of both her own work and that of Jekyll.

Although garden makers such as Margery Fish continued to perpetuate Arts and Crafts principles, many Arts and Crafts gardens gradually deteriorated during the inter-war years, slipping into a state of dormancy. As the country houses for which they were designed changed hands and changed functions, an element of obsolescence jeopardized the future of the gardens. Some country houses were divided, others became corporate or council headquarters. Often the essential unity between house and garden, and even between all the different parts of the house, was undermined by changes of use. Estates were split up and subsidiary buildings such as stables and lodge houses sold off. Division and neglect, however, were less damaging than wholesale changes in owners' taste. Gertrude Jekyll's garden fell into decline after her death in 1932, but the main bones survived until the 1960s, when they were wantonly destroyed on a whim. The aster beds and nut walks were laid to lawn, and a swimming pool was installed in front of the pergola. Jekyll's paths were removed, and the recent discovery of broken ceramic pieces used as hardcore beneath a modern path suggests a more barbarous wreckage of the fragments of her time.

No garden can be adequately safeguarded against the wishes of its owner, and until recently there was no protective legislation for private gardens in Britain. However, in the 1970s and 1980s, a succession of new books and exhibitions on Lorimer, Lutyens, Voysey,

Mackintosh, Ashbee, Baillie Scott, Greene and Greene, and a plethora of books on Frank Lloyd Wright, raised the level of appreciation of Arts and Crafts houses, causing many to be protected by statutory listing. As the status of the houses improved, restoration work gradually extended to encompass the gardens as well. Increasing sympathy with the ambitions of the Arts and Crafts garden as an integral part of the house and its lifestyle motivated many owners to begin to reinstate the outdoor rooms to their houses.

Garden restoration can be a very daunting business, fraught with philosophical as well as practical dilemmas. The Arts and Crafts garden, because it belongs to our recent history, is vested with its own particular advantages, problems and solutions. Documentation and surviving evidence on the ground is generally good by comparison with earlier gardens. The original structure often survives, not least because its removal would be such a monumental task: brick and stone paths, retaining walls, gateways and the remnants of formal hedges and vistas enjoy a permanence, even when partially obscured by decades of neglect or superficial changes. The probability of finding details of the garden, from the plan to the furniture, among the architect's drawings is better than for any previous period, and because the gardens coincided with an increase in the number of illustrated books and magazines, and in the use of photography (some houses were equipped with dark rooms), the accuracy and quantity of documentary evidence is often good. Paintings, too, record the planting and structures at their best. Where gardens continued into the 1920s and 1930s they fall within living memory, and many restorations have been enhanced by the detailed recollections of visiting former gardeners.

On the other hand, the Arts and Crafts garden was often equipped with ingenious inventions that test the resources of the conservator. Hestercombe has an irrigation system fed by a web of underground pipes. At Gravetye Manor Robinson installed a ram pump in 1884 that shot the overflow water from the lower lake up the hill to a reservoir above the kitchen garden. Neither system is viable without the devoted attention of an experienced plumber. At the core of garden restoration is the problem of how to treat the last vestiges of an original planting scheme. One of the few survivors of Jekyll's main border at Munstead Wood is a magnolia, now grown to two or three times the optimum size originally prescribed for it. Because it is so large it overshadows the east end of the border, compromising any replanting of that part of Jekyll's original plan, but to remove it would be a kind of sacrilege. Elsewhere in the garden the rootstock suckers of Jekyll's rhododendrons had grown to the thickness of a man's leg, starving the grafted sections and resulting in a miserable show of flowers, out of sight at the top of the bushes. They were pruned back with a chain-saw in the process of restoring and recreating the garden, and have since regrown to an acceptable size and shape.

Munstead Wood was not restored in a single sweeping statement. The decision to reverse the garden's development and to begin a return to the planning and planting of Jekyll's period wherever possible, was implemented in a series of gradual stages. The storms of 1987 and 1990 felled more than 130 trees, making feasible the clearing of the garden towards its original structure. According to the head gardener, Jekyll's borders are more easily maintained than a well-kept lawn. He tells the story of how the main borders were pegged out and two gardeners laboured for three days, rolling away the turf from the

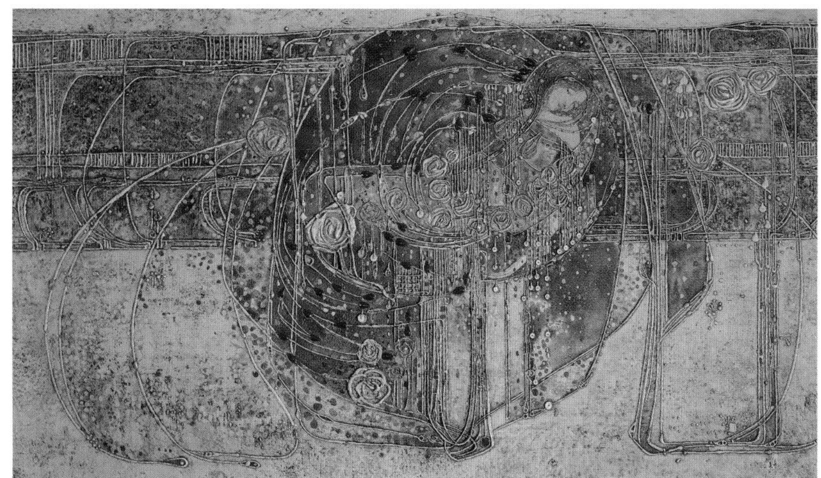

Left: *Above the drawing-room fireplace at The Hill House a gesso panel by Margaret Macdonald Mackintosh depicts a fairy-tale princess caught within a loose enclosure of wild roses.*

site of the garden walks while the owners were on holiday. On their return they awoke, heavily jet-lagged, to find the lawn they had left behind rolled up and arranged in rows like a terracotta Chinese army. Only one of the owners had been consulted before their departure. The new borders were heavily manured, in accordance with Jekyll's well-documented practice, and her planting was reinstated after a well-informed study of her photographs. The longer-term strategies of replanting important trees are combined with more detailed considerations: primroses found in the spring garden, for instance, are selected and their seed collected in an attempt to breed back to Jekyll's original strains. The restoration, like the original making of the garden, is seen as an ongoing process.

Although the economic and social conditions that generated the Arts and Crafts garden as an essential adjunct to an artistic country lifestyle have changed substantially, some of the creative and social propositions that concerned the garden maker have proved to be remarkably durable. The desire to abandon city life and escape to the country, a taste for indigenous plants and shrubs – for wild flowers, old-fashioned roses and cottage-garden plants – as well a slightly indulgent and essentially middle-class determination to preserve techniques in craftsmanship and building traditions perceived to be on the brink of extinction – are all as familiar today as they were a hundred years ago. It is notable that the Arts and Crafts manner of planting, in its own time and in the work of subsequent designers, with abundant drifts of flowers tilting the balance away from control towards a natural order, has been most brilliantly explored in the work of women garden makers. Today, Robinson's perception of the English flower garden and Jekyll's painterly preoccupations with colour and foliage form the basis of the 'English way of planting', which is constantly finding new expression in the work of new generations of garden writers and designers.

Footnotes

1 Francis Jekyll, *Gertrude Jekyll: A Memoir*, Jonathan Cape, London, 1934, p.174.
2 Wilfred Blunt, *England's Michelangelo, A Biography of George Frederick Watts*, Hamish Hamilton, London, 1975 p.231.
3 Quoted in Kay N. Sanecki, 'Hard Work in High Society', *Hortus*, Vol.1, No.2, 1987, p.66.
4 Lady Wolseley's bound volumes of gardening notes are in the archive collection of Hove Public Library, East Sussex.
5 Lady Wolseley, gardening notes, 1905.
6 Francis Jekyll, op. cit., p.174.
7 Robert Lutyens, *Sir Edwin Lutyens: An appreciation in perspective, by his son*, Country Life Ltd, London, 1942, p.79.
8 These figures are given in Lady Wolseley's gardening notes.
9 I am grateful to Jack Percival, gardener at Hidcote between 1932 and 1936, for these recollections.

SELECT BIBLIOGRAPHY

Allan, Mea *William Robinson 1838–1935* Faber & Faber, 1982

Amery, Colin, Richardson, Margaret, and Stamp, Gavin *The work of the English Architect Sir Edwin Lutyens (1869–1944)* Arts Council of Great Britain, 1981

Anderson, Dorothy May *Women, Design, and the Cambridge School* PDA Publishers, 1980

Angier, Belle Sumner *The Garden Book of California* Paul Elder & Co., 1906

Baillie Scott, M.H. *Houses and Gardens* George Newnes Ltd, 1906

Balmori, Diana *Beatrix Farrand's American Landscapes*, Sagapress, New York, 1985

Blomfield, Reginald, and Thomas, F. Inigo *The Formal Garden in England* Macmillan, 1892

Blomfield, Reginald *Memoirs of an Architect*, Macmillan, 1932

Bosley, Edward *Gamble House* Phaidon Press, 1992

Brooks, H. Allen *The Prairie School: Frank Lloyd Wright and his Midwest Contemporaries* University of Toronto Press, 1972

Brown, Jane *Gardens of a Golden Afternoon* Allen Lane, 1982

Brown, Jane *The English Garden in our Time* Antique Collector's Club, 1986

Burne-Jones, Georgiana *Memorials of Edward Burne-Jones* 2 vols., Macmillan, 1904

Callen, Anthea *Angel in the Studio. Women in the Arts and Crafts Movement 1870–1914* Astragal Books, 1979

Crawford, Alan *Charles Rennie Mackintosh* Thames and Hudson, 1995

Curtis and Gibson *The Book of Topiary* 1904

Davey, John (ed) *Nature and Tradition, Arts and Crafts architecture and gardens in and around Guildford* Guildford Borough Council, 1993

Davey, Peter *Arts and Crafts Architecture* (2nd edition) Phaidon Press, 1995

Eckstein, Eve *George Samuel Elgood* Alpine Fine Arts Collection, 1995

Elliott, Brent *Victorian Gardens* Batsford, 1986

Ely, Helen Rutherford *A Woman's Hardy Garden* Macmillan, New York, 1903

Fellows, Richard *Sir Reginald Blomfield: An Edwardian Architect* Zwemmer, 1985

Forsythe, Alistair *Yesterday's Gardens* Royal Commission of Historical Monuments, 1983

Fricker, Laurence *Beatrix Jones Farrand (1872–1959), Fifty years of American landscape architecture* Dumbarton Oaks, Trustees of Harvard University, Washington DC, 1982

Girouard, Mark *The Victorian Country House* Yale, 1971

Girouard, Mark *Sweetness and Light: The Queen Anne Movement 1860–1900* Clarendon, Oxford, 1977

Gradidge, Roderick *Edwin Lutyens: Architect Laureate* 1981

Greensted, Mary *The Arts and Crafts Movement in the Cotswolds* Alan Sutton, 1993

Hadfield, Miles *Pioneers in Gardening* Routledge & Kegan Paul, 1955

Hervey, John *Medieval Gardens* Batsford, 1981

Hitchmough, Wendy *CFA Voysey* Phaidon Press, 1995

Hobhouse, Penelope, and Wood, Christopher *Painted Gardens, English watercolours 1850–1914* Pavilion, 1988

Holme, Charles *The Gardens of England in the Northern Counties* The Studio, 1911

Hollamby, Edward *Red House* Phaidon Press, 1991

Hussey, Christopher *The Life of Sir Edwin Lutyens* Country Life Ltd, 1950

Griswold, Mac, and Weller, Eleanor *The Golden Age of American Gardens* Abrams, New York, 1991

Jekyll, Francis *Gertude Jekyll: A Memoir* Jonathan Cape, 1934

Jekyll, Gertrude *Wood and Garden* Longmans, Green & Co., 1899

Jekyll, Gertrude *Home and Garden* Longmans, Green & Co., 1900

Jekyll, Gertrude *Wall and Water Gardens* Country Life Ltd, 1901

Jekyll, Gertrude, and Elgood, George Samuel *Some English Gardens* Longmans, Green & Co., 1904

Jekyll, Gertrude *Colour in the Flower Garden* Country Life Ltd, 1908

Jekyll, Gertrude, and Weaver, Lawrence *Gardens for Small Country Houses* Country Life Ltd, 1912

Jekyll, Gertrude *Garden Ornament* Country Life Ltd, 1918

Jewson, Norman *By Chance I Did Rove* Privately published, 1973

King, Francis *The Well-Considered Garden* Scribner's, New York, 1915

Lethaby, W.R. *Philip Webb and his Work* Oxford University Press, 1935

Lethaby, W. R, Powell, Alfred, and Griggs, F. L. *Ernest Gimson, His Life & Work* Shakespear Head Press, 1924

Lutyens, Mary *Edwin Lutyens* John Murray, 1980

Lutyens, Robert *Sir Edwin Lutyens: An appreciation in perspective* Country Life Ltd, 1942

MacCarthy, Fiona *William Morris, A Life for Our Time* Faber and Faber, 1994

Mackail, J.W. *The Life of William Morris* Longmans, 1899

Makinson, Randell *Greene & Greene: Architecture as a Fine Art* Peregrine Smith Inc., Salt Lake City, 1977

Marix-Evans, J-P *Journal of an Ancient Manor* Unpublished manuscript in possession of the author

Masse, H.J.L.J. *The Art Workers' Guild 1884–1934* Art Workers' Guild, 1935

Massingham, Betty *Miss Jekyll*, David and Charles, 1966

Masson, Georgina *Dumbarton Oaks, A Guide to the Gardens* Dumbarton Oaks, Washington DC, 1968

Mawson, Thomas *The Art and Craft of Garden Making* Batsford, 1900

Mawson, Thomas *The Life and Work of an English Landscape Architect* Batsford, 1927

McCarter, Robert *Fallingwater* Phaidon Press, 1994

Muthesius, Hermann *The English House* Translation of 1904 publication, Crosby Lockwood Staples, 1979

Ottewill, David *The Edwardian Garden* Yale 1989

Parsons, Beatrice and E.T. Cooke *Gardens of England* Black, 1908

Pavord, Anna *Hidcote Manor Garden* The National Trust, 1993

Pevsner, Nikolaus *Pioneers of the Modern Movement* Faber and Faber, 1936

Robinson, William *The Wild Garden* John Murray, 1870

Robinson, William *The English Flower Garden* John Murray, 1883

Robinson, William *Garden Design and Architects' Gardens* John Murray, 1892

Robinson, William *Gravetye Manor, or Twenty Years' Work Around An Old Manor House*, (1911) Sagapress, New York, 1995

Ruskin, John *The Complete Works of John Ruskin* 39 vols., London, 1903–12

Saint, Andrew *Richard Norman Shaw* Yale, 1976

Savage, Peter *Lorimer and the Edinburgh Craft Designers* Paul Harris Publishing, 1980

Sedding, John Dando *Garden-Craft Old and New* Kegan Paul, 1891

Spielmann, M.S, and Layard, G.S *Kate Greenaway* Benjamin Blom, 1905

Streatfield, David *California Gardens: Creating a New Eden* Abbeville Press, 1994

Taylor, Geoffrey *Some Nineteenth Century Gardeners* Skeffington, 1951

Tipping, H. Avray *English Gardens* Country Life Ltd, 1925

Triggs, H. Inigo *Formal Gardens in England and Scotland* Batsford, 1902

Vallance, Aymer *William Morris. His art his writings and his public life* George Bell and Sons, 1897

Weaver, Lawrence *Small Country House of Today* Country Life Ltd, 1910

PICTURE CREDITS

Arcaid: pp:157 © Scott Frances/Esto; 159 © Richard Bryant

Architectural Association: p:156L © G Smythe

Bridgeman Art Library: pp:10: Musée D'Orsay, Paris; 20: Christopher Wood Gallery, London; 37: V&A Museum, London; 45: Mallett Gallery, London; 50: Maas Gallery, London

Christopher Wood Gallery: p:40

E.T. Archive: p:47

Frank Lloyd Wright Foundation, Scottsdale, AZ: p:156T © 1997

F. Warne & Co. p:24 © 1902, 1987

Glasgow School of Art Collection: p:176T

Glasgow Picture Library: p:178

National Portrait Gallery, London: p:114

Tate Gallery, London: pp:23, 26

GARDENS TO VISIT

BERKSHIRE:

Folly Farm, Sulhamstead.
Sir Edwin Lutyens and Gertrude Jekyll.
1906 and 1912.
Private house.
Open days through the National Gardens Scheme at the end of April, end of May, and end of June.

CHESHIRE:

Tirley Garth, Tarporley.
C.E. Mallows
1906–12.
Now the Tirley Garth Trust.
Garden open six days a year in May and June. Please telephone for details.
Tel. 01829 732301.

CUMBRIA:

Brantwood, Coniston.
Although this is not really an Arts and Crafts garden it is of interest because it was John Ruskin's home from 1872.
Open daily all year.
Tel. 015394 41396.

Brockhole, Windermere.
T.H. Mawson and D. Gibson.
From 1899.
Now the Lake District National Park Centre.
Open daily all year.
Tel. 015394 46601.

DERBYSHIRE:

Hardwick Hall, Doe Lea, Chesterfield.
'Old-fashioned' garden by Lady Louisa Egerton.
From 1860s.
Open daily end March to end Oct.
Tel. 01246 850430.

DEVON:

The Barn, Fox Holes Hill, Exmouth.
Edward Prior.
1897.
Country House Hotel.
Tel. 01395 224411.

Castle Drogo, Drewsteignton, nr. Exeter.
Sir Edwin Lutyens
1910-30.
National Trust.
Open daily except Fri., April to end Oct.
Tel. 01647 433306.

Dartington Hall Gardens, Dartington, Totnes, Devon.
Beatrix Farrand.
Continuing Arts and Crafts sensitivities from 1933.
Dartington Hall Trust.
Open all year.
Tel. 01803 862367.

ESSEX:

Easton Lodge, Warwick House, Little Easton, nr Great Dunmow.
Includes garden by Harold Peto.
1902.
Open through the National Gardens Scheme Sat. and Sun., 15 April to 9 July, 2–6 and by private appointment.
Tel. 01371 873305.

GLOUCESTERSHIRE:

Combend Manor, Elkstone.
Sidney Barnsley and Gertrude Jekyll.
1921–5.
Open day through the National Gardens Scheme at the beginning of July.

Hartbury House, nr Gloucester.
Thomas Mawson and Alfred Parsons.
1907.
Now the Gloucestershire College of Agriculture.
Open through the National Gardens Scheme towards the end of May and by private appointment. Please telephone for details.
Tel. 01452 700283.

Hidcote Manor, Hidcote Bartrim.
Lawrence Johnston.
From 1907.
National Trust.
Open daily except Tues. and Fri., April to end Oct. Also open Tues. in June and July.
Tel. 01386 438333.

Kelmscott Manor, nr. Lechlade.
William Morris' country home and garden.
1871-96.
Owned by the Society of Antiquaries. Open April to Sept: Every Wed., 11–1 and 2–5, and 3rd Sat. in each month 2–6. Thurs. and Fri. by appointment only.
Tel. 01367 252486.

Rodmarton Manor, nr Cirencester.
Ernest Barnsley.
1909–29.
Open Sats, early May to end Aug., 2–5.
Tel. 01285 841253.

Snowshill Manor, nr Broadway.
Charles Wade.
1919–23.
Architect's own garden.
National Trust.
Open daily April to end Oct. Closed on Tues. in April and Oct.
Tel. 01386 852410.

Upper Dorvel House, Sapperton.
Ernest Barnsley.
1901.
Architect's own garden.
Now a private house.

HAMPSHIRE:

Moundsmere Manor, Preston Candover.
Reginald Blomfield.
1908.
Open day at the beginning of July through the National Gardens Scheme.

HEREFORD AND WORCESTER:

Hergest Croft, Kington.
William Banks.
From 1896.
Open daily April to Oct.
Tel. 01544 230160

KENT:

Great Maytham Hall, Rolvenden.
Sir Edwin Lutyens.
1909.
(Inspired *The Secret Garden* by Frances Hodgson Burnett.)
Country Houses Association.
Tel. 01580 241346.

Red House, Red House Lane, Bexleyheath.
William Morris and Philip Webb.
1859.
Open one weekend per month by prior arrangement.
Tel. Edward Hollamby: 0181 303 8808.

Sissinghurst Castle Garden, Sissinghurst, Cranbrook.
Vita Sackville-West and Sir Harold Nicolson.
From 1930.
National Trust.
Open Tues.–Sun., April to mid Oct.
Tel. 01580 712850.

LONDON:

Myddelton House, Bulls Cross, Enfield.
E.A. Bowles.
From 1890s.
Public park open Mon.–Fri. (10–3.30).

Emslie Horniman Pleasance, East Row, Kensal Town.
C.F.A. Voysey.
1913.
To be restored.
Public garden open daily.

WEST MIDLANDS:

Wightwick Manor, Wightwick Bank, nr Wolverhampton.
Alfred Parsons and Thomas Mawson.
c.1890.
National Trust.
Open Thurs. and Sat., March to Dec.
Tel. 01902 761108.

NORTHUMBERLAND:

Lindisfarne Castle, Holy Island, Berwick-upon-Tweed.
Sir Edwin Lutyens and Gertrude Jekyll.
1911.
National Trust.
Open Sat.–Thurs., April to end Oct.
Tel. 01289 389244.

OXFORDSHIRE:

Buscot Park, nr Faringdon.
Harold Peto.
1904 and 1911.
National Trust.
Open Mon.–Fri. and 2nd and 4th weekends, April to end Sept.
Tel. 01367 242094.

SOMERSET:

Barrington Court, nr Ilminster.
Tate Forbes, Influenced by Gertrude Jekyll.
From 1917.
National Trust.
Open Sat.–Thurs., April to end Sept.
Tel. 01460 241938.

Hestercombe, Cheddon Fitzpaine, nr Taunton.
Sir Edwin Lutyens and Gertrude Jekyll.
1904–9.
Headquarters of the Somerset Fire Brigade.
Garden open to the public May to end Sept. Sat. and Sun.; all year Mon.–Fri.
Tel. 01823 413030.

Tintinhull House, Farm Street, nr Yeovil.
Dr S.J.M. Price from 1898.
Replanted by Mrs Reiss 1933.
National Trust.
Open Wed.–Sun., April to end Sept.
Tel. 01935 822545.

SURREY:

Goddards, Abinger Lane, Abinger Common, Dorking.
Sir Edwin Lutyens and Gertrude Jekyll.
1898–9.
Recently acquired by the Landmark Trust.
Tel. 01628 825925.

Great Tangley Manor, Wonersh.
Philip Webb.
From 1885.
Private house.

Munstead Wood, nr Godalming.
Sir Edwin Lutyens and Gertrude Jekyll.
From 1883.
Open days at end of April, end of May, and end of June through the National Gardens Scheme.

Phillips Memorial, Godalming.
Thackeray Turner and Gertrude Jekyll.
1913.
Public memorial garden.
Open daily.

Vann, Hambledon.
W.D. Caroe and Gertrude Jekyll.
1907–11.
Open days through the National Gardens Scheme and private visits by arrangement.
Tel. Mr & Mrs Caroe: 01428 683413

EAST SUSSEX:

Bateman's, Burwash.
Rudyard Kipling.
From 1902.
National Trust.
Open Sat.–Wed., April to end Oct.
Tel. 01435 882302.

Brickwall, Northiam, nr Rye.
17th century garden put in order by George Devey.
c.1860.
Although not an Arts and Crafts garden it was photographed by Rossetti and celebrated as a romantic, 'old fashioned' garden.
Open Sat. and Bank Hol. Mons., 2–5.
Tel. 01797 223329.

Gravetye Manor, West Hoathley.
William Robinson.
From 1885.
Country House Hotel.
Tel. 01342 810567.

Great Dixter, Northiam.
Sir Edwin Lutyens and Nathaniel Lloyd.
From 1910.
Garden now in the care of Christopher Lloyd.
Open Tues.–Sun., all year.
Tel. 01797 252878.

WEST SUSSEX:

Little Thakeham, Merrywood Lane, Storrington.
Sir Edwin Lutyens.
1902.
Country House Hotel.
Tel. 01903 744416.

WILTSHIRE:

Heale House, Woodford, nr Salisbury.
Harold Peto and Detmar Blow.
From 1901.
Open all year 10–5
Tel. Mr Guy Rasch and Lady Anne Rasch: 01722 782504

Iford Manor, Westwood, nr Bradford-on-Avon.
Harold Peto.
From 1899.
Architect's own house and garden.
Open daily May to Sept (except Mon. and Fri.), April and Oct. Sun. only.
Private visits by arrangement.
Tel. Mr and Mrs Hignett: 01225 863146

YORKSHIRE:

Newby Hall, Skelton, nr Ripon.
Ellen Willmott and later Major Compton.
c.1900 and 1923.
Open daily April to Sept (except Mon.) 11–5.30.
Group visits by arrangement.
Tel. 01423 322583.

SCOTLAND

FIFE:

Earlshall, Leuchars.
Sir Robert Lorimer.
From 1892.
Private visits by arrangement.
Tel.01334 839205.

Hill of Tarvit, nr Cupar.
Sir Robert Lorimer.
1906–7.
A bit of a hybrid as far as Arts and Crafts goes.
National Trust for Scotland.
Open daily all year.
Tel. 01334 653127.

Kellie Castle, Pittenweem.
Sir Robert Lormer.
From 1880.
National Trust for Scotland.
Open daily all year.
Tel. 01333 720271.

EAST LOTHIAN:

Grey Walls, Muirfield, Gullane.
Sir Edwin Lutyens.
1901.
Country House Hotel.
Tel. 01620 842144.

STRATHCLYDE:

The Hill House, Upper Colquhoun Street, Helensburgh.
C.R Mackintosh and Margaret Macdonald Mackintosh.
1902.
National Trust for Scotland.
Open daily 1.30–5.30, April to end Oct.

ORKNEY:

Melsetter, Island of Hoy
W.R. Lethaby.
1898.
Private visits by arrangement.
Tel. 01856 791352.

BELOW: *The Garden at Earlshall in Fife designed by Robert Lorimer from 1892.*

Index

Numbers in **bold** refer to pictures. The letter 'n' refers to footnotes.